MW01224349

HEAVEN'S PROMISE

THE SPICE FAMILY CHRONICLES

C.J. LOVIK

© 2019 C.J. LOVIK
ALL RIGHTS RESERVED

Preface

Although the storyline and the physical description of all the characters in this book are fictional, the characters are not. Each of the praiseworthy personalities in this book have been stitched together from people whom I have had the joy of actually knowing. Each unique character in this book is a composite of someone I am privileged to call a friend, and I'm happy to acknowledge.

Jeff, June, "Jumpin" Jason, Joey "Snow-brow" and Janelle Speichinger; Mike, Shannon, Justice, Jyles and my special cowgirl friend, Megan "Boots" Peterson; "The Three Magnificent Z's" and their parents Nick and "Pacing" Priscilla Anderson; The Doane family; The Campbell family; Ron and Tami Meier and the JV team; The Brogan family; Robb and Gina Peterson and "the wild bunch;" "The Oklahoma Princess" Tina Miller; "Chuck Wagon" Buck, Susan and Josh Keely; The Wrestling Orndoff's and the "Pink Princess;" Nathan "Two Desserts;" My daughter Elisa Lovik, who is the kindest person I know; and my beloved wife, Jo Ann, without whose encouragement and love this story would have remained unpublished, living only in my heart.

-C.J. Lovik

www.lighthouse.pub
A division of Rock Island Books

Visit our website
to purchase books and preview
upcoming titles.

Contact us at:
feedback@lighthouse.pub

Copyright © 2019, C.J. Lovik
All rights reserved

Table of Contents

Chapter 1

The Best Laid Plans

Dad arrived home late, hung his hat on the antler horns, that his great grandfather had fashioned, just inside the kitchen entrance, and sat down at the old oak table that had been in the family since 1895. Now most folks can't tell you when a prominent piece of furniture showed up in their home, but this very particular dining room table left little doubt about the matter.

Aunt Ida, who claimed the table had been hand crafted by her father, carved the year that she gave it to her nephew under the table. If you looked underneath either end of the rectangular, solid walnut table, you could see the date prominently displayed. The family never tired of chuckling every time anyone emerged from beneath the table saying or singing, "Thank you, Aunt Ida."

The youngsters in the family, and there was a parcel full of them, had not quite grasped the humor of the announcement and made it their business to tell every guest that happened to be sitting at the table that their Aunt Ida had given them the table and then gone to Heaven. Of course, there was no connection between the two events, but having it declared so authoritatively by a three-year-old guaranteed that Aunt Ida was still getting more attention in this life than she ever deserved.

The commotion John made in the kitchen had its desired effect. He could hear his wife, Janet, slipping down the stairs. Seconds later, she entered the room, rubbed her eyes and headed straight for John. John quickly rose to his feet. He knew what was coming and he wouldn't miss it for the world. Janet wrapped her arms around her husband and gave him an Eskimo kiss. Then just as quickly, she darted to the cupboard and began preparing John's favorite hot drink—a combination of hot chocolate, cinnamon and a half-teaspoon of vanilla. It was delicious, or at least John thought so.

"I have good news," announced John. Janet put the piping hot chocolate concoction in front of her husband, went to the opposite end of the table, put her two elbows on the table to prop up her chin, placed her thumbs behind her ears and wiggled them.

John chuckled "I can see you're all ears." They both laughed and then came the news.

John had ridden on horseback over sixteen miles to cast his ballot as the official representative of Elkin, North Carolina. "The vote was 15 to 3 against." John beamed. "The railroad spurs are not going through the Yadkin Valley."

The Northwestern North Carolina Railroad arrived near Elkin in 1890 and was now making plans to build spurs into the Yadkin Valley. John was not against progress, but had strong opinions about letting the "tentacles" of the railroad reach into areas that he believed would be spoiled forever by their presence.

John Spice was the son of a missionary, sent out by the Plymouth Brethren, and had spent the first twenty-three years of his life traveling all over

India and East Asia. He knew that a railroad was a two sided coin that could bring both prosperity, and at the same time, destruction of the old ways. Many were anxious to see the old ways disappear; John was not one of them.

John's great grandfather had been one of the earlier settlers to put down stakes near the Yadkin River that flowed through the most beautiful and rich farmland in the shadow of the Blue Mountain Ridge. A railroad would wipe away the rich tranquil lifestyle of every farmer in the valley and change the heritage and culture of the region forever.

It was 1911, and this was the third time in the past forty years that the railroad had tried to get permission to carve its way through the valley. John figured the battle was not over, but he was confident that it would not happen in his lifetime.

John's great grandfather had once owned nearly 500 acres of the rich farmland just on the outskirts of Elkin, North Carolina. Most of it had been sold off by the succeeding generations of relatives, all except for the original homestead. Great Grandpa Spice was a very successful farmer who had more children than anyone else in Yadkin County. Ten children, all boys! A farmer's dream!

The farmhouse constructed by Great Grandpa Spice was built for a very large family, or a small orphanage, depending on how you wanted to look at it.

THE BEST LAID PLANS

John Spice had dreams of returning to the mission field, a passion shared by his wife, Janet. They had taken up residence in Great Grandpa's farmhouse, now owned by John's father, as a temporary domicile. John had made plans to return to India to assist his mom and dad, who were training pastors to go into the rural area of India with the gospel.

Something happened to change all that when their first-born son, Charlie, was born with a congenital heart condition that was followed six years later with infantile paralysis, what we know today as polio. The combination of diseases had left Charlie crippled and immobile.

Apparently God had other plans for John and Janet Spice.

Charlie was the firstborn, but he was not an only child, not by a long shot.

John was determined to break the family record for producing offspring. With Janet's enthusiastic assistance, he had already "fathered" three girls and five boys, including Charlie. Now with "one in the oven," as they were fond of joking, number nine was well on the way.

Charlie was named after Janet's dad, as they agreed upon just after entering into the marriage. The other four boys were named Matthew, Mark, Luke and John Jr. Those were easy. It was the names of the girls that had stirred up the passions and created many a discussion into the wee hours of the night.

With a last name like Spice, John and Janet had decided to do something other family members had only dreamed of doing, but never mustered up enough courage to do. John and Janet had courageously decided early on to name each of their girls after the name of a spice.

Rosemary was the first Spice girl. Then came Cinnamon, followed by Ginger Spice. And then came trouble.

John, who had spent most of his life in India, wanted to name his fourth born girl after his favorite Asian Spice. John considered the Hindi name for clove, Lauṅga, but decided he much preferred the Malaysian word for Clove, Bunga Chingkeh.

Janet was having none of it. "This baby is not going to be born," she stubbornly announced, "until we can agree on a suitable name."

The normally very compliant Janet could not be persuaded to change her mind, despite all the eloquent pleadings by John, who apparently didn't see a problem in the world with saddling his newborn daughter with the name Bunga Chingkeh.

"Maybe we will have a boy after all," said John "and we could name him Zedekia."

Janet gave him an icy stare, placed both hands on the prominent bundle that was late for delivery and said, "*Daniel*, if it's a boy, just like we agreed."

John wasn't getting anywhere with his Malaysian Indian Spice name with Janet. Apparently she wasn't kidding about not having this baby until he changed his mind, considering she was already two weeks overdue. That evening, Janet served John his favorite hot drink, and within minutes they agreed on a suitable name for the next female Spice.

The following morning, *Cori Ander* Spice greeted the world with howls of delight. Evidently she was happy to have missed the appellation Bunga Chingkeh.

Cori grew up hearing the story over and over again of how she was spared by her mom from a fate worse than death. The boys picked up on the story and used "Bunga Chingkeh" as an expletive for anything unusual. If anything went wrong, they would say "Bunga Bunga" and laugh. Dad would just roll his eyes and try to ignore it. The Spice family lived in the rarified space somewhere between cheerful and joyful, and seldom wandered far out of that lane.

The one thing that did manage to trouble the entire family, especially John and Janet, was the deteriorating condition of their firstborn son, Charlie.

Charlie was almost eleven years old and for the past four years had been confined to his bed. Accommodations were made to make his convalescence as comfortable as possible. Everyone knew that things were not going to get better.

John had a talent for writing. If he could not be a missionary to India, then perhaps, thought John, he could be used to spread the gospel of Jesus Christ as a writer.

Years of submitting articles to Christian book companies, periodical and gospel tract publishers had yielded scant results. He had a few articles published over the past ten years, but nothing notable, and certainly nothing that would pay the mounting expenses of raising a large family in North Carolina.

Despite the lack of encouragement, John had decided that this was the talent he had been given, and he refused to bury it. John would continue to write and submit articles in the hopes that one day his work would be published.

In order to pay the bills, John worked a part-time shift at the small lumber mill in Elkin, and spent the rest of his time managing the ten-acre farm that had once sprawled over the Yadkin Valley for miles.

Ten acres was all he could handle, and with most of the other farmers in the valley tearing out their fruit trees to plant vineyards, the heritage Stayman Apples grown in the Spice orchard were in high demand. The orchard also had a couple a varieties of peach, apricot, plum and persimmon trees which provided a variety of fruit to be canned and made into jams and jellies.

Every year, the Spice family fruit stand was cleaned up and attended by either Matthew, Rosemary or Mark. Conveniently, its location was prime retail space, as it stood right next to the only road that connected over three dozen farms to the town of Elkin.

During apple season, their neighbors bought the Spice Farm Stayman Apples by the lug, knowing they were buying the best apples grown in North Carolina. The apple-butter made with Janet's special recipe was also a perennial favorite. Most of the neighbors were eager customers, knowing that the Spice family of eleven could use the small income the sale of fruit produced to keep the taxes paid, and all those growing children fed.

The Spice Family Fruit Stand was also where all the news of the local farm community was collected. One side of the fruit stand was devoted to posts and messages that all the farmers and their families were eager to stop and read. If a dog had been lost, or a horse, mule or Guernsey milk cow was for sale, the announcement was nailed on the side of the Spice Fruit Stand.

The latest post was from Wally McDaniel, who wanted everyone to know that he had increased the reward for the return of his favorite hunting hound. The description was detailed and included the scar on the left shoulder where "Eager" the hound had tangled with a coon when he was just a year old and was still learning the family business. The reward of two and half dollars was certain to keep everyone on the lookout for the missing hound dog.

Jeremiah 29:11-13

*For I know the thoughts that I think toward you,
saith the Lord, thoughts of peace, and not of evil,
to give you an expected end. Then shall ye call upon me,
and ye shall go and pray unto me, and I will hearken
unto you. And ye shall seek me, and find me,
when ye shall search for me with all your heart.*

Chapter 2

The Eagle's Nest

J ohn was a self-trained carpenter. He had honed his skills in India where he had few tools, coupled with lots of imagination and ingenuity. Bill Cummings, the proprietor of the lumber mill, told John he could have any lumber that was milled that did not make the "grade."

Nails were cheap, the lumber was free, and the labor was provided out of love.

The attic in the huge farmhouse clamored and clattered with activity. A very large window was installed a foot lower than normal on the side of the attic that faced the business end of the farm. From this window you could see just about everything that was going on in the farm below.

There was a view of the small pond, the garden, and the grassy knoll with the tire swing. The barn was also in view along with the small fenced coral that *Stubborn*, the family mule, and a couple of geese called home, and the smoke house where the wild game was cured. Off to the side, if you craned your neck, you could even see Janet hanging up the wash next to the area where their milk goat *Six-Pints* roamed on a rope tether.

It was the perfect Eagle's Nest.

A platform for a single mattress bed was built with casters on the bottom of the four bed posts so it might be rolled around to any spot in the extra-large attic. A larger table was also built and put on wheels so that it could be rolled sideways across and over the bed.

The walls of the attic were covered and wallpaper was applied. The floor was sanded and stained, and finally, a window was put into the roof so that stars could be viewed at night. No one in the community had ever mounted a "roof window," and most thought it was an exotic idea that must have come from India, which made it acceptable. It was not an idea that was going to be imitated anytime soon by the very practical farmers that populated the farmland, which graced the bountiful edges of the Blue Ridge Mountains.

"And one last detail," said John as he carefully cut and tied off the rope that was laced through a pulley system and hung just above Charlie's bed.

"What is that?" asked Janet.

"This is something Mark and Luke figured out." John said with a quick smile. Mark and Luke were the inventors in the family and were always working on some sort of contraption.

John opened the window and pulled the cord a couple of times. "CLANG CLANG CLANG!"

"What in the world is that noise?" asked Janet as she rushed to the open window.

"It is our alarm system," replied John.

"That racket would raise the dead," said Janet. "Exactly," said John. "Perfect."

Charlie was bundled up and carefully carried up to his new perch in the attic. His eyes got big as he surveyed the new accommodations. "This is great dad," he said smiling broadly.

Just before dinner time dad came up to help Charlie sit up in his bed. "What's going on dad?" Charlie asked with a surprised look.

"You'll see," said Dad.

Rosemary arrived with the red and white-checkered tablecloth and an arm full of plates. Ginger followed close behind with all the silverware and a vase full of sunflowers. Then came Dad again with Cori's high-chair, followed by Mom with a big pot of potato stew and some corn on the cob. Everyone made a couple trips up the stairs and then Mom did the Spice count, a routine that preceded all family gatherings, "nine, ten, eleven... where is Cinnamon?"

"Cinnamon," Mom yelled down the stairs, "you get yourself up here right now." Cinnamon was always the last one to show up, and the family had even memorialized her irritating habit with a song. Matthew, the second born, was the musician in the family and without a cue whipped out his *Matthias Hohner* harmonica and soon the whole family was singing, "She'll be coming around the mountain when she comes." Of course, this only encouraged Cinnamon, who seemed determined to show up just about everywhere at exactly the last minute or later if at all possible.

Everyone was in their place at the newly designed dinner table, spilling over onto a card table that was set up for the three youngest and one big brother to supervise. They were ready to inaugurate the first Spice Family Attic dinner. Everyone folded their hands as Dad offered a prayer and read a passage from Scripture.

It was a happy time in the sprawling, newly constructed and appointed attic. An old couch and stuffed chair, that had been donated by a neighbor, and a table for two with a checker board were all set up in one corner of the attic. Handmade figures, and "apple head" dolls filled an old cedar chest that had been turned into a toy box.

The favorite toy was a Kaleidoscope that was sent to all the Spice children on the Christmas of 1907 by their great Aunt Ida. The younger children had somehow gotten it into their heads that Aunt Ida had gone to Heaven. This only added to the amazing effect of endlessly viewing the ever changing wonders seen through a small window that changed the light in the room into a thousand sparkling colors and designs that the smaller children were convinced was a spy glass into Heaven. Adding to the enjoyment was the fact that the manufacturer of the device was H.M. Quackenbush. The Spice children just loved repeating the name with duck sounds added for comedic effect.

Everything about the attic beckoned you to stay and linger for a while. The biggest hit was the oversized picture window from which you could view the entire Spice Farm from the vantage point of a bird. And by the time everyone was sent to bed, the two older brothers had nicknamed the attic "Charlie's Eagle's Nest."

This pleased Charlie to no end.

The Attic instantly became the center of activity for the Spice family, exactly as John and Janet hoped it would. Charlie, who had spent the last four years in his solitary room, enjoyed a morning visit from Dad, Matthew, Rosemary and Mark who showed up every morning exactly an hour before breakfast for a devotional Bible study. Rosemary was the one given the job of delivering breakfast, lunch and dinner. She never stayed for more than a minute. And Mom, who might show up anytime of the day, always showed up in the evening to read him a short story and tuck him into bed.

Visits from mom and dad never lasted very long and were always interrupted by short bursts of "Hi Charlie!" through a hastily open and shut door as his brothers and sisters made their way to their own bedrooms.

That all changed when Charlie took up permanent residence in the attic. Charlie was now living in "Grand Central Station." The bird's eye view of the farm and a night-time view of the Heavens was an endless source of joy and conversation. Charlie loved his new room.

Usually one or two members of the Spice family were in the attic keeping Charlie company. On those rare occasions when Charlie found himself alone, he would always look out the window and watch the family drama play itself out on the farm below.

Charlie kept an eye on the property and was even instrumental in alerting his dad that a fox was approaching the hen house, or that *Matilda*, the American Milk, Goat was no longer tethered and heading for the fruit trees. Of course, the clang of the bell was always a shock to everyone, including the fox, who quickly vacated the premises whenever he heard it.

There was another bell that rang out at exactly the same time every Sunday morning. And even though the Spice family attended a small "Gospel Chapel" that met in the back of Bert Hamilton's Handy Hardware Store, they did love passing by the bell tower at Saint Katherine's Catholic Church and listening to the peeling of the bells.

Every Sunday as they passed the towering church, one of the Spice children would always ask, "Who is Saint Katherine?" This particular Sunday it was Ginger who asked, and received the answer she and everybody else knew she would. No matter how many times any of the children asked, they never grew tired of the answer.

John leaned back as he slacked the reins on Stubborn and caught Ginger's eye. She was standing up in the back of the Mitchell's Farm Wagon as if waiting to be awarded a prize.

"I don't know who Saint Katherine is Saint Ginger, but when I get to

Heaven I will ask around."

"OK Dad," Ginger replied with a smile and a giggle as she bounced playfully back to her assigned place on a layer of straw that cushioned the hemlock planks of the old farm wagon.

After church, the family would all change their clothes and get ready for the biggest meal of the week, Sunday lunch.

"Are we eating in the Eagle's Nest?" asked Mark.

"Yes we are Son. Now you take up the box with all the silverware and napkins, and while you're at it," Janet popped into the broom closet to grab the table cloth, "take this up with you."

Mark dutifully complied and returned a minute later asking if there was anything else he could carry up to the attic. "As a matter of fact there is," she said with a smile as she pulled her third born son in her direction and gave him a big kiss on the cheek. "Now you take that upstairs and share it with everybody."

"Oh Mom," Mark said.

"Here you go Mark," she said as she pulled a *roasted to perfection* turkey out of the oven. She continued, "Now put on these oven mittens and carefully take this to the attic, and no snacking on the way up."

Turkey was reserved for Thanksgiving and it was early September, something special was in the works and Mark knew it. He also knew that if he asked what it was he wouldn't get a straight answer. With bursting anticipation, he just gave his mom a big smile and carefully carried the 16-pound turkey, stuffed with his favorite dressing, up the stairs.

No one had to be called twice to this Sunday feast. The aroma of the roasted turkey was the only invitation any of the children needed, as even Cinnamon managed to find her seat before any of her sisters had even reached the top of the stairs.

Charlie was propped up, the table was slid into place and set, and all the fixings were carefully stationed in just the right spot around the turkey that was placed with care, along with the carving knife, in front of dad's place. Two candles were lit and Dad prayed a real long prayer. All the children looked at each other like it was Christmas morning. Mark was not the only one that had figured out that something was in the wind, something very special.

It was a delicious meal, eaten slowly, savoring every last morsel. The Spice family never starved, but many of their meals were seasoned with a twinge of hunger. With eleven mouths to feed, there was never enough, and never, ever left overs. Well hardly ever, as no one in the family would ever forget the day that dad decided to cook up a batch of bullfrog stew, which he claimed was the meal of Kings in India, a story no one believed.

This "meal of Kings" went into the dog dish and was rejected by Scruffy, and finally found a proper place in the garden as a snail repellant. Dad was never invited to cook again. And if anything strange ever showed up at the dinner table, all eyes would turn to Mom who would realize immediately that she needed to reassure all the Spicelings that what had been put before them was not something cooked up by Dad.

Psalm 31:7
I will be glad and rejoice in thy mercy:
for thou hast considered my trouble;
thou hast known my soul in adversities;

Chapter 3

A Place Prepared

Benjamin Franklin was appointed the first Postmaster General of the United States by the Continental Congress in the year 1775.

The first U.S. postage stamp was issued in 1847.

In June of 1856, the small town of Elkin, North Carolina built its first Post Office.

John Wanamaker, who served as the Postmaster General from 1889-1893, introduced rural mail delivery. He decided that it was a lot more practical and better for the country if one person delivered fifty letters, instead of fifty people living in rural America, travelling twenty-five miles round trip to pick up one letter.

On March 1, 1885, President Grover Cleveland appointed William L. Wilson Postmaster General. On October 1, 1896, General Wilson introduced rural free delivery (RFD) service to Charles Town, Halltown, and Uvilla in West Virginia—Postmaster General Wilson's home state. Within a year, forty-four routes were operating in twenty-nine states, including China Grove, North Carolina.

In 1904, Rural Mail Delivery made it as far as Yadkinville, North Carolina.

In the year 1910, John and Janet Spice were still picking up their mail once a month, or whenever they visited the small town Post Office in Elkin, North Carolina.

The following year, the post office began delivering mail to the 38 farmers that lived out on the rich farmland next to the Yadkin River.

In the minds of many of the farmers of the 20th century, rural population that made up over 65% of the United States, things were happening at breakneck speed. "Keeping up" with all the alterations and innovations was greeted with excitement, mixed with a touch of melancholy.

Watching the old paths and ways disappear was usually chronicled by the aging with "I can remember when." This replaced the old saying, "There was a time when." Changes were happening in front of their eyes and not just on the pages of a history book.

Letters arrived from India in bunches. John's parents, James and Anna Spice, wrote a letter to John and Janet every week without fail. But the letters always arrived in bundles, as many as five or six at a time. Janet would always read through them to make sure there wasn't any urgent news and then organize the letters by date in her very cluttered roll top desk. Every Sunday after lunch she would let the children pass the letters around so they could all look at the stamps.

The letters would finally end up with John, who would read them to the entire family. Since John had spent most of his life on the mission field in India with his parents, he provided background information about anything that was unfamiliar to the children. Family life centered around this weekly drama that drew the family together in ways that the modern family scarcely is able to comprehend.

There was no radio in the Spice home, and the reading of the letters from foreign parts, with descriptions and background added by Dad, was something everyone looked forward to. Even Janet, who had already previewed the letters, was drawn into the words on the pages of the letters that her beloved husband sprinkled so generously with his knowledge of India and artful storytelling.

The stamps and postmarks were viewed with great interest. The Spice children were more familiar with the profiles of King Edward the 7th, Queen Victoria, and King George the 5th than they were with the profiles of the past three Presidents of the United States. They all knew that India was a British colony, and could tell you all about the Indian Rupee and the "Anna," which was not only the name of their Grandmother, but also the name of the Indian form of currency.

John had not yet read the letter he held in his hands. Janet had purposely kept it from him. John held up the letter and waved it in front of everyone as if to demonstrate that it was the genuine article.

John began to read the opening greeting from his parents and then suddenly stopped reading and stood to his feet. "Bless my soul," he said half whispering and then with a hoot and a holler he made the big announcement to the whole family. "Grandpa and Grandma are coming home!"

John had figured that their children would probably never meet his parents this side of glory. Considering that possibility, he had made it a special point to pass as much of their legacy on in their absence. Although the children had never seen their grandparents, they were not strangers by any stretch of the imagination. They lived in the memories and hundreds of stories that had been told and retold by John and Janet.

Janet's mother had died of consumption when she was only three years old. She was raised by her father, who had since passed away, and by her dear Aunt Ida that lived in Missouri, but never visited. Janet had been adopted by John's parents, and Anna was the only real mother Janet had ever known.

The news that Grandpa and Grandma Spice would be coming to live with them was greeted without the slightest reserve. It was something they embraced with joy and enthusiasm, and as it turned out, for very good reason.

And this is where our story really begins.

The weekly correspondence between India and North Carolina went in two directions. James and Anna were well aware that their first-born grandson was not long for this world.

They had spent the last year turning over the responsibility of the Indian Gospel Mission to well trusted and trained Indian Christians. They had decided that it was time to be a missionary at home. This decision would end up blessing the Indian Mission which would flourish under Indian governance as well as the Spice family in North Carolina. The blessing would unfold in ways no one could imagine.

The letter announcing their arrival was dated July 20th, 1911. The letter was read in the third week of September. James and Anna would arrive well before Christmas.

The attention of the family coalesced around one single solitary, theme: *How to make Grandpa and Grandma feel at home.* Everyone got in on the act.

The largest bedroom—and the one facing the sunny south—was presently occupied by Matthew, who was the first one to decide that he was going to move in with Luke, his younger brother.

Luke thought the sun rose and set on his big brother Matthew, and was delighted at the prospect; although, it did create a momentary howl from John Jr. who had decided that Matthew should move in with him. Dad solved that problem by putting all three of them in the same room for a week, followed by a meeting to see how it was going. John Jr. accused Luke of snoring and was happy to retreat back to his own small room. Problem solved.

Memorabilia that is usually passed on from one generation to the next, never to see the light of day, was dug up and dusted off. John spent a week just cutting, assembling, and staining custom frames out of sugar pine to display all the newly framed memory pieces.

Matthew's room was now completely vacant. The first job was to sand and stain the oak floor. Everyone except Cori was given a sanding block and then lined up like racehorses at one end of the room. To make it interesting, Janet drew a chalk line for each child to follow as they scooted backward on their knees, scrubbing and swirling the wooden block with sandpaper neatly taped in place.

The Victrola was set up in the adjoining hallway and played "The Flight of the Bumble Bee" over and over again to everyone's delight. At the signal, the sanding race began in earnest, and within the hour the job was completely done. It's amazing what ten pairs of hands can accomplish thought Janet. Matthew was the first one to reach the finish line, followed seconds later by Rosemary.

Rosemary jumped to her feet when she was finished and said "Congratulations Matthew, you won fair and square." She extended her hand to Matthew who, without thinking, grabbed his sister's hand for a congratulatory handshake.

Matthew winced with pain and let out a loud and woeful cry, "Bunga Bunga!" as he begged to be released from the vise grip. Everyone stopped sanding and looked at Matthew and began laughing. "She got you that time," piped John Jr. Rosemary smiled, let go of her victim, and slapped her hands together sending a cloud of oak dust into the air. Rosemary was the one who milked Six-Pints, the family goat. Dad said Rosemary could crush walnuts with one hand—Matthew didn't doubt it.

John cleaned and did a final sanding of the oak floor, then stained and varnished it with great care. The windows were opened and the door was closed. Three days later the door was reopened, and except for cleaning off and re-varnishing a couple spots where the moths had landed, it was a perfect job.

"Hey Mom," said Ginger, "I can see my reflection on the floor."

Janet came over, placed her hands on Gingers tiny shoulders and peered over her head at the reflected image. "That's not you, Ginger." she teased.

"Who is it?" Ginger inquired. "That," said Mom, "is a very small angel that has come to make sure that everything is prepared for Grandma and Grandpa."

Ginger smiled, cocked her head and flapped her tiny arms. "Look Mom, the angel is flying."

The room was ready to be furnished; the only problem was they had no furniture—no bed, dresser, writing table or bookshelf.

The family made it a matter of prayer as mom scoured the local newspaper for any news of used cheap furniture. After a couple weeks of constant checking and making inquiries with her neighbors, she learned that there was going to be an estate sale in Elkin that Saturday morning.

Early Saturday morning, John loaded up the wagon with his family and headed for Elkin. They arrived early and found the location where the estate auction was going to take place. Soon, a pretty large crowd arrived and the bidding started. Everyone in Elkin knew everyone else, and everyone knew and admired the Spice family.

The Spice children had never been to an auction, and the fast-talking auctioneer, who they recognized as the Postmaster, was speaking a language they had never heard before. It was a linguistic experience that would not be soon forgotten. The Spice boys would imitate it whenever there was a chore or anything remotely unpleasant they wanted to pass on to someone else.

The bidding started with all the furniture in the living room. A grand piano was the first item to go up for bid, and it was soon apparent that the competition was going to be fierce. The piano sold for $100 dollars, a king's ransom in 1911. The two main actors in the bidding wars were the owner of the local furniture store, and the owner of the local general merchandise store.

The Spice family watched in amazement as the items up for auction fetched what they considered to be outrageous prices. With only ten extra dollars to their name, everything seemed out of their price range.

After hours went by, they finally came to the one room they had been waiting for—the master bedroom. The auctioneer was tired and so was everyone else. Half the crowd had gone home. "Alright," said the auctioneer "we are going to sell off all the bedroom furniture as one lot, and then we can all go home."

"Start praying," said John. Some of the kids bowed their heads and did as their father had requested. The auctioneer began to describe the 32 items that were all going up for sale at once.

Janet lifted up her left hand and silently mouthed a prayer and then shouted at the top of her lungs, "Hey Bob!"

Before Bob Hobbs, the auctioneer, could begin his auctioneering spiel Janet made her announcement. "You all know me and my husband John." He nodded. "Well, we just received news that James and Anna are returning home from spending almost thirty years on the mission field in India, and they have no furniture." Bob nodded again.

Janet continued, "I bid ten dollars—for all this bedroom furniture." Bob nodded again with a smile, certain he could get twenty times that amount without even trying.

"I have an opening bid for ten dollars do I hear fifty?" The crowd was silent. "Do I hear a bid for forty-five?"

Try as he might, he could not provoke another bid. Finally, in desperation he barked, "Do I hear fifteen dollars?"

There was not a sound as Bob pointed his gavel in the direction of the Spice Farm wagon.

"I see that hand," said the auctioneer, and everyone turned around to see little Ginger Spice with her hand up in the air.

"Honey put your hand down," waved Mom. Everyone laughed including Bob the auctioneer.

"Ten dollars going once, going twice, SOLD to the Spice family for ten dollars." The crowd erupted in cheers as they clapped and dispersed.

A few neighbors stayed to help John load up the wagon with more furniture than he knew what to do with.

On the ride home John was silent. Finally, he leaned over and gave Janet a big nudge, "You're pretty amazing," he said.

Janet smiled and mused, "I know."

"So tell me Janet, what are we going to do with all this extra furniture?"

Without missing a beat Janet said, "Sell it of course."

That is exactly what Janet did. When all was said and done she sold almost all the extra furniture and furnishings for a grand total of $124.57. After deducting the cost of advertising it in the classified section of the local newspaper, she had cleared a profit of $121.57. This was enough extra income to pay for a couple years of food and supplies. A windfall!

John and Janet were very careful to thank the Lord for all His benefits. John had grown up on the mission field and seen miracle after miracle unfold as the Lord supplied all their needs. John never worried about finances, but he was very concerned that the Lord get the credit for all the kindnesses he knew were from the loving hands of His Heavenly Father. This was one of the "life lessons" that was drilled into all the Spice children from birth. It was a lesson that had taken root and was producing fruit. The Spice family "almost" never complained, and constantly prayed that the "almost" would go away.

A beautiful Persian rug was placed in the center of the bedroom. Then came the big brass bed along with a polished cherry dresser and matching armoire with cedar lining. Finally, a walnut bookcase, matching writing desk, and oak roll top desk finished off the room.

"Looks like the royal suite at Windsor Castle," said John.

"The royal suite at Spice Castle," concluded Janet with a look of satisfaction. "I think Mom and Dad are going to love it," she concluded. She was right.

The Spice *farm* was turning yellow and orange as the crisp harbingers of fall made their presence known. The wind swirled the leaves around in a symphony that preceded the chill that was coming early that year. Farmers could usually tell what sort of winter it was going to be by the end of November, and it looked like the winter of 1911-1912 was going to be one for the history books.

Matthew and Luke were busy cutting, splitting and stacking wood. Janet took all the comforters, wool mittens and extra blankets out of the storage room and began distributing them to each child's bedroom. Rosemary was busy darning all the woolen socks that had been washed and sun dried. John busied himself putting all the tools where they belonged and tying down anything that might blow away. John Jr. helped the older boys carry wood into the house where it was neatly stacked in a large firewood box that would hold nearly a quarter cord. Luke checked all the storm windows to make sure they were all in good working order as Cinnamon swept the leaves off the front porch. Charlie carefully watched as his dad had instructed, looking for anything that might be missed as the family prepared for the coming storm and the severe winter that appeared to be on the near horizon.

It was just about dusk, and Janet had prepared a large pot of hot apple cider. Janet stepped outside the kitchen and rang the dinner bell. Everyone quickly finished their jobs and scrambled into the kitchen. As Mom began to ladle the hot apple cider into each child's mug, starting with the youngest, they were all jolted by the ringing of another bell. It was loud and it was persistent, something was amiss!

John immediately ran up the stairs wondering if Charlie was in distress. Once in the attic he saw his son with one hand on the rope that rang the Spice Family emergency bell, and one hand cupped on the picture window. John rushed to the window to see what it was that had alarmed Charlie.

"Look Dad," said Charlie excitedly, "I think its Grandpa and Grandma!"

John gazed out the window. "You're right," said Dad, "that's them alright? We will see you in a minute," and he rushed downstairs and out the front door to greet his parents, with the rest of the family in hot pursuit.

Philippians 4:19
But my God shall supply all your need according to his riches in glory by Christ Jesus.

Chapter 4

Homecoming

Dad arrived first and swept his mom up in his arms, spinning round and round. He finally set her down with a big kiss on the cheek and went for his dad. "Now, just wait a minute, Son," Grandpa said as he held up one hand. "You try that neat trick on me and we are both going to need back surgery."

Grandpa was not a large man, standing just over five feet, five inches tall. He didn't have an ounce of extra fat, and with his broad muscular shoulders and thick chest he looked a little like an up-ended bale of hay. John gave him a big hug and tried to lift him off the ground but was surprised when he found himself nearly a foot off the ground and looking straight into the eyes of his beloved father. "You may be six feet tall Son, but you will always be my little boy," Grandpa beamed as he gently put his son back on the well-trodden dirt path that led to the front porch.

"How did you get here?" John inquired, as the grandparents were busy hugging all the grandchildren they had only dreamed about for the past twelve years.

"We walked of course," said Grandpa, "how do you get anywhere?"

"It's an eight mile walk from the bus station," remarked Janet.

"Just a nice afternoon stroll for us" responded Grandma. "I used to walk the eight miles from Dad's farm to town three times a week and twice on Sunday when I was a lad," Grandpa remarked. "And besides, I wanted to see if anything had changed since I was last here over forty years ago."

"Well has anything changed?" asked John.

"The only thing that has changed, except for the new farm that they built up on Butler's Ridge, is that this road has grown by miles—or maybe my legs have just gotten shorter," Grandpa quipped. Everyone laughed.

The grandparents had put a name to each face and hugged every one of their grandchildren at least twice. The aroma of hot apple cider spiced with cinnamon left little doubt about what was next on the agenda as they all retired to the kitchen.

"Here, Grandpa, have a cup of apple cider," offered Matthew.

"That is very kind of you Matthew," he said as he sipped the cider. "There is one more person I must meet."

"Charlie?" said Matthew.

"Show me the way to the 'Eagle's Nest'," Grandpa gestured as he moved in the direction of the stairs.

Grandpa had obviously been reading the mail from the Spice family farm, thought Matthew. Up the stairs they went, and without a word Grandpa Spice greeted Charlie with a gentle hug that was followed by tears of joy.

"Charlie I am so glad to meet you on this side of Heaven." Grandpa said with a broad infectious smile. "Have a mug of hot cider," he offered as he helped Charlie sit up in his bed.

This side of Heaven, thought Charlie. The greeting stuck in Charlie's mind like peanut butter to the roof of your mouth, just like Grandpa wanted it to.

Grandpa had a nickname in India that roughly translated into English that meant "the big stick that plants the seeds."

Grandpa grew up on the very farm that Charlie could view for miles around as he gazed out his attic window. The farmhouse with the ten acres was actually owned by Charlie's grandpa and he knew every square inch of it by heart. And growing up on a farm, he knew all about planting seeds and then patiently waiting from them to grow. "Patiently waiting" as Grandpa was fond of saying, "is the hard part."

What did Grandpa mean when he said "this side of Heaven," Charlie wondered? He couldn't shake the idea out of his head. The "Big Stick" had poked a hole and planted a single seed into Charlie's mind, and it was already beginning to germinate.

Grandpa was a well-honed and very experienced evangelist. He had spent the last forty years training men how to handle God's Word, the importance of a personal walk with the Lord Jesus, and how to entice men to begin asking the important questions in life—questions that are rarely asked and hardly ever answered.

"I have something for you Charlie, I will bring it up this evening." With those enticing words, Grandpa got up and went back down the stairs.

It wasn't long before everyone including Grandpa was back up the stairs, along with the Victrola and a box full of carefully screened records. Fellowshipping in the attic had become a very familiar and pleasant pastime for the entire Spice family.

An extra couch had been added to the attic décor, along with a matching coffee table, a hand embroidered footstool, a bronze statue of a moose, a crystal cut glass oval basket—that was now filled with jelly beans, an antique clock with two golden angels on the top—that Janet had dressed modestly with black felt frocks, a picture of a brown and white horse hitched up and ready to plow, and finally, an *Ellen Clapsaddle* postcard announcing the 1907 new year that John had mounted on an oak plague. It was all part of the "booty" that John had dubbed "The Great Furniture Robbery of 1911," pulled off by "Calamity Janet" and her trusty sidekick "Ginger Spice."

Once you got tagged with a nickname in the Spice family it was hard to shake it, although it must be admitted that Janet loved the reference to Calamity Jane. She was not so fond of the obvious reference to the Wilcox Train Robbery of 1899 that made Robert LeRoy Parker, better known as

Butch Cassidy, a household name when it was made into a silent film in 1903 entitled, *The Great Train Robbery.*

Grandpa and Grandma had not yet been introduced to their new bedroom. As the Spice party wound down and the children began filing out headed to bed, Janet and John escorted James and Anna downstairs and introduced them to their "master suite."

Grandma could hardly contain herself as she was overwhelmed by the luxurious accommodations. Grandpa was also pleased and whispered in John's ear, "You *do* know who this room belonged to sixty years ago, don't you?"

"I have no idea," John said with surprise.

"This is my old room. I grew up in this very room." Grandpa said with a broad smile.

"Welcome back to the nest," John said with a grin.

It immediately became clear that Grandpa and Grandma had arrived with one single purpose in mind. They were on a mission. The mission included every single member of the Spice family, but it most especially included Charlie.

James and Anna were probably the most hospitable people you could ever meet, and they had also learned the fine art of being guests. They lived their lives out in deeds matched by few words. They never offered advice unless it was requested, and never, ever navigated themselves between their son and daughter and their children. They were "home" to serve the Lord and they seemed to know exactly how to do it without ever ruffling feathers, undermining the authority of the parent, adding to the confusion, or becoming the source of irritation to anyone.

The task was made much easier as the household of John and Janet Spice was the most joyful, peaceful, and loving family to ever live in the shadow of the Blue Ridge Mountains.

There was no mistaking the fact that James Spice was on an urgent mission. Had the Lord, or one of His angels, told James what was coming up next in the lives of the John and Janet Spice family? No one ever asked, but looking back on the events that followed, you could sure see God's fingerprints all over the days that were to come. Glorious days!

Before James went to bed, he pulled a large book out of his suitcase and quietly made his way into the darkened attic. Charlie was asleep. Grandpa placed the big book on the stand next to Charlie's bed and headed down the stairs. It had been a long day and James was very tired.

The following morning, John got up early to find his dad already nursing a cup of coffee, sitting next to the small fire he had started an hour earlier. "You're up early," said John.

"I am still on India time," responded James.

James was not one for laying out a big plan all at once, as he had learned to do things in small bites. "Son," said James, "would it be alright if I spent about an hour a day reading to Charlie and the rest of the kids?"

"What a great idea, Dad. When would you like to do that?"

"You tell me, Son, when would be the best time?"

"How about after dinner when all the chores are done. When would you like to start?"

James looked at John with a twinkle in his eye and asked if it would be all right if he started that evening after dinner.

"How would you like to join Charlie, Matthew, Rosemary and I in our morning Bible study?" asked John.

"Love to," James said. "When?"

John pulled out his pocket watch and said, "About an hour and a half from now."

The father and son spent the next hour catching up on what was happening in the Bombay Mission.

John 14:1-3

*Let not your heart be troubled: ye believe in God,
believe also in me. In my Father's house are many mansions:
if it were not so, I would have told you.
I go to prepare a place for you. And if I go and
prepare a place for you, I will come again,
and receive you unto myself;
that where I am, there ye may be also.*

Chapter 5

Learning to Listen

That evening just after dinner, Dad made the announcement that as soon as all the dishes were washed and put away, everyone was to meet upstairs for a "sunanā sunanā."

Rosemary asked the question that was on everyone's mind: "What is a *sunanā*?"

Dad leaned over to whisper in Rosemary's ear, loud enough for everyone to hear: "The sooner you get these dishes cleaned up, the sooner you will find out."

"Right Dad," said Rosemary who then began immediately organizing the cleanup crew, who all pitched in double time.

Grandpa made his way up the stairs to get ready for the mass migration of Spices into the attic.

"Hi Grandpa," Charlie saluted.

"Namastē," greeted Grandpa. Charlie just stared not knowing how to respond. Grandpa came over to Charlie's bed and lifted the big brown book he had placed there on the nightstand the night before. "Have you looked at the book yet?" "Yes sir," said Charlie. "I looked at all the pictures."

"Namastē," said Grandpa, "is the Indian way to say 'hello.' Can you say it?"

"Namastē," said Charlie, who was happy to have discovered the meaning of the mysterious foreign greeting.

John, Janet, Anna and all the Spice children began trudging up the stairs and tumbling into the big attic. They each found their own special spots around and on Charlie's bed.

When everyone was seated, Charlie lifted his hand up, faced it palm out as if he was greeting a Cherokee Chief and said "Namastē Namastē, greetings white man."

Grandpa's laugh was instant and contagious. John and Anna immediately caught the humor and joined into the laughter. Ginger and John Jr. then began laughing, not really knowing why. Finally, Charlie, who didn't know what he had said that was so funny, joined into the chortling.

Everybody else just silently looked at each other. Janet crossed her arms and asked, "Just exactly what are we laughing about?"

"My dear Janet," said Grandpa, "Namastē is Hindi for 'hello'."

"And you taught that word to Charlie?" she said.

"That I did," said Grandpa, still chuckling.

Janet's smile quickly became a chuckle that soon was promoted to a belly laugh. "Charlie, you are priceless," she finally blurted out as she slowly gained back her composure.

It took a couple of days before Charlie figured out what he had said and why it was so funny. No explanation besides the laughter was forthcoming that evening. The spell of laughter was broken when Rosemary, who was no nonsense and had worked up a mild glow getting the entire kitchen in order, asked, "So what is a Sunanā Sunanā?"

Dad squared off face to face with Rosemary and put his index finger behind his right ear and wiggled it: "Sunanā one." He then did the same thing with his left ear: "Sunanā Two."

Rosemary cocked her head and said "Ears?" Dad then added, "Are for?" Rosemary thought for a second and then said, "Listening, listening!"

"You are so smart Rosemary Spice," chimed Grandma, with a hearty "I second that motion," by Janet.

Grandpa was a skilled storyteller. His voice ranged from high tenor to deep baritone and he used it like a musical instrument. He soon had everyone's raft attention as he began to read Bunyan's classic tale, *Pilgrim's Progress*.

After the reading, Grandpa left time to do some explaining, and then invited questions. All John Jr. and Ginger knew was that they were on

Grandpa's knees listening to a story that included them, and that was all they needed to understand.

With "Christian," the main character in Bunyan's *Pilgrim's Progress*, making a dash for the Shining Light on the horizon, the evening ended. Everyone went to bed knowing that having Grandpa and Grandma under their roof was a thing of wonder—a gift they would never, ever forget for as long as they lived. John and Janet could not have been more pleased than if the Lord had sent the Angel Gabriel himself, to grace the Spice household.

James Spice was the youngest of ten sons. He was born in 1845. The Great American Civil War began just months after his 16th birthday. All his brothers—except for Nathaniel, who was born blind—joined the Confederate Army.

James served with distinction under General Braxton Bragg. He soon was given the name James "bullwhip" Spice. When James was twelve years old, he was given a bullwhip by his uncle, who delivered the first beef cows to the Spice farm just four years before the Civil War. The bullwhip was used as a "pastoral tool" to herd the cattle by prodding them with the loud noise made by snapping the "cracker."

The beef cows only lasted two years. The passion for cracking a bullwhip lasted all through James' youth and his early years as an adult. James had developed "whipping" into a skill that was nothing short of expert. He could stun a rabbit at twenty feet and break ten bottles set up on fence posts in less than three minutes.

When he joined the Confederate Army his sergeant told him to give his bullwhip away. As the Sergeant was just finishing up with his orders, a raven landed on a lower branch about twenty feet away. With a single stroke James cracked his whip, instantly striking the bird and sending it to the ground. "That's quite a talent son," said the sergeant, who hated ravens and thought they were bad luck. He then smiled and said, "You can keep it."

James and all his other brothers joined up with General Braxton Bragg, except for Daniel, the eldest, who was determined to serve with General George Picket.

Daniel died in the Battle of Gettysburg in 1863. Daniel was not the only brother who would die in the Civil War. When it was all over, in 1865, only six brothers returned home to the farm in Yadkin Valley, and two were badly wounded and spent years recovering. It was a terrible time—a time James Spice could never forget.

James Spice had married Anna, the eldest daughter of circuit riding Methodist preacher, in 1872. In 1880 they packed up their first-born son, John, who was now three years old, and boarded a steamer to the British Isles. They lived in a community with the Christian group known as the "Plymouth Brethren" where James deepened his faith, memorized the Bible, and became forever devoted to the Lord Jesus Christ, who he always referred to as the "Greatest Friend a sinner ever had."

In 1882, the family of three boarded a British Schooner in London and sailed to the western coast of India, landing in Bombay in early 1883. James and Anna Spice spent the next twenty-eight years preaching and teaching the gospel of Jesus Christ in Bombay, the most populated city in all of India. The horrors of the American Civil War and the impoverished diseased streets of Bombay in the late 19th century had one thing in common: death was all around them.

James Spice knew all about ministering to the dying, and did not shrink from bringing the gospel of life to those whose existence in this life was a sad saga of what he called "hopelessly fading into the dark abyss."

You might think that being surrounded by these constant reminders of the "devil's big lie" would have worn James down and cast a shadow on his soul, but it did not. James was a man filled with love and hope. Where did all this hope and optimism spring from? As James was fond of saying, "I am constantly being lifted up by the hands that bear the emblems of glory." James Spice was a man who had truly met the Savior.

Charlie had met the Savior when he was eight years old, and was baptized the following year in the Yadkin River. John had spent at least one hour a day leading all his sons and daughters in a family Bible study. In addition, each day began with a Bible study that included the older children: Charlie, Matthew and Rosemary.

After the morning Bible study, Grandpa decided to take a walk by himself. He had a favorite place up the road that no one knew about. After about thirty minutes of trudging, he stopped and viewed a giant Autumn Blaze Red maple tree. "Well I can see you have done a lot of growing since I last sat under you," Grandpa said. The maple was in its full glory of blazing red leaves. Grandpa approached the tree and began poking around. "Now where is that log I used to sit on when I was a kid?" he asked as he investigated around the tree. "There you are," he said as he rolled the log up on its end and seated himself.

Grandpa sat on the log that he had placed up to the trunk of the maple tree and leaned back. He looked down the road in both directions. "Well, Lord, it's me again," Grandpa folded his hands and bowed his head. "Lord, I know you're just about to take Charlie home, and don't get me wrong, I do know how glorious that is going to be," Grandpa paused. "But Lord, I was hoping you might just delay his homecoming a little while longer so I might get to know him a bit and give his brothers and sisters some encouragement, with your help of course. I sure would appreciate it, Lord."

Grandpa looked up at the red blazing leaves and bowed his head one more time, "and Lord, thank you for this reminder of your precious blood and the Heaven it purchased for all your children, including Charlie."

Grandpa made his way back home, just in time to find a hot cup of coffee and a two gingerbread cookies on a porcelain blue Christmas plate that pictured a lad sailing toward a lit up chapel on a starry night. The calendar on the plate was from 1907.

"I see Aunt Ester is still sending you Christmas plates," remarked James.

"That is the only one that survived the afternoon that Ginger and Cinnamon decided to fix us lunch using all the plates I had hanging on the wall," replied John.

"What happened?" asked Grandpa.

"Ginger tripped over Scruffy and what you're looking at is the sole survivor."

Janet then asked, "We have been looking all over for you Dad, where have you been?"

"Oh I have been having a little chat with my best friend," Grandpa replied.

"Hope you said hello from me," said Janet, smiling.

"I figure that is something you can do yourself," said James with a chuckle. Janet smiled.

Rosemary and Cinnamon were busy making ginger cookies, while Ginger was busy eating them almost as fast as they came out of the oven. "Ginger you're going to make yourself sick, that is your last cookie."

"But Mom, Ginger needs ginger," she protested.

Janet sighed—another one of John's jokes coming back to haunt her. "Last one, Ginger."

"OK, Mom," moaned Ginger, who considered it her right of birth to devour anything with ginger in it, especially ginger cookies.

Grandpa laughed at the antics of his "grand girls." "There is nothing quite as tasty as a homemade ginger cookie washed down with a hot cup of coffee," he said with a big smile, lips covered with ginger crumbs.

Grandpa sat in the kitchen for a while and then quietly got up and went up the stairs to see Charlie. Charlie was alone in the attic, as the rest of the children were getting ready to do their homeschool work and clean up their rooms for the late morning inspection that took place just before lunch. If the room did not pass muster, you missed lunch. "The secret to a child's clean room is through their stomachs," Janet quipped.

Proverbs 17:17
A friend loveth at all times,
and a brother is born for adversity.

Chapter 6

Getting Ready to Go

"N amastē Charlie," said Grandpa as he slid beside his grandson. "Namastē Grandpa," Charlie said without the "big chief" voice or the raised hand.

"Figured that out did you?"

"Yep, there are Indians from North Carolina like the Waccamaw, Creek, and Cherokee, and then there are Indians from India."

Grandpa had learned that the best conversations started with a question.

"What have you been thinking about Charlie?"

Charlie was silent for a minute and then said, "Grandpa, what did you mean when you said you were glad to meet me this side of Heaven?"

Grandpa immediately took control of the conversation, and answered his grandson's question with another question. Waiting a spell in order to let Charlie's question drift off a bit, he finally asked, "What do you think Heaven is like, Charlie?"

Charlie thought for a moment and then said, "I was meaning to ask you the same question."

"Have you been wondering about it?"

"Yes," said Charlie.

"Well, Charlie, since neither of us has been to Heaven, we will have to find our answers in the Bible."

"What about in *Pilgrim's Progress*?" asked Charlie.

"Well now that's a thought," said Grandpa. "I am almost positive that the man who wrote *Pilgrim's Progress* got all his ideas from the Bible. We can look at what Mr. Bunyan has to say about Heaven, but we need to make sure it is in the Bible. Agreed?" asked Grandpa.

"Agreed," said Charlie.

"OK, where do we start?" asked Grandpa.

"Is Heaven real, like North Carolina, like our farm?" asked Charlie.

"Now that is a very good question. Yes, Heaven is real. In fact, it is even more real than North Carolina or this farm."

Charlie thought for a moment, "I thought maybe it was kind of smoky like a cloud."

Grandpa laughed, "No it's more real than anything you can imagine."

"But what about me when I get there, won't I be sort of misty?" asked Charlie.

"You mean like a ghost?" inquired Grandpa.

"Sort of," said Charlie.

As Grandpa began to thumb through his Bible, he asked his grandson a question, "Charlie, what part of you is going to live forever?"

"Dad and I were talking about that the other day," said Charlie. "My body is going to die but my spirit lives forever."

"That's right Charlie, and did you know that your body cannot live without your spirit?"

Charlie had a puzzled look on his face. Grandpa let his grandson think about it for a while and then asked, "Charlie, before you contracted polio, did you learn to ride a bike?"

"Dad gave me a bike for my 7th birthday, it's the blue bike that Cinnamon is learning to ride."

"Did you learn to ride the bike?"

"Oh yes," said Charlie.

"Is the bike alive?"

Charlie looked puzzled, "It's just a bike Grandpa."

"Your body is like the bicycle," said Grandpa. "You make it 'come to life' when you are on it pedaling it and controlling the handle bars to make it go where you want to go."

Charlie thought about it for a minute and then mustered up a smile.

"Grandpa, I think my bike has a flat tire."

Grandpa laughed and quipped, "And mine is getting rusty, and the pedals are about to fall off." Grandpa and Charlie had a good laugh.

Grandpa figured that he wanted this lesson to settle into his grandson's mind. But before he left, he wanted to clear up the one question Charlie seemed to be stumbling over.

Grandpa opened his Bible to Zechariah six as he told Charlie to pay special attention. Then Grandpa slowly read the following passage from Zechariah chapter six, verses one through three.

And I turned, and lifted up mine eyes, and looked, and, behold, there came four chariots out from between two mountains; and the mountains were mountains of brass. In the first chariot were red horses;

and in the second chariot black horses; And in the third chariot white horses; and in the fourth chariot grisled and bay horses.

Grandpa stopped reading and looked into the eyes of his grandson to get his full attention. "Now let me ask you a question Charlie, are you ready?"

Charlie nodded his head.

"What color were the first horses pulling the first chariot?" Grandpa asked. "Red," responded Charlie enthusiastically.

"And the color of the second horses pulling the second chariot?" he asked again.

"Black," responded Charlie.

"And the third?" asked Grandpa.

Charlie thought for a minute. "I think they were white horses," he finally responded.

"And what about the horses pulling the fourth chariot?"

"I don't know Grandpa," Charlie answered.

"I am not sure I do either: I will do some research and we can try and figure that out together," Grandpa chuckled.

"Now let me ask you one more question. Are you ready for this one, Charlie? It's a tough one," Grandpa challenged.

"I'm ready," Charlie said.

Grandpa put his hand to his chin and stroked his whiskers, "Any smoky misty horses or ghost horses in this Bible verse?"

"No Grandpa."

"Were the chariots see-through smoky chariots?"

"No," said Charlie, trying to figure out what Grandpa was getting at.

Grandpa continued to read from the book of Zechariah 6:4-5.

Then I answered and said unto the angel that talked with me, What are these, my lord? And the angel answered and said unto me, These are the four spirits of the Heavens, which go forth from standing before the Lord of all the earth.

As Grandpa finished reading, he looked at Charlie to see any signs that he had understood the lesson.

Charlie thought for a minute and then said, "OK, I get it; spirits are real, not smoky ghosts."

"You got it," said Grandpa with a broad approving smile.

Grandpa began writing a list of Bible verses, saying each one out loud. "Let me see: Job 33:4, Psalms 104:4, Ecclesiastes 3:21, oh, and here is a great verse, Ecclesiastes 12:7; then there is John 4:24, Hebrews 1:7 and finally, John 6:63."

Grandpa handed Charlie the list of Bible references and promised him that tomorrow, about the same time, he would come to visit Charlie again, and they would talk about Heaven's "Super Blue Bicycle." In the meantime, Charlie was to read all the verses Grandpa had written on the list.

Charlie eagerly looked at the list as he reached for his Bible, "don't forget about tonight," Charlie reminded.

"Yes, we need to find out what happens to Christian as he journeys to the Celestial City, don't we?"

Charlie nodded.

"See you at dinnertime Charlie."

"How do they say goodbye in India?" Charlie asked.

"Alavidā," said Grandpa.

"Alavidā Grandpa," replied Charlie.

Charlie found the verses Grandpa had written down and began to read them carefully. If he was going to Heaven, he wanted to find out as much as he could about where he was going and what it would be like.

Job 33:4
The spirit of God hath made me,
and the breath of the Almighty hath given me life.

Psalms 104:4
Who maketh his angels spirits;
his ministers a flaming fire:

Ecclesiastes 3:21
Who knoweth the spirit of man that goeth upward, and the
spirit of the beast that goeth downward to the earth?

Ecclesiastes 12:7
Then shall the dust return to the earth as it was: and
the spirit shall return unto God who gave it.

John 4:24
God is a Spirit: and they that worship him must
worship him in spirit and in truth.

Hebrews 1:7
*And of the angels he saith, Who maketh his angels spirits,
and his ministers a flame of fire.*

John 6:63
*It is the spirit that quickeneth; the flesh
profiteth nothing: the words that I speak unto you,
they are spirit, and they are life.*

Chapter 7

God's Pond

s Grandma took Charlie's lunch up to the attic, the rest of the children poured outside to get some exercise. "I think they call this recess at the Elkin School-House," Janet said to Grandpa James.

Grandpa soon joined in on the fun and found ways to interact with all his precious grandchildren. Cinnamon was trying to teach Scruffy to roll over and play dead, while Scruffy was more interested in sniff-following bugs around the garden.

Matthew was inspecting his tree house, along with Mark and Luke.

John Jr. was busy on the swing, yelling at the top of his lungs for somebody to come and push him.

Rosemary was busy collecting fallen leaves for her scrapbook, and Cori was busy finding the most comfortable place in the bundle of blankets to snuggle up to her mom.

Grandma came out the front door and sat down on the porch swing. John went into the house and fetched a blanket, then returned to cover up his mom's legs with the quilted blanket as he joined her on the swing.

Charlie watched it all from his perch in the attic. Just then, the Spice family alarm bell rang as Charlie yelled out the window at the top of his lungs, "Ginger is headed for the pond."

Grandpa James knew exactly how dangerous that pond was, having almost drowned in it himself when he was just a toddler, over sixty years ago. In a flash, he sprinted toward the pond and scooped up Ginger as she gurgled and flailed, sending up a boiling swirl of bubbles and mud.

John arrived about ten seconds later, his face white as a ghost, "is she alright, Dad?"

"Close call," said Grandpa. "If Charlie had not spotted her when he did, this would have been a very sad day."

Ginger began to cry. "Yep, she is back in good form," said Grandpa, as he handed the wet wailing bundle off to his son.

A few seconds later Janet showed up and took charge of Ginger. "She will never do that again," she said.

"This next summer we will teach her to swim," said John. They all agreed.

Everyone was called inside and invited to go to their rooms with instructions to spend some time thinking about what had just happened, and what might have happened. They were encouraged to each find a Bible verse that fit the situation, and be ready to read it before dinner. Gently, they were all reminded that God had given them two eyes so that they would not only look after themselves but also see the needs and struggles of others. A timely reminder from Mom and Dad that they were all responsible for each other and needed to keep an eye out for trouble.

Janet, Anna and Rosemary spent the rest of the afternoon working on a very special dinner and making a big chocolate cake with a double recipe of frosting.

The aroma of roast beef and mashed potatoes curled up the stairs and drifted under every door in the house. The announcement was crystal clear; something delicious was about to transpire.

The dinner table was set and everyone arrived without an invitation.

John took charge as he led the family in a heartfelt prayer, thanking the Lord for preserving Ginger that afternoon. Ginger was hoisted up on John's shoulders and everyone clapped and cheered.

Ginger announced that she was going to learn to swim next summer, but until then, she promised never to go near the pond again, unless she was with one of the big boys, or Mom and Dad. That reassuring news was greeted with claps of approval.

Next, all the children read the verses they had discovered that afternoon. Each child had carefully considered the tragedy that had almost taken the life of Ginger.

Of all the verses read, Matthew found the ones that everyone would remember.

Psalms 69:1-2
Save me, O God; for the waters are come in unto my soul.
I sink in deep mire, where there is no standing:
I am come into deep waters, where the floods overflow me.

Acts 9:41
And he gave her his hand, and lifted her up, and when he had
called the saints and widows, presented her alive.

As Rosemary was about to polish off the last small morsel of roast beef and Luke finished off the final mouthful of mashed potatoes, Janet slipped quietly from the table and emerged about a minute later with the largest chocolate cake that anyone in the Spice family had ever seen before. It was crowned with a big, light red Christmas candle that was traditionally reserved for Christmas Eve. Everyone understood that this was something special.

As she stepped over the threshold that led into the attic, she began singing, "For he's the jolly good fellow that no one can deny." Everyone joined in the celebration and added their own individual gusto to the song. The cake was placed in front of Charlie. On cue, Ginger sprung from her seat and put her tiny arms around her big brother and kissed him a half-dozen times, and then jumped into Grandpa's lap and repeated the drama. Finally, she returned to her seat as Janet wept silent tears of joy. Charlie blew out the candle and flashed his best big brother smile. Joy overflowed the hearts of the entire Spice family that night.

Grandpa let the meal settle, along with the events of the day, and finally was invited to continue reading John Bunyan's *Pilgrim's Progress*. The story ended that evening with Christian being pulled out of the Swamp of Despond.

"Then Help said, 'Give me your hand.' So Christian gave him his hand and set him on solid ground."

As Grandfather read these last words for the evening's reading of Bunyan, John and Janet looked at each other. There were too many coincidences in this day to ignore. God had orchestrated the entire day to bring himself glory in ways that were yet to unfold. John and Janet were not the only ones to understand that this Spice symphony was being directed from above, as Grandpa closed the book and lifted his eyes upwards and mouthed a silent, "Thank You, Lord!"

That evening brought with it no terrors in the night. No bad dreams, or night sweats. All had been calmly placed in the hands of their loving Heavenly Father. There was not one member of the Spice family that night that had not come to the realization that God loved them "real good," as their dad had so often reminded them—real good indeed!

The next day was uneventful as Spice days went. The quiet pace of the day was a nice change from the high drama that had been laced with high blood pressure and throbbing adrenaline. It was to be a quiet day, but not one without importance.

After the morning Bible study and a hearty breakfast, Grandpa slipped out and made another silent trip to the Autumn Blaze Red maple tree. It was there that Grandpa poured out his heart in praise and thanksgiving to the Greatest Friend a sinner ever had. Fortified by the prayers of the morning, Grandpa James made his way back to the farmhouse and up the stairs to find his place by the side of his grandson Charlie.

Psalm 91:11
For he shall give his angels charge over thee,
to keep thee in all thy ways.

Chapter 8

The Big Change

randpa had no sooner sat down when Charlie reminded him that this was the day he was going to tell him about the "Super Blue Bicycle."

Grandpa opened up his Bible and turned to 1 Corinthians 15:50-54 and began reading to Charlie.

1 Corinthians 15:50-54

Now this I say, brethren, that flesh and blood cannot inherit the kingdom of God; neither doth corruption inherit incorruption. Behold, I shew you a mystery; We shall not all sleep, but we shall all be changed, In a moment, in the twinkling of an eye, at the last trump: for the trumpet shall sound, and the dead shall be raised incorruptible, and we shall be changed. For this corruptible must put on incorruption, and this mortal must put on immortality. So when this corruptible shall have put on incorruption, and this mortal shall have put on immortality, then shall be brought to pass the saying that is written, Death is swallowed up in victory.

Grandpa kept his Bible opened and put it in his lap.

"Have you been thinking about that Super Blue Bicycle, Charlie?"

Charlie nodded, "I have been wondering how it is different from my old blue bicycle?"

"Tell me about your old blue bicycle, Charlie."

Charlie looked down at his crippled legs covered by a blanket. "It's broken and it never worked right."

"Two flat tires, Charlie?" Grandpa replied.

"Yep, two flat tires with missing spokes and no pedals," said Charlie.

Charlie paused for a minute and then continued, "Dad says I will get a new body that works perfect when Jesus comes to get us and take us to Heaven."

"That's right," said Grandpa.

"But if I am already in Heaven with my spirit body, do I still get a new body?" Charlie asked.

"These are all good questions, Charlie. Let me tell you how it works. When you die and lay down the old broken down blue bicycle, your Spirit man goes to be with Jesus. And then one day while you're in Heaven, you might be walking down one of the streets in Heaven with one or two of your friends, and you will hear the voice of Jesus say 'Charlie, follow me!'"

Charlie interrupted, "What about my friends?"

Grandpa chuckled, "Your friends will hear their names called also and so will tens of thousands of saints in Heaven that have all been waiting to get their new bodies."

Charlie smiled as he imagined himself walking in Heaven.

"Now, Charlie, here is where it really gets interesting. As you're traveling with Jesus, you start seeing the earth come into focus as you get closer and closer, and then just before you land on earth, Jesus stops in midair."

"Is this where the Christians on earth are changed into their new bodies and fly up to meet Jesus?" asked Charlie.

"No," said Grandpa, "this is where you and all your tens of thousands of new friends fly down like an eagle ready to pounce on a rabbit. But instead of a rabbit, it is your new body that comes out of the grave and shakes hands with your spirit man, and before you can blink, your new body and your spirit man become one brand new Charlie Spice, just like it says in 1 Thessalonians 4:13-16, verses 13 through 16.

Would you like me to read what the Bible says about that?

"Yes," said Charlie, "I would."

Grandpa picked up his Bible and began reading.

1 Thessalonians 4:13-16

But I would not have you to be ignorant, brethren, concerning them which are asleep, that ye sorrow not, even as others which have no hope. For if we believe that Jesus died and rose again, even so them also which sleep in Jesus will God bring with him. For this we say unto you by the word of the Lord, that we which are alive and remain unto the coming of the Lord shall not prevent them which are asleep. For the Lord himself shall descend from Heaven with a shout, with the voice of the archangel, and with the trump of God: and the dead in Christ shall rise first:

Grandpa waited a few minutes for Charlie to take it all in and then asked, "And then do you know what happens Charlie?"

"Not exactly," said Charlie, who was still absorbing all this astounding information.

Grandpa began thumbing through his Bible and finally found the passage he was looking for. "Let me read you a story from the Gospel of Luke."

Luke 17:11-18

And it came to pass, as he went to Jerusalem, that he passed through the midst of Samaria and Galilee. And as he entered into a certain village, there met him ten men that were lepers, which stood afar off: And they lifted up their voices, and said, Jesus, Master, have mercy on us. And when he saw them, he said unto them, Go shew yourselves unto the priests. And it came to pass, that, as they went, they were cleansed. And one of them, when he saw that he was healed, turned back, and with a loud voice glorified God, And fell down on his face at his feet, giving him thanks: and he was a Samaritan. And Jesus answering said, Were there not ten cleansed? but where are the nine? There are not found that returned to give glory to God, save this stranger.

Charlie listened to the story but couldn't figure out what Grandpa was trying to tell him.

"So Charlie let me ask you a question. How many lepers were healed by Jesus?"

"Ten," Charlie replied.

"And how many returned to thank Jesus for what he had done for them?"

"Only one," said Charlie.

"Pretty sad, don't you think?" asked Grandpa. Charlie shook his head in agreement.

"So now that Jesus has given you a new body, what is the first thing you're going to do?"

Charlie instantly got the point. "Oh! I get it. I am going to fly back up to where Jesus is and thank him over and over again," said Charlie imagining the scene in his mind.

"That's right, and do you think you will have any company?" Grandpa asked.

"I think everyone who got a new body is going to fly back up to thank Jesus," said Charlie.

"Every last one of them, including you and me," said Grandpa.

Charlie was taken back.

"Are you going to be there too, Grandpa?" Charlie hadn't thought of that.

"Well, unless Jesus comes and takes me away to be with him before I die."

Charlie smiled with delight.

"Now, Charlie, what do you think happens next?"

"We all fly with Jesus back to Heaven with our new bodies," Charlie announced.

Grandpa again opened his Bible to the book of First Thessalonians, Chapter four and began reading to Charlie.

1 Thessalonians 4:14-18

For if we believe that Jesus died and rose again, even so them also which sleep in Jesus will God bring with him. For this we say unto you by the word of the Lord, that we which are alive and remain unto the coming of the Lord shall not prevent them which are asleep. For the Lord himself shall descend from Heaven with a shout, with the voice of the archangel, and with the trump of God: and the dead in Christ shall rise first: Then we which are alive and remain shall be caught up together with them in the clouds, to meet the Lord in the air: and so shall we ever be with the Lord. Wherefore comfort one another with these words.

"Don't you think you should wait until everyone gets their new blue super bicycle?" asked Grandpa.

Charlie smiled, "So next, Mom and Dad and all the rest of the family get changed and fly up to meet Jesus."

Grandpa paused and smiled. "That could happen, or maybe they will have already received their new bodies along with you and me." Charlie hadn't considered that possibility, and it shocked him at first, but then it gave him some comfort.

"So Mom and Dad might be in Heaven with me in Spirit bodies before we go and get our new bodies?"

"It is possible," said Grandpa, "but then again, Jesus could come at any time; He could come right now, or tomorrow, or next week, or in a hundred years. The only thing I know for sure is that one day He is coming because He promised He would, and He never breaks His promises."

Just then, Grandpa and Charlie heard some loud clatter coming from the front porch. Charlie looked out the window and saw Luke with a fishing pole resting over his right shoulder. He was waving up to Charlie, who waved back. Grandpa looked at his watch, "Talk about keeping promises, I have to keep the promise I made with Mark and Luke to show them my favorite fishing spot on the banks of the Yadkin River."

Before he left, Grandpa wrote three passages down on a piece of paper and handed it to Charlie.

"Charlie I want you to read these passage over a couple of times. Tomorrow I want you to tell me about the Super Blue Bicycle and these verses will give you some clues."

"Thanks, Grandpa," said Charlie, as he eagerly took the paper and immediately began looking up the references.

1 Thessalonians 4:16-18

For the Lord himself shall descend from heaven with a shout, with the voice of the archangel, and with the trump of God: and the dead in Christ shall rise first: Then we which are alive and remain shall be caught up together with them in the clouds, to meet the Lord in the air: and so shall we ever be with the Lord. Wherefore comfort one another with these words.

Chapter 9

Fishing on the Yadkin River

I t had been sixty years since Grandpa had done any fishing on the famous Yadkin River. Dad had told Mark and Luke about his dad's fishing exploits. John had exaggerated the stories, and with each telling, the fish got bigger and the adventure more exciting. Like riding a bicycle, fishing the Yadkin River was something you just never forget how to do.

"Every great fishing trip starts with a bucket of fine, moist compost and plenty of worms and grubs," said Grandpa as he handed Mark a shovel. The boys troweled through the edge of the garden looking for earthworms, and within fifteen minutes had enough to last everyone the entire day. Matthew decided at the last minute to join in on the earthworm hunt and was easily persuaded to come along on the fishing expedition.

Mom came out the kitchen door carrying four sack lunches and two canteens full of spring water. The troops were ready to make their assault on the unsuspecting whoppers that lurked in the Yadkin River, just waiting to be hauled up as trophies by the Spice boys, who couldn't imagine anything going wrong with their plans.

Grandpa wet his finger and lifted it up to the wind. "Perfect day for fishing," he said. It was overcast with a slight drizzle and a gentle breeze. Fishing was good all year long in the Yadkin River, but if you were fishing for dinner instead of just the sport of it, you needed cold water and lots of clouds in the sky. These are exactly the conditions you would find at the Yadkin River in late autumn, just before winter. All the conditions were ripe for a great fishing expedition.

With buckets and poles and a box full of lures, hooks, and extra line, the three boys and an old man headed west toward a special spot that Grandpa had kept a secret since childhood.

Grandpa was a skilled fly fisherman, but decided that trying to teach three boys how to fly fish was something better suited for the pond and not an outdoor adventure bursting with expectations of a bountiful fish fry.

The conversation on the two-hour hike to the fishing spot was lively and hopeful as all fishing trips are in the beginning. *It was a good sign*, thought Grandpa.

As the boys approached the highly anticipated, special fishing spot, Grandpa began whispering to the boys and taking exaggerated soft steps toward the rock outcropping that bordered the fishing spot.

"Why are we whispering?" Luke asked.

"We don't want to scare the fish off." Grandpa said. "Now let's all head for that spot behind the rock and out of sight of the river."

Grandpa motioned as they all silently crept behind the rock and sat down. "Fish can hear the vibration of your footsteps," Grandpa explained. "If they think you're a bear or an otter, they will hide in the rocks. Now," said Grandpa in a whisper, "this is where you come to untangle your lines. And don't make any unnecessary noise while you're fishing; use hand, signals if you want to communicate. If you wave your hands then I will know it means you need help, and I will be along as soon as I can. One more thing," said Grandpa, "stay at least fifteen feet apart from one another, and try not to get your lines tangled."

The Spice boys had done a lot of fishing, but felt like they were learning things they never imagined. They had never considered that fish knew a thing or two about not getting caught by overzealous young anglers. Grandpa was already making a big impression before they had even gotten their lines wet.

"Now, boys, I want you to follow me." The boys followed as Grandpa backtracked, keeping about fifty feet away from the river's edge, and marched the boys a couple hundred yards down river. "OK," he said, "this is a good spot."

"For fishing?" Luke asked.

"No," said Grandpa, "this is a good spot to let all your lines drift out in the water to get wet, and then reel it back in."

Grandpa could see the boys were confused. "Boys we need to get the lines wet and do a couple casts. Dry line gets tangled easy, and so we need to carefully let the fishing line out and let it get wet—then wind it back in a couple times so everything works smoothly. We're doing this down river so we don't scare off all those fish in my fishing spot that are just waiting

for you to catch them." With all the lines tested and the bugs worked out, everyone was ready to find the juiciest night crawler and catch their first fish.

"One more thing, boys," said Grandpa, "fish are fishers also, and they like to catch their dinner by hiding in places where the water is not running fast—like next to a log, so they don't wear themselves out trying to swim against the current. They wait for something that looks good to eat to pass by and then they dart out and swallow it. So look for spots where you can let your bait drift by them." The boys had no idea there were so many tricks to fishing, and were taking it all in like little sponges.

The part of fishing that involved water was about to begin.

With a splash, Matthew's line was the first in the water. Grandpa came alongside and gave him a few pointers and then moved down the line to Mark. By the time he got to Luke, Matthew had caught his first fish, and it was a big one. The way it was trailing through the water and fighting, Grandpa immediately knew that Matthew had caught himself a large bigmouth bass. The fight for survival went on for about five minutes and finally, Matthew pulled his prize to shore. It was a female about two feet long and weighing well over eight pounds. Grandpa helped Matthew take the hook out of the fish's mouth and held it up for Mark and Luke to see.

"Matthew, we need to put this one back in the water," said Grandpa. "Why?" asked Matthew.

"Two reasons," said Grandpa. "The first reason is that this is a female about to lay her eggs; the second reason is that we are fishing for dinner, and big-mouth bass taste like mustard on mud." Matthew watched with interest as Grandpa showed him how to release a fish back into the river.

The next one to catch a fish was Luke. Grandpa came along side and helped Luke untangle his line and unhook the 12-inch small-mouth bass. Grandpa showed Luke how to put the stringer through the fish's mouth and out the gills. He found a good strong straight stick and shoved it into the soft wet riverbank and tied it off. The small-mouth was then put in the water where he would stay fresh and alive until they were ready to return home.

Just then, Grandpa heard a squirrel making a racket, along with a couple of orange crowned northern cardinals. Grandpa immediately recognized the signs—an intruder was nearby. He remained still and watched as a black bear stood up on its hind legs. He could see a white star on its chest. Grandpa nudged Luke, who was busy baiting his hook for his next conquest, "look where I am pointing." Luke looked and then grabbed Grandpa's arm with a tinge of fear. "Nothing to worry about Luke, we have invaded his fishing spot and he is just checking to make sure we don't stay too long." With that, the elusive and very shy black bear lumbered off and out of sight.

Matthew no sooner had his line in the water when he caught another fish. This time it was a sunfish, a close relative to the bass, but much smaller and not much of a fighter. Matthew pulled it in and carefully took the hook out of its mouth. "Can I keep this one Grandpa?"

"Well," said Grandpa, "do you know what kind of fish this is?"

"No sir," said Matthew. "You have caught yourself a beautiful sunfish—beautiful to look at and just awful to eat."

"Mustard on mud?" Matthew asked.

"More like mush weed with small bones," said Grandpa.

Matthew carefully reintroduced the sunfish to the river just like Grandpa had taught him. "Good lad," said Grandpa.

There was a quiet spell and then the sun came out for about a half an hour, and warming up the top of the water. "Fishing is about to get real good," encouraged Grandpa. Sure enough, within the next half an hour they had caught a dozen fish. Five were "keepers."

Grandpa figured they were going to need to come home with at least 20 fish to feed the whole Spice family, so decided he had better get busy and catch some dinner.

With the boys all within earshot, Grandpa found a small tributary and hiked up the steam for about a quarter of a mile until he found the perfect spot. These streams were loaded with trout, and within a half an hour he had a stringer with six rainbows, two brooks, and one brown trout.

When he returned, he found that Matthew had caught two nice sized, small-mouth bass. Luke had caught three more small-mouth bass and a sunfish that was too far gone to put back in the river, so they left it on a rock as a peace offering for the bear.

Mark was the quietest of all the Spice children. *A thinker,* Grandpa observed. Without alerting anyone to his success, he had managed to catch six, very nice, small-mouth bass and one medium sized big-mouth bass.

Grandpa gave the boys the wave signal and they all retreated to behind the big rock where they had a late lunch. As soon as Matthew had finished his sandwich, Grandpa said, "You boys keep fishing, Matthew and I are going to take a quick hike up river."

Grandpa led the way and within about fifteen minutes had located a perfect spot on one of the tributaries of the Yadkin. A perfect place for trout fishing. With little instruction, and within about five minutes, Matthew had hooked a very large rainbow trout. It gave Matthew a good fight before it was finally pulled up on the sandy shore of the small brook that fed into the Yadkin River. "Do we keep this one Grandpa?" asked Matthew. Grandpa"You just caught the most delicious fresh water fish in the entire state of North Carolina."

"It's a keeper?" asked Matthew. "It will make a meal fit for a king," answered Grandpa.

The fishing expedition was a resounding success, and would be remembered for years into the future. Everyone gathered around to admire the catch of the day. It was going to be a fish feast that would not be forgotten for a long time. Everyone relished the fish stories. The bear that Grandpa pointed out to Luke just before it retreated to the brush, had grown by feet and hundreds of pounds—proving to Grandpa that a young boy's mind is filled with measuring devices unknown to most grown-ups.

The four worn out fisherman arrived back home just before dusk. The night had turned strangely warm, and Janet and Anna had decided that it would be a great night for eating outside. All the arrangements had been made. The cook fire was blazing, and a good four inches of charcoal supported a half-dozen pine logs. The fish were seasoned and put in the well-buttered pans to be fried up to perfection. Charlie was carefully carried to a lounge chair that had been especially prepared for him, and was bundled up in blankets.

The fish were cooked with care by Anna and Janet, and devoured by each member of the Spice family with noises that were "cook's music" mouth-watering testimonials to the finest cuisine in Elkin, North Carolina. Matthew put two pan-fried fish on his plate, a small-mouth bass, and the rainbow trout he had caught with Grandpa in the brook above the Yadkin

River. It was then that he decided to become a fly fisherman on the trail of winding brooks, with irregular bottoms, stumps and drops where the small eddies secreted the most delicious fish to ever grace a hot iron pan. Matthew had discovered the many wonders of the rainbow trout.

Mark 1:17
And Jesus said unto them, Come ye after me,
and I will make you to become fishers of men.

Chapter 10

Marshmallows and Memories

T he nights grew longer as autumn raced toward an early winter. The moon that night was an orange sliver sweeping through the Heavens like a sickle. The black nights spread over the Spice farm that was tucked just inside the shadow of the Blue Ridge Mountains, far away from the artificial lights of civilization. Like diamonds on black velvet, they glistened and pulsed with the unrelenting message that God was the fashioner of works that were wondrous to behold.

The fire crackled as the Spice children poked it to find the perfect spot to roast the marshmallows.

There were no marshmallow plants in North Carolina, or at least none that Janet knew about. What there was in North Carolina was plenty of eggs and gelatin. Janet had found an old recipe under the chapter simply titled "Confections" in the cookbook that had been given to her by her aunt. She had learned to make marshmallows, a talent that was appreciated by each and every one in the Spice family. Janet had improved the recipe by adding a little honey.

Matthew kept the marshmallows he had carefully skewed on the end of his hardwood stick well away from the flames. The heat from the fire caramelized the exterior of the marshmallow and just when the molten interior was about to drop off the stick he would pop them in his mouth and hold them between his teeth so it would not burn his tongue. Then, when the temperature of the molten candy marvel had reached just the right temperature, he would curl it into his mouth with his tongue and slowly chew the savory treat. The other Spice children had not learned this trick and were constantly blowing out the flaming marshmallows, and then letting them cool before devouring them.

Cinnamon had finished off her last marshmallow and had found her favorite spot where she "generaled" the comet counting. "There is one!" she would yell. "That's eight so far tonight." John Jr. and Ginger tried to join the club but were rebuffed by Cinnamon.

Determined to make a contribution to something as obviously vital as counting falling stars, Ginger and John Jr. set up their own visual command center right next to Cinnamon and began calling out numbers that were not sequential, or related to falling stars—except in their over-aerated imagination. And to make the matter intolerable, the numbers they so robustly announced were always greater than Cinnamon's.

This created a situation that Cinnamon was sure needed immediate arbitration from Mom, who—with the wisdom of Solomon—moved John Jr. and Ginger to the other side of the yard, where they could keep track of half the activity in the Heavens while Cinnamon retained her exclusive franchise to the other half.

Grandpa James and Anna observed this mini-drama without interfering and with obvious delight. It was just then that Scruffy came and sat at the feet of the two Grandparents. Grandpa reached down and scratched her ears. From here, Scruffy had the best view of all her charges.

Scruffy was not your run of the mill mutt. She was a mutt with a proud and distinguished historical past. Scruffy was the eighth generation Scruffy, preceded by seven other female Scruffys. The story gets a little confusing, and admittedly, holes in the genealogy are filled with unsubstantiated facts, but the gist of it goes like this.

When Robert Spice went off with his brothers to join the Confederate Army, he was followed by his dog Scruffy, a female Irish wolfhound. It was against regulations for soldiers to have a mascot or a pet, but it so raised the morale of the soldiers that the rule was rarely enforced.

Scruffy had lived through the entire Civil War without ever missing a meal or being injured. The same could not be said for her master Robert, by the time the war was over, he had carved Union lead out of his leg and forearm, broken his shoulder, and suffered a wound that left the butt end shape of a Colt Revolving Carbine imprinted on his forehead.

When asked about the impressive scar, Robert would smile and say the butt of the Colt Carbine Rifle that was imprinted on his forehead was a sign of God's care and favor. He would then tell the tale of the rifle pointed at his head that would not fire. "Instead of a lead 'Minie' between my eyes, I now proudly bear the marks of divine providence with little pain and a grateful heart." Robert Spice was a poet, and his Civil War ballads never became very popular as everyone was determined to forget the tragedy.

The gruesome war that haunted the memories of at least two generations was over, and Robert and Scruffy were on their way back home to the peaceful lush valleys that gently graced and overflowed the Blue Ridge Mountains.

On his long march home, Robert and Scruffy passed through Greensborough in Guilford County where they spent a couple nights licking their wounds and collecting rations for the long walk home.

It was behind the newspaper offices of the Greensboro Patriot that Scruffy had a brief romance with a big black Labrador. Robert had gone into the newspaper office with a copy of a letter he had written to the Colt Manufacturing Company thanking them for designing a rifle that was so unreliable. The paper published the letter, and exactly nine weeks later—in the middle of July, in the year 1865—the Scruffy dynasty began.

Since that famous date, the head of the Spice family, whoever wore that mantle, was responsible for picking out the best female "Scruffy" to carry on the family tradition. This was not a job that was taken lightly, as everyone of voting age in the Spice family considered themselves a "dog-breeding expert."

As fate would have it, the only two male dogs within sniffing distance of the 500-acre Spice Farm was a purebred Labrador and a Bull Terrier. There was no evidence of the Bull Terrier in Scruffy's bloodline. Each succeeding generation looked less and less like a Wolfhound and more and more like a Labrador. The history of Scruffy became a matter of fact that was passed along to each succeeding generation of Spices.

The last big "Scruffy" decision was made by Grandpa Spice, who picked out the best female in the litter. The great, great, grand-daughter of that decision now lay happily at his feet.

John was on the mission field in India when someone from the Spice family did the litter picking duties that produced the current Scruffy, and no one knew exactly who it was.

What everyone in the Spice family knew for sure was that their Scruffy had the Civil War hero's bloodline coursing through her veins. The only remnant of the original Scruffy were the pronounced Wolfhound ears.

Scruffy had taken her place as the head of the canine dynasty that had ruled the Spice Farm for three generations.

The Civil War Hero legend conferred with lavish praise on the original Scruffy was invented out of whole cloth. As Grandpa would say, "In matters of family tradition, the best thing to do is to gild the edges." His son John had done his best to do exactly that. Scruffy was not just a dog, she was a living legend.

Scruffy was a great watchdog, and no man or beast entered the Spice Farm without its notice and heralding bark. Scruffy would first raise the hackles on her neck and stiffen up as she stood completely still. After she identified the intruder, she would bark persistently until she was told to sit down and be quiet, which she obediently did. She was a great family dog that was loyal and trustworthy. She could also be pretty intimidating if you found yourself between her and her adopted family.

And this fact became the gristle of what turned out to be a perplexing mystery.

Psalms 119:104-105

Through thy precepts I get understanding: therefore I hate every false way. Thy word is a lamp unto my feet, and a light unto my path.

Chapter 11

Beatles with Lanterns and the Stranger

H ow had the stranger arrived on the property without a sentry's alarm from Scruffy? Even when the stranger presented himself to shake Grandpa's hand, Scruffy made no protest. She just sat there as quiet and contented as could be.

It was a strange clue that would be woven into the story of the curious event that was about to take place that beautiful autumn night on the Spice Farm.

The stranger was not menacing in the least. In fact, you might say he was strangely serene.

Both Grandpa James and his son John had lived on the mean, unforgiving streets of Bombay where misjudging someone could cost you your life. A place where demon possession and the dark evil passions of man were perpetually on display.

Grandpa had a gift for sizing people up from a long distance away. It was mostly a spiritual gift, mixed with the experiences of life, that had placed James Spice on the highway crowded by men on their way to the gates of hell.

Grandpa immediately stood up and took the measure of the man while shaking his hand and welcoming him with warmth—the family trademark.

As he rose to his feet, Grandpa noticed the next thing that was out of place. Not only was Scruffy, the famous family watchdog, not watching; there was a strange phenomenon that had apparently followed in the wake of the mysterious stranger.

All the Spice children were immediately enthralled with the cloud of "fireflies" that had suddenly began casting a green luminous light in a synchronous symphony. Grandpa noted later that he had never witnessed anything like it before.

The "luminous beetle," as Grandpa like to call them, were a perennial favorite on the Spice Farm, usually showing up in late June and disappearing as the temperature fell in early August. It was now early October, and "Fireflies" were strangely out of place.

To make matters more perplexing, these particular fireflies were not the ones that regularly visited the farm. These fireflies were blinking in harmony with one another and they were all overhead. The "luminous beetles" that were common in the summer all stayed near the ground and hardly ever out of reach.

Grandpa James, Grandma Anna, Janet and John gathered around the stranger to greet him and to try and figure out what this was all about. They offered him dinner, which he gladly accepted, although, they noticed after he had gone that the plate he had received, with such obvious pleasure, was untouched—except for the warm slice of Janet's special Ginger Bread.

"My name is James Spice," Grandpa said, "and what is your name?"

"My name is Ariel," he replied. "And who do we have over here?" he asked as he walked over to greet Charlie.

"That is my son Charlie," said John, who was not going to let this man out of his sight until he figured out why he was on the Spice Farm after sun down in the middle of nowhere.

"Hello Charlie," the man greeted. "My name is Ariel, and I am happy to meet you." Charlie smiled.

The number of fireflies had multiplied, and the green light cast a glow over the farm. The Spice children were mesmerized. They had never seen anything like it and were not likely to ever see anything like it again.

The man had a charm and grace about him that was disarming. He obviously meant no harm, but why was he here? This is the question that all the adult Spices were asking themselves as they followed him over to the place where he had planted himself, right next to their son Charlie.

Charlie was distracted by the fireflies, but after a few words of conversation, he became strangely fixated on the stranger. He asked a lot of questions and seemed genuinely interested in Charlie's responses. They laughed together. James and John listened intently but could not make out a word that was spoken between them.

John had asked the man what he was doing in the area, and the man simply replied that he was a surveyor. John soon gave up asking questions, as all the answers were vague and strangely off. Neither James nor John sensed any dishonesty in the man, and his responses were all clearly meant to be truthful, yet they revealed nothing that the two men considered "normal."

After about a half an hour, the man greeted James and John and said that he needed to go. He turned around and said to Charlie, "I will back in these parts about this time next year, Charlie; I will come back and visit you then." Charlie smiled. "And when I come next time, Charlie, I will bring some of my surveying tools for you to look at." Charlie was delighted.

The man then turned to Grandpa James and said something he would never forget. "James," he said, "your request has been granted." With those simple words, he walked under the cloud of fireflies. He took a minute and looked at all the Spice children as they danced around the fireflies, jumping up in the air to try and catch them with jars they had retrieved from the kitchen. He then waved at John and Janet. Then, in an instant, the light from the fireflies disappeared, and the mysterious stranger was nowhere in sight.

John and Janet rushed into the void of darkness that appeared after the green lights from a myriad of "glowing beetles" had disappeared, and led all their children to the front porch where they were kissed and sent to bed.

No one said a word as Grandpa bundled up Charlie and followed John up to the attic where Charlie was tucked into bed for the night. Charlie, who had been noticeably worsening in the past couple of weeks, was strangely revived. Something had happened, but no one yet had figured out exactly what it was.

Something had happened—something strange... and perhaps wondrous.

After the children were all put to bed, the four adults immediately gathered together in the living room where John lit a cozy fire that signaled it was going to be a long evening.

"What just happened?" Janet insistently asked. No one said a word. "Who was that man?" she asked again. No one said a word.

Finally, Grandpa James turned to Janet and said, "My dear daughter, I would like to tell you a story that may shed some light on what you just witnessed this evening."

Grandpa began his story as he grabbed Anna's hand with both of his and squeezed it affectionately.

"Your Mom and I arrived in the port city of Bombay in the year 1883. Our Christian brothers and sisters had given us enough money for the Schooner passage, with some left over to rent a small apartment and buy enough food to last the three of us a month. They then pledged to send

us a small remittance each month, which we were to use to support ourselves while we got settled. Then, I was to find a part time job and begin establishing a mission."

John interrupted, "Dad, I don't remember ever hearing this story."

"Here it is Son," he replied, "you lived it." John perked up trying to retrieve his memories as a four-year-old in Bombay India, without much success.

"Anyway," Grandpa continued, "we had been in Bombay for over six weeks, and I had not found a job. We checked the harbormaster's post office every day to see if the promised funds had arrived. Now, not to labor the point, but we were all three of us experiencing that gnawing that comes from days of not eating. Mom had saved out one big last meal, and we decided to eat it that night.

"Mom cooked it all up, and although it was plain fixings, it seemed like a banquet to us. We had just finished our prayers when there was a knock on our door. Before a morsel was eaten, I rose and answered the door.

"The man who greeted me at the door was dressed in rags and his face was dirty. 'Sir,' he said, 'I am very hungry and was hoping you could give me a meal,' he pleaded. Mom, over-hearing the conversation, said, 'James, please invite the stranger in.' 'Please come in sir,' I said, as I opened the door and showed the stranger to the small dining room table. Anna had scooped the food off her plate, onto my plate and placed it before the stranger.

"The stranger sat down and seemed to beam as he devoured every last morsel that had been set before him. He then rose from the table, and as I escorted him out the door he turned to me and said, 'Thank you, James.' I was shocked, as I had not given the stranger my name, and yet he seemed to know me.

"As I walked back into the house, my Anna was weeping. 'It will be alright, Anna,' I said, 'the Lord will provide for our needs.

"Anna rushed to my arms and kissed my neck and said, 'James, the Lord has already provided.' I looked up and there on the table were seven gold coins sitting where the stranger sat.

"I went to the table and picked up the seven coins and jangled them in my hand. 'Anna,' I said in a subdued voice, trying to curb my enthusiasm, there is enough money here to pay the rent and buy all the provisions we need for two years, with money left over.

"We both stood there speechless with tears streaming down our faces. By the next morning, the pantry would be overflowing with food."

Anna moved close to James and put her head on his shoulder. "That was the first and last time we ever worried about anything except the souls of men," James said.

"That's right," said Anna, "I will never forget that day for as long as I live."

Janet was stunned. "So you're saying that man was, what?"

Anna took Janet's hand and said, "An angel perhaps."

"What did he say his name was?" interrupted John.

Anna answered, "He didn't." John apologized, "Sorry, Mom, I meant the name of this evening's stranger."

James piped up. "He said his name was Ariel,"

Then added, "I think that is a Hebrew name."

John went to the bookshelf that was in the corner of the living room and started scanning though his books. "Where is that book?" he said as he rustled through the hundreds of books he had collected in the past twenty years.

"Found it," John said as he returned to his chair next to the fireplace. John opened the book titled *10,000 Hebrew Name Origins and Meanings* by Rabbi Jonathan Kleppar. John thumbed through the pages. "Found it... Ariel," he said, "looks like it is the name of an angel that is connected with health and healing, and it also means the Lion of God."

By this time, Janet was beside herself. Tears streamed down her face as she turned the idea over and over in her mind. Did she dare to dream that a

Heavenly messenger had touched her beloved son Charlie?

The four exhausted Spice's got on their knees and one by one poured out their hearts with praise and petitions, and then went to bed.

It was early in the morning before Janet finally fell asleep. As the room began to brighten with the rays of the morning sun, she was up and on a mission. She immediately scurried to the kitchen and made a cup of hot chocolate, Charlie's favorite. Then, she was up the stairs with her special treat carefully cradled between both hands.

"Charlie, Charlie," whispered Janet as she gently shook her son out of his sleep.

"Mom?" replied Charlie as he opened his eyes and began to rub them. "Is something the matter?" asked Charlie.

Janet helped Charlie sit up and arranged the pillows behind his back. "I brought you a cup of hot chocolate," she beamed.

Just then, John, who was a light sleeper, slipped into the attic and went to the side of his son and wife.

"Charlie," said Dad, "we want to ask you a few questions." Charlie was puzzled but nodded his head.

The first question did not seem strange to Charlie, although it should have. "Charlie," asked Dad, "how do you feel?"

Charlie looked at his dad and said, "I was thinking about the same thing."

"What do you mean?" said Dad.

"Well," continued Charlie, "last night, just after that man came to visit..." "Ariel?" interrupted Dad.

"Yes," nodded Charlie, "he put his hand on my forehead and I felt a tingling." "Tell us about it," said Janet.

Charlie thought for a minute and said, "It was a warm tingle that started at my head and went down to my stomach."

Janet pulled the cover sideways off Charlie's legs, half hoping to see a miracle. She was disappointed. Charlie's legs were still atrophied and lifeless, but the rest of him seemed strangely revived.

The two parents did their best to pry every scrap of information they could out of Charlie, who now was beginning to wonder what was going on.

John and Janet told Charlie to try and get some more sleep, as they slowly and quietly went down the stairs and into the kitchen. "What do you think John?" asked Janet.

"I think that whatever happened it seems to have lifted Charlie's spirits and perhaps his body."

Janet thought for a minute, and replied "I think we are all letting our imaginations run a little too wild. Perhaps the night air lifted Charlie's spirits and the stranger was just that: a surveyor who had lost his way and looking for a free meal." John smiled and said nothing.

Just then, Rosemary came into the kitchen with a big smile on her face. "Dad, that was quite a night wasn't it?"

"That it was," said Dad. "By the way, what did you think of that stranger?" he asked, clearly looking for another perspective besides the one settled on by his wife, Janet.

"You mean strangers don't you Dad?" Janet perked up, "You mean there was more than one?" she asked intently.

"There were thousands and thousands of them, all glowing and blinking," Rosemary said, as she twirled around the kitchen floor and jumped in the air to catch the illusive fireflies. "You know Grandpa calls them 'beetles with lanterns,'" she concluded.

John laughed. "Rosemary, we are talking about the man that came to visit us about the same time the beetle lamps showed up."

Rosemary, while still twirling and jumping said, "What man?"

Janet rushed into the conversation. "Stop fooling around, Rosemary; your Dad asked you a direct question." Rosemary was stunned and stopped her dance of the fireflies and stood motionless in the middle of the kitchen— miffed and a little deflated. "Honest Mom, I didn't see any man."

Just then, Matthew walked into the kitchen. He was immediately cornered by his mom and told to think back carefully to the previous night and described the man that came to visit. Matthew looked confused and perplexed. "Mom are we talking about last night with the fish fry and the fireflies?"

"That's right," Mom said, impatiently waiting for an answer.

Matthew replied carefully, "Mom, I saw the fireflies; I saw you bring an extra plate of food outside; I saw you all huddle around Charlie, but I never saw a stranger."

The next fifteen minutes were spent interrogating every child that made their way into the kitchen. Each reported their perspective on the night of the fireflies, but none of them saw the stranger.

Grandpa James and Grandma Anna entered the kitchen to find everyone in an uproar. Janet was obviously struggling to make sense of what had happened the previous evening, perplexed that the evidence pointed in the direction of a Heavenly visitor.

Finally, John took his obviously shaken wife in his arms and asked, "What is troubling you Janet?"

"If it was an angel, why didn't he heal Charlie?" she whispered just loud enough for Grandpa James, who had come to her side, to hear.

Grandpa replied, "Janet, angels are God's messengers."

Janet wiped her eyes, looked at John and asked. "What was the message?"

John shrugged his shoulders, "I have no idea." Janet moaned and quietly slipped out of the kitchen and into her room where she had a good, long cry.

"Leave her be," advised Grandpa, "she needs some time to sort out her expectations about God."

John nodded, "You're right Dad," John said as he tried to normalize the situation, sending each child to do their morning chores.

John and Janet had no idea why the visitor had come, but there was one person that did. Grandpa James had it all figured out before he had gone to bed at just before midnight the previous evening... or at least he thought he did.

Psalm 91:11
For he shall give his angels charge over thee,
to keep thee in all thy ways.

Chapter 12

The Gift of Time

T he messenger had delivered an answer to the prayer James had prayed under the *red blazing* maple tree the previous day. He had just one question he needed to ask Charlie before he made up his mind with absolute certainty. He was determined to ask the question as soon as he could. So as soon as it was convenient, Grandpa walked out of the kitchen and up the stairs to see Charlie.

"Namastē," said Charlie with a big grin as soon as Grandpa's face appeared above the threshold of the attic stairs.

"Namastē," replied Grandpa delighted, by the greeting.

Grandpa slipped beside Charlie. "Hey Grandpa, I think I figured out the Super Blue Bicycle."

"Have you now?" said Grandpa. "I can't wait to hear about all your new discoveries. But before we talk about the Super Blue Bicycle, I want to ask you a question."

"Sure," said Charlie.

The previous evening Ariel and Charlie had a conversation that lasted about fifteen minutes. James was close enough to hear the conversation, but he could not make it out. James could speak three languages—English, Hindi and German—but for the life of him, he could not make out the language that passed between Charlie and Ariel the previous evening.

And it was not just Ariel that was speaking an "alien" language, Charlie was speaking it also.

"Charlie, do you remember the conversation you had with Ariel the other night?"

"Oh yes," said Charlie.

"Can you tell me what it was about?"

Charlie smiled, "Grandpa, Ariel doesn't live in North Carolina."

"Where does he live then?" asked Grandpa.

"I am not sure, but he was telling me about it and it really sounded wonderful."

"Did you ask him the name of the place?" asked Grandpa.

"Yes, and he told me that next time he came to visit me he would show me exactly where it was. I think he is going to bring a map."

Grandpa paused and thought about the next question he was going to ask. "Charlie, what else did he tell you?"

Charlie paused to collect his thoughts, "He said that I should keep reading the Bible and that I should not become discouraged."

"Did he say anything else?"

"Well he did say something strange, Grandpa, that I wanted to ask you about."

"What was that?"

"He said that he had visited you in India once—a long time ago. He told me that I was supposed to mention it to you and then you would remember."

Grandpa was stunned and silent.

"Do you remember him Grandpa?"

"Charlie, I remember him like it was yesterday," said Grandpa with a grin.

"He said you would remember. Was he a friend of yours?" asked Charlie.

"A better friend than I ever imagined," said Grandpa.

"We will all be friends," said Charlie.

"Yes, we will," said Grandpa, "precious, wonderful friends!" said Grandpa.

"Can we talk about the Super Blue Bicycle now?"

Grandpa took a deep breath and patted Charlie on the shoulder. "I think this would be a wonderful time to talk about the Super Blue Bicycle," Grandpa said.

Grandpa opened his Bible and turned to the New Testament Gospel of Luke, Chapter 24. "Charlie, I want you to open up your Bible and read along with me," invited Grandpa. Charlie rustled through his Bible and found Luke 24 and followed along as Grandpa read the story out loud.

Luke 24:1-8

Now upon the first day of the week, very early in the morning, they came unto the sepulchre, bringing the spices which they had prepared, and certain others with them. And they found the stone rolled away from the sepulchre. And they entered in, and found not the body of the Lord Jesus. And it came to pass, as they were much perplexed thereabout, behold, two men stood by them in shining garments: And as they were afraid, and bowed down their faces to the earth, they said unto them, Why seek ye the living among the dead? He is not here, but is risen: remember how he spake unto you when he was yet in Galilee, Saying, The Son of man must be delivered into the hands of sinful men, and be crucified, and the third day rise again. And they remembered his words.

Grandpa stopped reading and looked at Charlie, and asked, "What have we learned so far, Charlie?"

"Jesus rose from the dead after three days," said Charlie who was very familiar with the Bible story.

"So, Charlie, what sort of body did Jesus have after he rose from the dead?"

Charlie thought for a minute and finally said "Jesus had a 'risen from the dead body.'"

"That's right, Charlie. And what do we call this kind of body?"

"I don't know, Grandpa."

Grandpa smiled. "Charlie, we call this a resurrection body."

Charlie's eyes got big. "Like the body I get when I come back to the earth and shake hands with my new body that comes out of the grave?"

"That's the one!"

Grandpa returned to reading the narrative from the Gospel of Luke.

Luke 24:9-17

And returned from the sepulchre, and told all these things unto the eleven, and to all the rest. It was Mary Magdalene and Joanna, and Mary the mother of James, and other women that were with them, which told these things unto the apostles. And their words seemed to them as idle tales, and they believed them not. Then arose Peter, and ran unto the sepulchre; and stooping down, he beheld the linen clothes laid by themselves, and departed, wondering in himself at that which was come to pass. And, behold, two of them went that same day to a village called Emmaus, which was from Jerusalem about threescore furlongs. And they talked together of all these things which had happened. And it came to pass, that, while they communed together and reasoned, Jesus himself drew near, and went with them. But their eyes were holden that they should not know him. And he said unto them, What manner of communications are these that ye have one to another, as ye walk, and are sad?

Grandpa stopped reading and asked Charlie to tell him about what he had just read. Charlie recounted the events that happened without any difficulty. Grandpa continued to read the account from the Gospel of Luke.

Luke 24:18-31

And the one of them, whose name was Cleopas, answering said unto him, Art thou only a stranger in Jerusalem, and hast not known the things which are come to pass there in these days?

And he said unto them, What things? And they said unto him, Concerning Jesus of Nazareth, which was a prophet mighty in deed and word before God and all the people: And how the chief priests and our rulers delivered him to be condemned to death, and have crucified him. But we trusted that it had been he which should have redeemed Israel: and beside all this, today is the third day since these things were done. Yea, and certain women also of our company made us astonished, which were early at the sepulchre; And when they found not his body, they came, saying, that they had also seen a vision of angels, which said that he was alive. And certain of them which were with us went to the sepulchre, and found it even so as the women had said: but him they saw not. Then he said unto them, O fools, and slow of heart to believe all that the prophets have spoken: Ought not Christ to have suffered these things, and to enter into his glory? And beginning at Moses and all the prophets, he expounded unto them in all the scriptures the things concerning himself. And they drew nigh unto the village, whither they went: and he made as though he would have gone further. But they constrained him, saying, Abide with us: for it is toward evening, and the day is far spent. And he went in to tarry with them. And it came to pass, as he sat at meat with them, he took bread, and blessed it, and brake, and gave to them.

And their eyes were opened, and they knew him;
and he vanished out of their sight.

Grandpa stopped reading. "Charlie, this is where we have to start being detectives and begin looking for clues about what the *resurrection body* is going to be like."

Charlie had been paying close attention and immediately volunteered one clue. "The resurrection body can make itself invisible." Charlie announced with some pride.

"Well, to be very precise, the resurrection body can vanish and reappear somewhere else," added Grandpa.

"Oh," said Charlie, not fully grasping the difference between disappearing and vanishing.

Charlie noodled on that for a minute, then asked, "Is my resurrection body going to be exactly like the resurrection body of Jesus?"

Grandpa replied, "That is a good question, Charlie, and the answer is *no*. Jesus is God, and no man, or angel, or any other creature can ever have a body exactly the same as God—but we will have a body that is *like* the resurrection body of Jesus."

Grandpa thought for a moment, not wanting to introduce anything confusing into the conversation.

"Charlie, did the lightening bugs show up here on the farm in late July like they usually do?"

"Yes, they did," said Charlie. "Dad took me outside, and we all watched them and collected them for hours."

Grandpa looked outside just as the sun had screened itself behind a cloud. "Charlie can you see the sun outside?"

"Dad told me never to look at the sun because it is too bright and it might blind me."

"That's right," said Grandpa, "do you see it through the clouds?"

Charlie peered out the window with his hand cupped over his eyes. "Yes, I see the sun," Charlie said.

"Charlie, the lightening bug is *like* the sun. But the glowing beetle is *not* the sun, even though they are alike in some ways. Do you understand?"

Charlie perked up. "Because Jesus is God, and we are people *he* created to be like Him, but not Him."

"Could not have said it better myself," Grandpa said as he continued to read the account from the Gospel of Luke.

Luke 24:32-37

And they said one to another, Did not our heart burn within us, while he talked with us by the way, and while he opened to us the scriptures? And they rose up the same hour, and returned to Jerusalem, and found the eleven gathered together, and them that were with them, Saying, The Lord is risen indeed, and hath appeared to Simon. And they told what things were done in the way, and how he was known of them in breaking of bread. And as they thus spake, Jesus himself stood in the midst of them, and saith unto them, Peace be unto you. But they were terrified and affrighted, and supposed that they had seen a spirit.

"Grandpa, will we be able to walk through walls?" Charlie asked.

"I am pretty sure that with your new heavenly resurrection Body you will be able to walk through walls on earth, should the need ever arise."

"What about in Heaven, can I walk through walls in Heaven?"

"Hmmm," said Grandpa, not wanting to dampen the enthusiasm that Charlie was nurturing as he considered his new Heavenly glorified body.

"Well, Charlie, I guess you will have to wait until you get to Heaven to give that a try, but I would start out with a slow walk before I took a run at any walls in Heaven." Grandpa laughed and shook his head as he considered that Heaven was full of children who were probably asking questions just as humorous as Charlie was asking down here on earth.

Grandpa continued reading Luke's account.

Luke 24:32-37

And he said unto them, Why are ye troubled?
and why do thoughts arise in your hearts?
Behold my hands and my feet, that it is I myself:
handle me, and see; for a spirit hath not flesh
and bones, as ye see me have. And when he had
thus spoken, he shewed them his hands and his feet.

"Charlie, this is the next big clue." Grandpa said.

"I am going to still have flesh and bones?" Charlie asked.

"That's right Charlie."

Charlie was having trouble understanding how this could be possible. Grandpa offered a word of encouragement, "Charlie, the flesh will be nothing at all like the flesh you have now, and the bones will never break and are nothing like the bones you have now. Let me read you what the Apostle Paul said about this in 1 Corinthians 15." Grandpa turned in his Bible and read out loud.

1 Corinthians 15:38-44

But God giveth it a body as it hath pleased him,
and to every seed his own body. All flesh is not the same flesh:
but there is one kind of flesh of men, another flesh of beasts,
another of fishes, and another of birds.
There are also celestial bodies, and bodies terrestrial:
but the glory of the celestial is one, and the glory
of the terrestrial is another. There is one glory of
the sun, and another glory of the moon, and another glory
of the stars: for one star differeth from another star in glory.
So also is the resurrection of the dead. It is sown in corruption;
it is raised in incorruption:
It is sown in dishonour; it is raised in glory:
it is sown in weakness; it is raised in power:
It is sown a natural body; it is raised a spiritual body.
There is a natural body, and there is a spiritual body.

"Charlie, the thing you need to understand is that God is going to give you the perfect body for the place he has prepared for you. It will be a body like the body of Jesus. It will be a body with flesh and bones, but nothing like the flesh and bones you now have. We don't know a lot about it now, except that we know it is a body that is created for us by Jesus, and that means it will be perfect."

Charlie was happy with the answer and ready to move on with the clues about the resurrection body.

Grandpa continued reading from the Gospel of Luke, chapter 24.

And while they yet believed not for joy, and wondered, he said unto them, Have ye here any meat? And they gave him a piece of a broiled fish, and of an honeycomb. And he took it, and did eat before them.

Grandpa stopped reading and looked at Charlie. "I really like this part, Charlie."

"Why?" asked Charlie.

"Because your Grandma Anna makes the best lemon meringue pies on two continents, and I love eating them."

Charlie was miffed. "Is Grandma going to be cooking pies in Heaven?"

Grandpa laughed. "Heaven is going to have food that will make your Grandma Anna's delicious lemon meringue pie taste like frog guts by comparison."

Charlie was shocked. Grandpa had arrested his attention and they both laughed. "In other words, Charlie, we will be eating and drinking in Heaven. And not just ordinary food like we eat down here on earth, but the food of angels."

Grandpa continued, "The resurrection body is going to be a mystery until we are clothed in it, and then we will fully understand because we will see Jesus in His *glorious* body, and we will be like Him. That is a mystery, but we can think about the few clues God has left for us to discover—in order to help us be patient while we wait for God to work out His perfect *redemptive* plan."

Grandpa leaned over and gave his grandson a kiss on the forehead as he left the room, down the stairs and down the path to the big red blazing maple tree.

Ephesians 5:15-16

See then that ye walk circumspectly, not as fools, but as wise, Redeeming the time, because the days are evil.

Chapter 13

The Bullwhip

T he Spice children were all busy doing their morning chores as Grandpa waved and headed out to the dirt road in front of the farm. Grandpa could not wait until he arrived at his favorite spot and immediately began a conversation with the Lord.

"Thank you, Lord, for answering my prayer and sending one of your ministering angels to let me know you had heard my request. Thank you for giving Charlie another year to spend here on earth with his family. And most of all Lord, thank you for giving me time to spend with my grandson."

As Grandpa James was singing and praying he felt something brush up against his leg. He looked down to see a hound dog that was anxious to make his acquaintance.

"How are you, boy?" Grandpa said reassuringly as he reached down to stroke his neck and shoulder. The dog let out a whelp. Grandpa stopped to more carefully examine the animal and discovered raised welts all over his body; the dog had been badly beaten and mistreated. He was limping badly and looked like he had not eaten in weeks.

Grandpa decided to head back home without stopping at the maple tree in order to immediately tend to the needs of this poor animal that was obviously in great distress. The dog had a brown leather collar with about four feet of rope attached. The end of the rope was frayed and wet. It did not take Grandpa long to figure out that the animal had been tied up and mistreated, but had just recently escaped and was looking for someone to give him assistance.

Just then a rider on a horse came galloping up the lane.

"You got my dog," said a strapping young lad who looked to be in his early twenties.

"Your dog?" asked James.

"That's right, *gramps*, now hand him over, or I will horse whip you right here on the spot."

The young ruffian began to pull something out from the left side of the saddle. Grandpa prayed it was not a revolver and smiled when a coiled up bullwhip appeared instead. The young man began to back the horse up in order to make room for the lashing he intended to deliver to James if the dog was not immediately turned over to his custody.

Grandpa was a peaceful man, but he was not a pacifist. He had survived hand to hand combat in the bloodiest war to ever take place on American soil, and considered it the sacred right of every man to defend himself when all other options had been explored. As far as Grandpa James was concerned, the young ruffian had run out of options, and the only one left was a life lesson the young tuff would not soon forget.

James may have been seventy years old, but he was as strong as a mule and still quick on his feet. Grandpa quickly grabbed the horse by the reins, next to the bit with his right hand, and then swung around to grab the end of the bullwhip with his left. With a mighty jerk, he unseated the young ruffian, who was determined to hold on to his whip. Rider and bullwhip were both sent tumbling to the ground.

With that, he let the horse loose, waved his hands, and shouted loudly. This sent the horse galloping off down the road.

"Now to deal with you," said James as he quickly closed the space between himself and the young man who was temporarily stunned, spewing profanities, and getting ready to stand up. Before the young man could find his footing, Grandpa James gave him a thumping that sent him back on his hands and knees, loosening his grip on the bull whip. Grandpa James grabbed the bullwhip and took three paces back.

The hound dog followed James—cowering in fear and looking for comfort. Obviously this young ruffian was the source of the poor dog's welts and gross mistreatment.

Grandpa backed up and gave the bullwhip a couple of strokes and then sent a stinging crack that snapped the end of the whip that grazed the rascal's backside. The young lad screamed in pain.

"That will give you something to remember next time you take a whip to a dog," said Grandpa. Another stroke of the whip sent the young man's cap sailing off his head. The young ruffian put his head between his knees and began crying, begging for mercy.

Grandpa knew his type and was not moved by pleas or tears made in the middle of defeat by an oversized bully that just moments before was threatening his life.

"If you are not up and chasing your horse by the time I finish counting to five, I will give you a horse whipping that will leave you scarred for life."

Anyone who was acquainted with Grandpa James knew he wouldn't follow through on the threat. The only thing that mattered to James was that the ruffian was convinced by the burning sensation on his posterior that this particular old man meant business.

The young rascal got up and tottered to get his balance as he uttered more profanities. Grandpa stroked the whip and let it just touch the side of the lad's boots. The lad danced as if on hot coals. One more quick stinging crack to the bully's calf, just above the boot, was enough, and no other stimulation was needed as the ruffian began running and yelling for his horse—that didn't seem in any hurry to be caught, leaving his cap and his bullwhip behind.

With the bull whip now curled and hanging over his shoulder, James

turned his attention to the cowering and shaking hound dog.

"I am sorry boy," Grandpa said in a soft soothing whisper, "no one is ever going to hurt you again. Now, let's take you someplace where I am sure you will be loved and cared for." The hound dog knew he had been rescued and showed his gratitude and relief by wagging his tail and licking James' hand as he followed him back to the Spice Farm without any prodding.

The two made their way back to the farm as James watched the young rider chase his horse up into the hills and out of sight. He knew he would never see him again, as cowards rarely return for a rematch. *No one is going to believe this story*, he thought to himself. "James 'bullwhip' Spice to the rescue," he said out loud as he chuckled.

Arriving on the farm with the brown hound dog was an immediate sensation. Scruffy was the first one to sound the alarm, and then the rest of the children streamed in from all corners of the farm to see Grandpa and the hound dog.

John opened the front door and took the measure of the dog as he marched toward his dad with a hot cup of coffee in his hands. "Here Dad," he said as he handed him the hot cup of coffee with a pinch of cinnamon. "You look like you could use it."

"Sorry, Son," said Grandpa. "I know you have enough mouths to feed but I just couldn't leave this poor injured animal out on the road." John sized up the animal, giving it a careful once over, as the Spice kids began petting and comforting the poor beast.

"Whoever did this should be horsewhipped," said John in disgust.

"He was," said James with a chuckle as he dropped the bullwhip to the ground.

Grandpa treated his son to the abbreviated version of the adventures of James "bullwhip" Spice. "You're getting too old for that sort of thing, Dad; we are going to have to take your bullwhip away from you," John chuckled.

"I wish you would," Grandpa laughed, as John continued to inspect the animal.

"You see this scar on the right shoulder?" Grandpa leaned over and looked.

"Yes, and he has a couple dozen more—thanks to this bullwhip."

"Actually, Dad, this scar is about three years old. It was a gift from a fully grown raccoon delivered to Eager when he was only a pup."

"Eager?" inquired Grandpa James.

"Yep, Dad, I would like you to meet Eager McDaniel. . . , the dog with the two dollar and fifty cent bounty on his head."

"Jeff McDaniel?" asked Grandpa.

"Jeff died last winter and this dog belongs to his son, Wally."

"Little Wally McDaniel?" asked Grandpa.

John laughed. "Dad, *little* Wally is six feet, two inches tall, and weighs over three hundred pounds."

Grandpa slapped his knee and shook his head, "Time does fly by," he finally said.

The next half hour was spent cleaning up Eager and making sure he had a big dinner. Grandpa had insisted that John go along with Matthew and Luke, who were keen on returning Eager to their friend, Wally McDaniel. "And take your rifle," said Grandpa. "If that rascal *does* return, he will have company."

Grandpa made his way into the house, up the stairs, and into the attic where Charlie was waiting for him.

"I saw the man running after the horse Grandpa. And I saw the dog," Charlie said excitedly. Grandpa spent a few minutes to tell his grandson about the high adventure that had taken place that morning.

Charlie's eyes got big as he listened with the ears of his big imagination—hearing the sound whip as it cracked on the thief's backside, and sending him running after his horse.

Proverbs 12:10
A righteous man regardeth the life of his beast:
but the tender mercies of the wicked are cruel.

Chapter 14

Who is Going to Heaven?

Afolloter listening to Grandpa's adventure with the bullwhip, Charlie asked a strange question. "Grandpa do you think that man is going to Heaven?" Grandpa thought for a moment as he constructed in his mind the possibilities this opened for helping Charlie understand Heaven.

"Charlie, let me ask you a question," said Grandpa. Charlie perked up—he liked Grandpa's questions. "So, let's imagine that you're in Heaven and you have a dog," Grandpa began.

"Are there dogs in Heaven?" Charlie beamed with his eyes wide open.

"Well, I am not sure about that," Grandpa said, "but let's just imagine there is a dog that is your companion in Heaven."

"What kind of dog?" asked Charlie. Grandpa was beginning to think he might have picked the characters for his story more carefully, but it was too late, he was stuck with the dog.

"OK, Charlie, for the sake of my story, let's say it's a glowing Heavenly dog."

"Glowing!" said Charlie. "Can I pet it?"

Grandpa began to chuckle; this story had clearly gotten away from him. "Yes, and you're petting your glowing dog in Heaven, and a bandit comes in your house and steals your dog."

Charlie was miffed. "Why?" he asked, then paused and said, "Grandpa,

I don't think they let dog thieves in Heaven."

"Charlie, you're exactly right. There are no dog thieves in Heaven."

Grandpa recovered himself from the story that was clearly going to end in a train wreck unless he did some quick thinking and fast explaining.

On the small table next to Charlie's bed was the big brown book, *Pilgrim's Progress*. He carefully slid it onto his lap and thumbed through the pages until he found the paragraph he was looking for. "Ah, here it is," said Grandpa as he began to read.

PLIABLE: "Come, neighbor Christian, since it is just the two of us, tell me more about the wonderful things that await us when we arrive at the place we are going."

CHRISTIAN: "I can better conceive of them with my mind than talk about them. But since you are interested, I will read to you what it says in my Book."

PLIABLE: "And do you think that the words of your Book are true?"

CHRISTIAN: "Yes, very sure; for the words were written by the One who cannot lie."

Charlie interrupted, "That's God, right? Christian is talking about the Bible, isn't he, Grandpa?"

"That's right," said Grandpa, "God cannot lie and His Book is always true." Grandpa, continued to read.

PLIABLE: "Well then please tell me about the things that are waiting for us when we arrive at the Celestial City."

Charlie interrupted again, "The Celestial City is Heaven, right Grandpa?" "That's right," said Grandpa as he continued to read.

CHRISTIAN: "There is an endless kingdom to be inhabited, and everlasting life to be given to us so that we may live in that kingdom forever."

PLIABLE: "Well said, and what else?"

CHRISTIAN: "We will be given crowns of glory and clothing that will make us shine like the sun!"

Charlie interrupted again, "Is that why the dog glowed in Heaven?"

"We will talk about that later," said Grandpa, realizing that he had dug a hole for himself that was getting bigger every minute. "Now pay attention," encouraged Grandpa.

PLIABLE: "This sounds very pleasant. What else?"

CHRISTIAN: "We will be with Seraphim and Cherubim, and creatures that will dazzle your eyes when you look at them."

Grandpa, anticipating the question, said, "Seraphim and Cherubim are special angels I will tell you about another time," and he continued to read.

CHRISTIAN: "You will meet with thousands that have gone before us to that place."

Grandpa paused. "And this is the part of the story I wanted you to pay attention to," said Grandpa, as he started reading the paragraph over again, inserting Charlie's name into the story for the best effect.

"Charlie, you will meet with thousands that have gone before you to that place; none of them are hurtful, but all of them are loving and holy— every one walking in the sight of God, and standing in His presence with acceptance forever."

Grandpa closed *Pilgrim's Progress* and put it back on the nightstand. Sensing he had a second chance to clear up the muddle he had made with his story of the glowing dog, Grandpa continued asking Charlie questions.

"Charlie, what do you think Heaven would be like if God allowed horse thieves, and dog thieves, and murderers, and gossipers, and drunkards, and bullies and..."

Grandpa paused as he tried to recall some other criminal class when Charlie piped up with "Chicken thief."

"That's right, Charlie," Grandpa continued, "bullies, and chicken thieves, and pirates, and swindlers, and cheaters ,and liars, and any other sort of wicked person into Heaven?"

Charlie thought for a minute as he recalled all the stories contained in the letters from Grandpa over the years describing the mean and violent streets of India. "It would be like Bombay," Charlie said.

"Yes, it would be like Bombay, or Calcutta, or San Francisco, or any other city in the world that is filled with sinners," replied Grandpa.

"Charlie, Heaven has been especially prepared by Jesus for His special friends. Friends that have been born again and have a new nature that is free from all sin. Everyone in Heaven has been changed by Jesus so that they will all get along in Heaven without any fighting, stealing, jealousy, hatred or lying."

"And no sickness either!" declared Charlie.

"That's right, Charlie, no sickness or disease is allowed in Heaven."

"So no dog thieves in Heaven." Charlie summarized.

"Only ex-dog thieves go to Heaven." Grandpa added. "Charlie, we are all sinners that could never enter Heaven unless God did a work in our hearts and then changed us so that we would fit into the Heaven he made especially for us."

"Charlie, tell me about that time you cut a wedge out of the molasses cookies your mom made and then squeezed them back together so no one would know you were stealing cookies?"

"You know about that?" Charlie sheepishly replied.

"I sure do. And I know about the time you killed a chicken with your father's new axe and then lied about it, and about the time you 'borrowed' Rosemary's silver dollar and spent it on candy at the Mercantile in Elkin."

Charlie bowed his head in shame.

Grandpa reached over and gently grabbed Charlie's wrist and continued, "And what about the time I stole my father's watch and tried to trade it for a fiddle? Or the time I told my mom I was going to feed our two mules, when I was really going behind the barn to smoke a corncob pipe I had swiped from Uncle Todd. And then there was the time I told my Aunt Mary that I had memorized the Ten Commandments when I hadn't. She gave me a dollar, but I never spent it because I was so ashamed."

Charlie looked up surprised. "You did all those bad things Grandpa?"

"Charlie, those are only the things I can talk about; I have done things that I am so ashamed of; I could never speak about them out loud."

Grandpa leaned over and gave Charlie a hug. "Charlie, you're a young sinner, and your Grandpa is an old sinner." As it turns out that, is the best part of the story." Charlie looked surprised.

Grandpa reached for his King James Bible and handed it to Charlie. "I want you to look up these verses and read them to me."

"Look up Ephesians 1:7 and read it out loud."

Charlie did as his Grandfather requested and read.

"In whom we have redemption through his blood, the forgiveness of sins, according to the riches of his grace";

Grandpa then quoted Ephesians 2:13, *But now in Christ Jesus ye who sometimes were far off are made nigh by the blood of Christ.*

"Look up Colossians 1:14, Charlie."

Charlie quickly found the passage and read it out loud, *"in whom we have redemption through his blood, even the for-giveness of sins:"*

Grandpa then quoted 1 Peter 1:18-19, *"Forasmuch as ye know that ye were not redeemed with corruptible things, as silver and gold, from* *your vain conversation received by tradition from your fathers; But with the precious blood of Christ, as of a lamb without blemish and without spot:"*

Charlie read 1 John 1:7, *"But if we walk in the light, as he is in the light, we have fellowship one with another, and the blood of Jesus Christ his Son cleanseth us from all sin."*

"Very good," said Grandpa, "now I want you to listen carefully to the next two verses I am going to read to you." Charlie handed Grandpa the Bible, who opened it up to the book of Revelation and began reading Revelation 1:5, *And from Jesus Christ, who is the faithful witness, and the first begotten of the dead,* "And the prince of the kings of the earth. Unto him that loved us, and washed us from our sins in his own blood."

Grandpa then closed his Bible as tears began to flow down his cheeks and he quoted from memory Revelation 5:9, *"And they sung a new song, saying, Thou art worthy to take the book, and to open the seals thereof: for thou wast slain, and hast redeemed us to God by thy blood out of every kindred, and tongue, and people, and nation;"*

Grandpa concluded, "You see, Charlie, Jesus came to die for sinners so they could go to be with him in Heaven. So let me ask you a question, Charlie," said Grandpa.

"OK," said Charlie.

"What word showed up in all those verses we both read?"

Charlie didn't need to think twice, and immediately answered, "blood."

"So let's see if we understand this," Grandpa said.

"No dog thieves are going to Heaven! Only ex-dog thieves that have been washed clean by the blood of Jesus.

"No liars are going to Heaven, except all those ex-liars who have been born again and had their sins washed away by the blood of Jesus."

"And certainly no cookie thieving, chicken killing, money stealing boys are going to Heaven, except for those that have trusted in the Lord Jesus Christ, been born again, and washed clean as newly fallen snow by the precious blood of Jesus."

Grandpa hugged his grandson and wiped his own tears; then he wiped Charlie's, and asked Charlie one last question.

"Charlie, why should God let you into Heaven?"

Charlie smiled, "Because of the blood of Jesus," he said without a doubt in his mind.

Romans 3:23-24

For all have sinned, and come short of the glory of God;
Being justified freely by his grace through
the redemption that is in Christ Jesus:

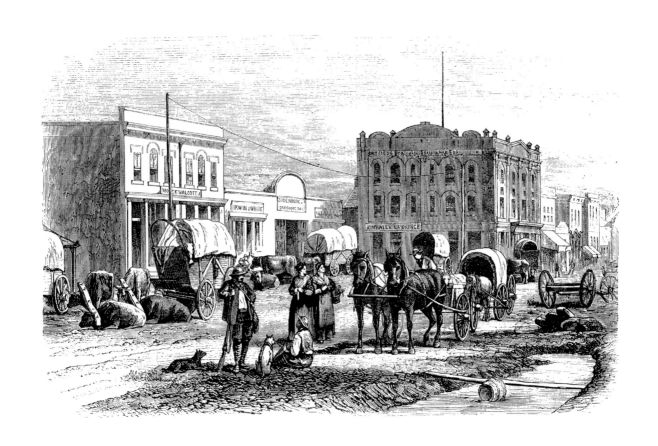

Chapter 15

The Big Trip to Town

I t was going to be a very special day. Anna, Janet, Rosemary, Ginger, Cinnamon, Cori and Matthew were all about to take a trip into Elkin. John was up before dawn to feed Stubborn, the mule. By the time Janet got up and fixed everyone a very early breakfast, John had hitched Stubborn to the farm wagon, greased the wooden wheels, oiled the wagon tongue gears, and adjusted the brakes.

"Should I grease you up too, Stubborn?" John teased, as the mule's ears went back for just a second before returning to normal.

Stubborn was born on the Spice Farm and had been in the family for about ten years. He was as steady as mules came. Most of the farmers in the valley used horses to pull their wagons, but the Spice family had always been partial to mules. Stubborn had started pulling the Spice family farm wagon when he was about five years old. Mules were easier to keep than horses; they were stronger, ate less food, and were much more surefooted than a horse. Mules also lived about five years longer than a horse and were usually slower. Stubborn was the exception to the rule and was anxious to get wherever he was going as fast as possible. Stubborn did not like to be passed by other wagons and thought himself quite superior to a horse.

Janet came to the barn with a cup of piping hot coffee for John. "Where did you put your rifle, John?" she asked. "It isn't hanging over the fireplace." "It will be in the wagon before you leave along, with a box of extra ammunition," said John, who hoped Janet would not notice the rifle leaning up against the shutter, next to the window.

"Oh, and before I forget, Janet, I have something for you." John reached into his pocket and pulled out five silver dollars and handed them to Janet.

"Is this the reward money for finding Eager?" she asked, with her eyes wide open.

"Yep," said John as, he stepped to the back of the farm wagon, raked out the old straw, and replaced it with fresh straw.

"I thought the bounty was $2.50," said Janet.

John kept working as he replied, "Wally was pretty impressed when he heard about how Grandpa had rescued his favorite dog from the young scoundrel, so he doubled the reward. He called it a 'combat bonus.'"

Janet smiled and replied, "That was very generous of him, John."

"Yes," said John, "I protested but Wally is bigger than I am, and after a couple minutes of arguing, it was clear to me that I was going to take the reward, or else."

"Or else what?" Janet laughed, knowing what a lovable character Wally was.

"Or else he was going to sit on me," John replied. They both laughed as Janet jingled the five silver coins in her hand.

Janet went back into the house, but before she opened the door she spotted the rifle. She checked it and happily discovered that it was not loaded. Janet decided not to scold John, who was usually pretty careful about keeping anything dangerous out of the path of the youngsters.

Janet was a crack shot and could out-shoot any man in the valley. "That's what happens when a dad who always wanted a boy raises you," Janet would reply. She was a tomboy, until she laid her eyes on John Spice and immediately decided to explore her "everything nice" feminine side. But make no mistake about it, Janet could out-ride, out-shoot, and out-fish just about anyone in the Yadkin Valley.

The sleepy town of Elkin was only about eight miles away. No one ever took a trip into town without taking along the family rifle.

The Spice family took a trip to Elkin once a week to attend church, and had developed a plan in case anything went wrong on the journey to and from town. They knew every neighbor that lived on, or near, the road that led to Elkin.

Janet had made it a point to visit all her neighbors at least once a year with a tin of cookies, always allowing enough time to pass an hour or two in sweet fellowship. She considered this her special time to turn neighbors into friends.

Janet Spice was admired and loved by just about everyone. Thanks to her, if they ever did break down, they were never more than a mile from a friend of the family who would be more than willing to help out.

In the winter, John always made sure they had plenty of extra blankets in the wagon—along with an axe, some dry wood, matches, a lantern with extra wicks, and a good supply of kerosene. John was a man that believed in being prepared.

John had done another thing to tilt the odds in favor of surviving, should anything go wrong. Charlie, at John's request, had been told to watch out the window and count the number of wagons that go by the farm. Charlie took this chore very seriously and kept tabs from sun up to sun down for over a week. He carefully counted all the wagons that passed by the Spice Farm going in either direction. On average, John and Charlie had figured out that about 16 wagons passed by going in both directions between rising of the sun and its setting. Most crossed the path of the Spice Farm in the late morning and just before sundown.

John had instructed Janet that if she was ever alone in the wagon and she broke down that she was to stay in the wagon with the rifle and wait an hour—knowing that the chances were very good that a neighbor would rescue her. The exception was if it was close to sundown, and then she was to make her way to the closest farm with the rifle and the mule in tow.

John had done one more thing to ensure a timely rescue, should something go awry. He had turned this particular strategy into a game that was played by the Spice children, who never guessed it had a serious purpose.

John had timed the trip by wagon from his farm to Elkin, on several occasions, in order to calculate the average amount of time the trip took. The trip to Elkin took just under three hours. He knew the distance between the farm and the town was less than eight miles, so he divided three hours by eight and came up with twenty-three minutes, give or take a minute or two. Once he had calculated the distance and the speed, he spent one Sunday afternoon with Matthew and Mark collecting the biggest river rocks they could find—sixteen of them to be very precise.

The following Sunday, they all loaded up the wagon to go to church about an hour earlier than usual. On the way to Elkin, John checked his watch and stopped every twenty-three minutes and carefully put the rocks by the side of the road. One rock marked one mile. Twenty-three minutes later he stopped and put two rocks by the side of the road that marked two miles, and so on, until he got to four miles; then he did the same thing only in reverse. By the time the wagon got to the fourth rock, they knew they were half way to town. The next marker of three rocks told them they had only three miles to go.

All the Spice kids had this figured out after a couple trips to town and made it their business to calculate the distance in miles to wherever they were headed. Janet knew that these mile markers would tell her which way was the shortest way to travel for safety in an emergency—home or Elkin.

It was a brisk and chilly October morning. Janet bundled everyone up and helped huddle them all together in the farm wagon. "OK Mom," yelled Janet, as she checked the rifle to make sure it was loaded and tucked carefully by the place that had been especially prepared for it next to the seat.

Anna scrambled to the wagon with Cori in her arms. Matthew was the designated man for this trip and very happy to be going into town. His job was to keep track of all his little sisters and to assist with the chores that waited for them at the end of their journey. These chores included making sure Stubborn had food and water while the girls went shopping.

Taking a trip to town was not something that was ever taken lightly. It was a taxing six-hour round trip from the Spice Farm to Elkin and back. There had to be a good reason to take this trip, and there was.

Anna had been promising Janet that if she ever had the opportunity, she would teach her how to cook John's favorite Indian recipes. Janet was a great cook, with a limited menu. She could cook up mouth-watering blueberry muffins and pancakes. She knew how to roast lamb to perfection, grill beefsteaks, and smoke venison. She was the bacon and eggs "queen of the kitchen," with absolutely no idea how to prepare anything even remotely exotic.

Janet was looking forward to learning how to carve new pathways into the loving heart of her husband, who had grown up on, and never stopped talking about, the famous dishes served and seasoned with the exotic hot spices of India.

Anna had spent the last two days scouring the kitchen to try and find the ingredients she needed to begin Janet's "delicious dishes from India" culinary training, with no success. Anna had made a list and was hoping they would find most of the ingredients at Dick Grier's Grocery store in Elkin. If not, they would order what they needed from the "Hornet's Nest"—the nickname given to Charlotte, North Carolina after the Civil War. Charlotte was the largest city in North Carolina.

Janet was confident they could find everything they needed in Dick Grier's Grocery store. Dick Grier regularly advertised his grocery business in the *Elkin Times*.

There was a picture of Dick Grier seated on his delivery wagon hitched up to his favorite cow. The ad read "the best little grocery store in the best little town in North Carolina." Dick Grier promised to deliver groceries anywhere within the city limits of Elkin, within three minutes.

The population of Elkin was just under 900 in 1911. Whenever Janet did any shopping at Dick Grier's Grocery she would kiddingly ask Mr. Grier when he was going to expand his grocery delivery service out to the Spice Farm. Dick would always say, "As soon as I can teach my cow to fly." He would then look at his watch and say, "Janet, I wouldn't hold my breath."

Janet would always laugh, and the younger children would always ask if cows really could fly. Janet would just look at her little darlings and make a funny face and cross her eyes—her way of asking, "What do you think, dopey?"

Life was simple in 1911.

The Spice kids had seen the picture in the Elkin Times of Dick Grier with the wagon hitched to the milk cow and were keen on convincing Dad to harness Lulu Belle, their milk cow, to the farm wagon. Dad just laughed, looked at the picture in the *Elkin Times* and said it must be a publicity stunt.

In India, cows were used to pull wagons all the time, but John knew it was not a job for a lactating cow.

Milk was a vital and important staple of the Spice family. John was full of fun, but he drew the line when it came to risking the welfare of his family. He was not going to gamble losing milk production by harnessing his prize Guernsey milk cow to a wagon that was pulled very nicely by Stubborn the mule. As John was fond of saying, "There are some things you just don't mess about with unless you are determined to find trouble."

Proverbs 31:14-20

She is like the merchants' ships; she bringeth her food from afar. She riseth also while it is yet night, and giveth meat to her household, and a portion to her maidens. She considereth a field, and buyeth it: with the fruit of her hands she planteth a vineyard. She girdeth her loins with strength, and strengtheneth her arms. She perceiveth that her merchandise is good: her candle goeth not out by night. She layeth her hands to the spindle, and her hands hold the distaff. She stretcheth out her hand to the poor; yea, she reacheth forth her hands to the needy.

Chapter 16

The Merchants

T he Spice expedition arrived just as the little town of Elkin had stirred from her sleepy rest. "Open for Business" signs were popping up all over town, as doors were swung open and the citizens of Elkin were invited to fill the cash registers and moneyboxes of the eager merchants.

No business was more eager for customers than Dick Grier, who was busy putting out all his sales signs and bins of overripe produce.

The best maintained water trough in town was in front of the Burt's Livery stable next to the *Elkin Times*. Stubborn needed no guidance and immediately parked in front of the water trough. He patiently waited to be unharnessed and tied to the hitching post where he could drink his fill and wait for the hay and grain treats that always came his way.

Stubborn was one of the quickest mules in the country and certainly one of smartest; He had figured out that the sooner he arrived, the sooner he was fed.

Matthew attended to Stubborn while Janet, Anna, and the rest of the Spice girls made their way to the grocery store. "Meet you in the Mercantile in about an hour," shouted Janet, as she made her way down the boardwalk.

"OK, Mom," Matthew shouted back.

Matthew and Burt had become friends over the years, and Burt loved listening to Matthew play the harmonica. "Did you bring your mouth organ, Son?" asked Burt as he arrived with a feed bag for Stubborn the mule.

"Yes sir," Matthew replied.

"Well then sit yourself down and play a spell," said Burt.

Matthew loved an appreciative audience and smiled as he pulled his Hohner harmonica from his pocket. Matthew found a bale of hay, made himself comfortable, and asked Burt what song he would like to hear. Of course, he knew the answer because it was always the same. "Why don't you play 'The Bonnie Blue Flag?' requested Burt.

Burt was seventy years old and had served with Robert E. Lee in the Civil War. Burt had never gotten over the fact that the South had lost the war and considered the present condition a temporary truce. He was just waiting for Southern reinforcement, and listening to "The Bonnie Blue Flag" always got Burt to "recollecting."

When Matthew finished the song, he knew he was going to be listening to a true story—only slightly embellished by a tough old southerner, who was going to go to his grave with that tune on his lips.

It was safe to play "The Bonnie Blue Flag" in Burt's Livery Stable, but Matthew had been warned by his dad to never play that song in public.

Passions ran deep and wide in the Yadkin Valley. Even after forty years, there was a growing tension between the South that wanted to get on with their lives, and the South that would never, ever forget the most tragic event that ever happened in American history.

Matthew waited for Burt's story to begin to flag off, and then he would always play something lively like "Eatin' Goober Peas." A few more tunes later and Matthew knew it was time to meet his mom at the Mercantile.

"Gotta go," said Matthew as he headed toward the Mercantile Store.

"See you before you leave, and don't worry, I will keep Stubborn good company while you're gone," said Burt.

"Thank you, Burt," Matthew replied.

Matthew had been well trained to never address an adult by their first name. Burt would never tell anybody his last name, and made a big fuss if anyone called him Mr. Burt. If you called him "sir," he told you to call him Burt, and so it was considered good manners by the Spice family to just call Burt, *Burt*. According to Dad, "Burt is the exception that every rule is required to have, which doesn't change the rule.

While Matthew was playing his harmonica and listening to old war stories, the Spice girls were busy picking out all the ingredients required to prepare their first exotic Indian meal.

Grandma Anna had something in common with her husband James. Neither had grandiose ideas and always approached life and ministry by laying the foundation slowly and carefully. Grandma had one single recipe in mind, knowing that if it were successful, the rest would follow effortlessly.

John and his father, James, loved *Indian Butter Chicken*. It was a chore to prepare, it kept well and would provide many very delicious meals.

"Can you find any red kashmiri chili powder, Janet?" asked Anna, whose eyeglasses were almost twenty years old. "My eyes are not working like they used to," she said as she tried to read the labels of all the spices and sauces hidden on the top shelves of Dick Grier's Market, with little success. "Janet, you will have to be my eyes today," she quipped.

"I found a jar of *Uncle Bob's Jump Up and Down Chili Powder*," said Janet with a chuckle.

"That will have to do," said Anna as, she looked into her wicker basket and counted out the ingredients she had gathered so far.

"Let me see... ginger, garlic, turmeric, mint, cucumbers, cashew nuts, a half-dozen tomatoes and six, big onions. Looks like we need to find some *kasturi methi*," Anna said.

"Speak English, Mom," said Janet.

"Sorry darling... That would be," Anna stopped to think and then said, "dried Fenugreek leaves."

"Dried *fenugreek* leaves," repeated Janet. "Found it. What's next on our list?"

"Do you have brown sugar at home?" Anna asked.

Janet looked at Rosemary, who was hanging on her right arm. "Rosemary, any brown sugar left at home?"

"Not much, Mom," said Rosemary, who had learned how to make molasses and ginger cookies and had become the guardian of the brown sugar bowl.

"Better buy ten pounds," said Janet. Rosemary smiled and raised her eyebrows as she calculated about how many ginger cookies that would make.

"I found a large tin of curry," Janet said.

Curry was actually not an Indian spice but a combination of Indian spices concocted by the British to season food so it tasted "Indian."

Anna thought for a minute. "Yes, let's go ahead and put that in our basket."

As she continued checking her list of ingredients, she asked, "Janet, do you know how to make yogurt?"

"And he (Abraham) took butter, and milk, and the calf which he had dressed, and set it before them; and he stood by them under the tree, and they did eat." said Janet.

"I figured as much when I met your milk goat, Six-Pints, said Anna.

"First came Six-Pints the nanny goat, and then came the cheese, and then the yogurt," said Janet, who paused and then continued. "I taught John how to take down and clean his Winchester bolt-action single-shot 22 caliber long rifle, and he taught me how to make yogurt and cheese."

Anna laughed, "Sounds like a marriage made in Heaven." Janet just smiled.

"Looks like all we need is a boneless chicken," said Anna.

"Plenty of those on the farm," said Janet.

Just then, Cinnamon, who had been quietly watching all the gathering of ingredients with great interest, said, "But Mom, all our chickens on the farm have bones." Janet gave her a squeeze and smiled as Grandma laughed out loud.

Rosemary jumped into the conversation trying to explain to Cinnamon the perplexing mystery of the boneless chicken. Cinnamon's mind was made up and no amount of explaining was going to "pop the cork" of her understanding. Cinnamon's boneless chickens became a humorous family joke that lasted a lifetime.

All the ingredients were gathered for preparing *Butter Chicken*, chutney, spiced yogurt drink, crepes, flatbread and chicken kabobs.

The wicker basket, full of the special ingredients, along with fifty pounds of flour, fifty pounds of rice, twenty-five pounds of black lentils, ten pounds of goober peas—better known as peanuts, ten pounds of Brown Sugar, ten pounds of white cane sugar, and a few other odds and, ends were paid for and then carefully piled in the corner behind Dick Grier's hardwood counter that boasted a brand new cash register.

The next stop was the Mercantile, where Janet found Matthew looking at the new arrival of hunting rifles. Janet gave Matthew and Rosemary each a Barber Quarter Dollar and commanded them with a big wave to pick out anything they wanted in the entire store. Matthew and Rosemary laughed, knowing that there were not too many things of interest to them in the Mercantile that cost 25 cents or less.

Cinnamon was given two Liberty Head nickels and told to find something for herself and Ginger. Cinnamon needed no guidance, she headed straight for the candy counter where she and Ginger argued over whether they should invest their small windfall on peanut butter peach Blossoms or red bird peppermint puffs.

Just then, Matthew showed up with a selection that he proudly showed to his mom. "Good choice," said Janet as she admired the hickory hand carved double flute recorder. "Matthew, I want you to go to the counter and pay for your flute. Then I want you to go hitch up Stubborn, and carefully load all the supplies we purchased at Dick Grier's. Pack everything carefully in the front of the wagon, and cover it with the blanket that's rolled up in the corner of the wagon. When you're done, bring the wagon in front of the Mercantile."

"OK, Mom," said Matthew, as he showed her the price tag on the double flute.

Janet read the price tag, "Thirty-two cents!" she said in mock surprise. Janet fished seven Indian Head pennies out of her pocket and said, "I must love you real good." She handed the coins to Matthew and then gave him a big hug.

"Thanks Mom," beamed Matthew, as he headed for the brass plated cash register guarded by Elmer, the proprietor of Smyth's Mercantile.

Janet and Anna made quick work of picking out a deep cooking, cast iron pot, a flat griddle with a hardwood handle, a big spice box containing 12 smaller spice boxes, a tea canister and a tea-kettle, assorted tin pails, pans and basins, six pie pans, a meat grinder, a chopping knife, two new frying pans, three sugar boxes, three bread pans, and a couple of crock-pots.

Elmer Smyth was a fastidious tight-fisted little man who had just one thing on his mind, and that one thing was commerce. To be more accurate, it was the accumulation of wealth that motivated Elmer, and everyone in town knew it.

Elmer was a thin man without an extra pound of fat or ounce of grace. Elmer never gave anything away and extended credit to only the most prominent citizens of Elkin. Elmer was one of the richest men in Elkin and wanted everyone to know it. John and Janet always referred to him as "poor old Elmer" and prayed for him regularly. They invited him to church on a regular basis and his answer was always the same. A curt and unambiguous "NO!"

Janet arrived at the cash register and greeted Elmer with a smile. Elmer nodded and began adding up the total. "I will need some help getting this all into my wagon," said Janet.

Elmer nodded and glared at Janet, "I do not extend credit."

Janet looked at Elmer and asked with the most charm she could muster. "Elmer, when has the Spice family every asked for credit?"

Elmer was un-chastened by the comment as he tallied the total. "That will be ten dollars and three cents." Elmer announced.

Janet rummaged in her pocket and pulled out a Liberty Head double eagle twenty dollar gold coin and handed it to Elmer, along with three Indian Head pennies. Elmer's mouth dropped open as he looked up at Janet.

The Spice family was one of the most loved families in Yadkin County, and also one of the poorest, as far as how this world measures riches.

"I would like my change in gold, not silver," said Janet, who was enjoying the moment.

Elmer fumbled around and finally made change for Janet. "Here you are Ma'am," said Elmer, "two Half Eagle Liberties."

The sight of a twenty dollar gold piece was not something he saw every day, and when he did see one it was usually in the possession of someone of considerable means.

"Bumper crop?" inquired Elmer, as he helped move the merchandise from the counter to the covered boardwalk in front of his store.

"Gold Mine." said Janet in a secret whisper meant for only the ears of Elmer. Anna, who was following the drama, gave her a gentle jab in the ribs with her elbow. Janet was quick witted and responded to Anna out loud so Elmer could hear it, "Elmer is trustworthy; he won't jump our claim."

Anna shook her head thinking this was a joke that could backfire.

Janet knew that Elmer was too tight lipped to ever say anything to anyone else and too honest to ever be a threat. "And besides," said Janet, "I am tired of being treated like an 'Irish potato farmer' just off the boat."

Anna laughed and said, "I need to keep in mind that I am not in Bombay, India anymore."

From that day forward, the Spice family was treated like royalty at the Smyth Mercantile. The next time they invited Elmer to go to church —instead of the terse "NO!"—they received what John later called "a very polite 'NO', smothered in honey with a cherry on top."

Matthew arrived with the wagon and helped load up all the sundries and supplies. The girls were bundled up as Janet began to drive the wagon back to the Spice Farm. Before leaving town, Janet had two stops to make.

"I will be back in a minute," said Janet as she locked the brake on the wagon, hopped down, and headed for the Elkin Post Office. She returned with a sack full of mail, including what looked like the monthly rejection letter from another publisher her devoted husband and part-time author had recently sent in for consideration.

Janet stepped back into the wagon with a helping hand from Anna, released the brakes, and said, "Here you go, Matthew," as she pulled a bag of saltwater taffy out of the back of the wagon. She then pulled a Morgan silver dollar out of her pocket and handed the bag and the silver coin to Matthew. "now matthew," instructed Mom, "go give this to Burt, and immediately return before he tries to return the silver dollar."

Matthew did as he was instructed and returned immediately to the farm wagon. "Hike, Hike!" yelled Janet. Stubborn immediately began pulling the wagon and they were well on their way before Burt could raise an objection.

"Whoa," Burt yelled, but Stubborn would not stop.

Stubborn had been raised by Janet and John, who both loved horses, but loved mules even more. Stubborn had never been mistreated and had bonded as only a mule can to both Janet and John, with a special affection for Janet. Stubborn would obey the voice commands of John, or Matthew, or any of the other Spice children, but his loyal heart belonged to Janet; if she said, "Hike," which is mule language for "Giddy-Up," then "Hike" it was.

Burt had been a generous and kind friend who had made it a point to assist the Spice family in a hundred ways over the years, without expecting anything in return. Janet would always say that someday she was going to start settling the score, and today seemed like a good day to start.

Burt arrived on the road outside his Livery Stable just in time to see all the Spice children waving him an enthusiastic good-bye. His voice commands had no effect on Stubborn, and he was too old to run after them, so he just smiled and waved back.

"Seems like the Spice family has come into a small fortune," said Anna, as they settled into the long ride home. Janet just smiled.

Matthew, hearing the comment, piped up, "the great furniture robbery of 1911." Anna looked puzzled.

Janet laughed, "I will tell you about it on the way home."

And so she did. Kept reminding her daughter-in-law how good and faithful the Lord is.

Proverbs 31:10-12

Who can find a virtuous woman? for her price is far above rubies. The heart of her husband doth safely trust in her, so that he shall have no need of spoil. She will do him good and not evil all the days of her life.

Chapter 17

The Turkey Shoot

atthew was the first one to notice that something was not right. "Mom, you're going the wrong way."

Janet smiled, "Wrong way to where?"

"Wrong way to go home," said Matthew. "Oh, that wrong way," said Janet. "Well it just so happens," she said, looking at her pocket watch, "that it's only a quarter after twelve. I want to arrive home at just after sun down, around seven thirty, and it takes three hours to get home. So tell me, Matthew, how much time in between when we need to leave Elkin and when we need to get home?"

Matthew did some quick calculations and said, "Little over four hours."

"That's right Matthew."

Janet pulled the half page advertisement that she had cut out of the newspaper and handed it to Anna. Anna put on her glasses and began to read the announcement:

TURKEY SHOOT
Starts at 1:30 at Col. Darnell's Farm
Sponsored by the Elkin School Board
Shoot Gun &
Long Rifle Competition

One Dollar Contestant Fee

Donated Prizes include

$$First Prize$$

Ten dollars & a half side of Beef

$$Second Prize$$

Five dollars & 22-caliber rifle

All proceeds go to the Elkin School Board

to buy McGuffey Readers and slate tablets

The news caused instant excitement and a little confusion. "Are you going to shoot a turkey, Mom?" asked Rosemary.

Janet explained that a "turkey shoot" was a name given to shooting contests. "I will probably be shooting the holes in playing cards," Janet said with a smile. "And you all know how much I hate gambling cards." she added with a grin.

The Spice family arrived at the Colonel Darnell's Farm along with a half-dozen other wagons, at least ten riders, and dozens of pedestrians. The Annual Elkin Turkey Shoot was an event that emptied the town of Elkin every first Saturday in October between 1 p.m. and sundown.

Just about everyone in Elkin showed up for the event that had turned into a cross between a county fair and a shooting contest. Booths were set up where farmers sold everything from peach jam to smoked venison. Last year they had introduced a dunking pool where, for a nickel, you had three chances to put the mayor of Elkin into a cattle trough full of cold water.

A big sign announced that the potato sack race would begin at one o'clock. Matthew and Rosemary were all wide eyed and infected with the "pleeze-can-we-pleeze-can-we" bug as they asked mom to be allowed to enter the race.

"Rosemary, you are in charge of Ginger, and Matthew, you are in charge of Cinnamon," Mom said firmly. Grandma who was holding Cori said she would supervise the girls while Matthew and Rosemary ran the potato sack race. "You all stick together and do what your Grandma tells you to do. Is that clear?" "Yes Mom," the kids all said in unison.

As Janet headed to the field where the Turkey Shoot was being held, she passed a beanbag toss, a pie eating contest, and a barbershop quartet. This is turning into a real circus, she thought to herself.

"Hello Janet," sounded a familiar voice.

Janet turned around to try and locate the greeter. "Hello Sally,"

"I am surprised to see you here," said Sally.

"I am going to enter the Turkey Shoot," said Janet. "Howdy Janet," came another voice from the crowd. "Who is that?" Janet asked. Sally piped up, "That's Bill," said Sally who fished her husband out of the loitering crowd.

"You here for the Turkey Shoot?" asked Bill.

"Yep," said Janet.

"So am I," said Bill.

Bill and Sally Simpson had just moved to Elkin from Virginia. Bill had inherited his Uncle's small farm just a couple miles outside of Elkin and was struggling to make a go of it. They had four kids—all boys, all freckles, all redheads, and all under six years old. Sally had her hands full.

Bill and Sally had started attending the Gospel Chapel started by the small group of Plymouth Brethren that met in the back of Bert Hamilton's Hardware Store. Sally and Janet had become friends, and Janet had played the role of "older sister" to Sally, who had grown up in the city and was having some difficulty getting used to rural life in North Carolina.

"I was just getting ready to do some target practice before the shooting contest begins, said Bill . Would you like to join us, Janet?"

Janet hesitated, "I need to go pay the entry fee first. "I will meet you over there in about five minutes."

Bill Simpson, being new to the Yadkin Valley, did not know anything about Janet Spice's reputation as the best crack shot in the Yadkin Valley. She really did not need to do any target practice; nevertheless, she was happy that John, knowing that she was going to show up for the Turkey Shoot, had sent her to town with a small box of ammunition.

Janet purchased her contestant ticket for the Turkey Shoot and headed toward the practice target range. The range had been especially set up for contestants to make sure their rifles were all in good working order and the sites adjusted for the length of the target range at hand.

"Hello again," said Bill Simpson. Sally and her boys made themselves comfortable as Bill adjusted the sites on his Sharps model 1874. Janet had heard about the Sharps sniper rifle but had never seen one in person. It had a reputation for being the most accurate long-range weapon of the time. "What you got there Janet?" said Bill as he looked at the 22 caliber Remington long rifle that Janet was holding. "That's a nice rifle," said Bill, trying to be kind and encouraging, while wondering to himself why Janet was wasting her hard earned money entering a shooting contest she had no chance of winning.

Bill Simpson pointed out the blue bottle that was on top of the wooden plank held up by two saw horses, along with a couple dozen other bottles of various colors and sizes. The target was about 500 feet away. He then pointed out the blue pillbox which was obviously the hardest target to hit. Bill lifted his rifle to his shoulder and carefully squeezed off a shot. The lead nicked the plank right next to the blue pillbox that wobbled and then fell over, making it half the size it was when it was standing up.

Without really thinking about it, Janet took aim—and wasting no time—pulled the trigger that sped the bullet which shattered the tiny blue pillbox into a dozen pieces.

Bill was astonished. "Where did you learn to shoot like that?" he asked.

"Just a lucky shot I guess," she said, avoiding the temptation to puff herself up any more than she already had.

Bill took a couple more shots with his Sharps. After adjusting his sites, it was obvious to Janet that she had some serious competition. Janet thrived on competition. All her life she had been beating boys at their own games, and loving it. As she grew in her faith as a Christian, she began to wonder if maybe she didn't love it too much.

Bill invited her to take a couple more practice shots, but she declined. She had nothing more to prove and wanted to save her ammunition for something that would feed her family, not her pride.

Sally never said anything to Janet about how things were going, but Janet could spot the signs.—the ill-fitting shoes, the over-mended shirts, the sallow faces and the forced smiles. This was a family in some distress.

The large man with the official vest and the bullhorn announced that the Turkey Shoot was about to begin for the long rifle shooter.

The qualifying round was simple. Glass bottles were set up on a plank that was sitting on two sawhorses. The shooters had three tries to hit at least one bottle. Once you hit one bottle, you were qualified for the next round.

The first shooter hit the bottle on his third, and last, try. The next three shooters were disqualified. Of the twenty-three contestants, only nine went to the next round.

The second qualifying round was equally as simple, as the target was moved another 150 feet away from the shooter.

Hitting a bottle at 750 feet with any rifle was difficult. By the time this round was completed," the number of contestants was down to four.

The next target was a paper target with printed bold numbers on it. Each contestant drew three numbers out of a straw hat. The object was simple: shoot out the numbers you drew, that were on the large target. The one who shot out the most numbers won the contest that were.

The Turkey Shoot had been a tradition that was only eight years old, but in that time, no one had ever hit all three numbers.

By this time, a large crowd had gathered to watch the match. Janet was obviously the town favorite among all the women. The men in town were cheering for any man that would put things back the way they always were before "Calamity Janet Spice" had shown up to disturb the natural rhythm of things.

Janet bristled at the prospect of losing this contest to a man, and was determined to give all the women of Yadkin Valley something to smile about. It was her duty.

"Ladies first," said the town councilman who was conducting the shooting contest. Janet raised her rifle and shot out the first number she had drawn from the hat... then the second... and then the third.

The crowd gasped with amazement, followed by cheering and clapping. "Way to go, Mom!" Matthew yelled as loud as he could, as the Spice girls enthusiastically jumped up and down.

The next two shooters did not even come close to hitting the numbers they had drawn.

The next shooter was Bill Simpson. He took careful aim and hit his first number. Then he nicked the second number, and the shooting stopped as the judge was called in to apply the rules. If half the number was gone it was a hit, and if not, it was a miss. The judge took his magnifying glass and marched to the target. The number Bill was supposed to hit was the number sixteen. "All that is left is the loop on the six," said the Judge, "it is a hit." The men of Elkin sent up a shout.

Bill's next shot was taken with care as he aimed at the number three. He squeezed the trigger and the three disappeared. Hoots and hollers, along with flying hats, instantly filled the atmosphere of the shooting range.

The judges huddled. There was no way to split the prizes in half, so it was determined that the contest would continue.

One of the judges was sent out into the field with a sack full of bottles as the announcement was made.

Each contestant would have three bottles tossed into the air. The one who shot down the most bottles in flight would win the shooting contest.

"You go first," said Janet.

"Thank you, Janet," said Bill.

The first bottle was thrown, and Bill shot it out of the air just when it reached its zenith. The next bottle was thrown and shot down with the same accuracy. The third bottle was thrown in the air, and you could hear the bullet glance off the bottom of the bottle, but it did not break.

"That's two for Bill Simpson," said the judge.

Janet loved shooting at moving things, and moving bottles were easier to hit than the dirt clods her dad had taught her how to explode in mid-air. She looked back at her family who was cheering her on. Then she looked at the Simpson family and immediately knew what she was going to do.

The first bottle went flying through the air and Janet effortlessly shot it down. The second bottle went up in the air, and Janet purposely nicked it without breaking it. The third bottle went up, and Janet missed it by a mile.

The men of Elkin erupted in cheers and shouts. Bill Simpson was the new town hero—a reputation that would help him get through some of the tough times coming. The merchants in town never tired of retelling the story of what happened that day, and would often add a few extra items to his shopping bag at no charge.

As soon as the crowd had finished shaking Bill's hand and congratulating him, he made his way over to Janet, who had re-gathered her family around her and was about to head home. "Janet," said Bill, "I don't know if I beat you fair and square or not; I just know you're the best shot—man or woman—I ever met."

Sally, who had no doubt about what just happened, interrupted the conversation by giving Janet a big hug around the neck. "Promise me, Janet, that you and your family will join us for a roast beef dinner next week after church."

"I promise," said Janet.

While Bill was getting his wagon loaded with the beef, and now ten dollars richer, Janet was marching her family to the wagon with a brand new 22 rifle and a five dollar gold piece.

"When is your birthday, Matthew?" asked Mom.

"Next Wednesday," said Matthew. "Happy birthday Matthew," she said as she handed him the brand new 22 rifle.

Matthew was beside himself and didn't know what to say. "Sorry you came in second place, Mom," he finally muttered.

Janet looked at him with her funniest face and her eyes crossed, which was what she always did when any of her kids said something that sounded goofy. "And just what would you do with a half side of beef?" she said. They all laughed as they headed home.

1 Thessalonians 5:11-13

Wherefore comfort yourselves together, and edify one another, even as also ye do. And we beseech you, brethren, to know them which labour among you, and are over you in the Lord, and admonish you; And to esteem them very highly in love for their work's sake. And be at peace among yourselves.

Chapter 18

The Divine Appointment

J ohn, James and the boys all pitched in and did the morning chores. At noon, they had all gathered on the front porch sipping cider and eating the cucumber and beef sandwiches that Janet and Anna had prepared the evening before their big trip into town.

Suddenly, they heard a wagon approaching. "That can't be Janet," John said, looking at his watch. Luke, who was the runner in the family, lit off the porch and headed for the open gate that marked the entrance to the Spice Farm. Out of breath, he came running back with news. "It is Mr. McDaniel," said Luke as he caught his breath.

Within a minute or so, Wally McDaniel, his wife, Marie, and their dog, Eager, all showed up on the Spice Farm.

"Hello, Charlie," Wally said with a wave of his hat.

"Good to see you again so soon, Wally and Marie," said John. "What brings you out this way?"

"Oh this and that," said Wally.

It soon became apparent that Wally had come to visit with James and to personally thank him for rescuing his favorite dog, who was already showing the effects of Wally's famous affectionate care, along with regular meals.

"Where are the women folk?" Wally asked.

HEAVEN'S PROMISE - THE SPICE FAMILY CHRONICLES

John explained that they had all gone to town and would be back just before sunset.

Marie, hearing the news, called Wally aside for a brief pow-wow. "Marie has a great idea!" Wally announced with pride.

Wally was a late bloomer and had just gotten married to Marie the previous summer. Marie was the daughter of an immigrant family that had arrived from Italy about ten years ago. She was a dark-haired beauty who was full of energy—just what Wally needed.

Marie was from a large family, and though she loved farm life with Wally, she missed all the bustle of a big, loud family. Wally and Marie were planning and hoping for a many children, but so far it was just the two of them.

"Marie and I would like to cook you folks an Italian dinner tonight."

John looked at James as James looked at Wally, who was every bit of three hundred pounds. He was all the testimony they needed to be convinced that Marie was an excellent cook who believed in large portions. "That would be wonderful," said John, "but I doubt we have the ingredients for an Italian dinner. Janet and the kids are going to be tired when they return home."

Wally and Marie huddled again. "Marie has another great idea," announced

Wally. "We will go on back home and do the cooking and return here just before sundown."

"That's a lot of work for you and Marie. Are you sure you have the time?"

Wally stood up straight and smiled. "Got all the time in the world."

Marie piped up, "Thank you John; I love cooking for a large family."

"OK then," said John, who was delighted at the prospect of not having to prepare a meal himself, as he had promised Janet he would.

Wally McDaniel was not the most ambitious farmer in the valley, and as it turned out, he didn't have to be. His dad had worked the farm for fifty years and saved every penny he ever made. He managed to put a modest amount under the mattress every year, which added up over time. Although Wally McDaniel was not the richest man in Yadkin County, he was probably the most prosperous farmer. And that suited Wally just fine, as he decreased the farm workload and increased the hunting and fishing.

The Spice family had never eaten an Italian dinner. They spent the rest of the afternoon noodling on every delicious possibility the imagination served up.

John and the boys had prepared the dining room table for the big event. Grandpa had made a special place for Charlie, who was bundled up and carried to his special spot. "This is going to be a wonderful evening," said Grandpa.

"I know," said Charlie, "I heard Mr. McDaniel and Dad talking about it."

The rest of the Spice boys, who were bundled up on the porch, began stirring as Wally McDaniel and Marie drove their wagon to the front of the house, unhitched their two horses, and called the boys over to help unload the back of the wagon.

The boys helped Marie carry all the prepared food to the house, where she lit the stove and immediately took charge of the kitchen. Marie was a woman that created her own head winds, and was a marvel to her husband. Wally would just watch her go to work with amazement and some pride. "Ain't she a marvel!" said Wally, more than once.

Everything was ready for the big meal. The aromas that filled the house were new and inviting. The boys were all taking deep whiffs of the delicious vapors that lifted off the simmering sauces. Marie said the recipe for the spaghetti sauce was a family secret that had been handed down over untold generations.

Just then, Luke entered the house with news that Mom was only about a quarter of a mile down the road.

John called all the boys to the front porch with instructions that they were to unload the family wagon and put everything into the pantry so it could be sorted out the following day.

The remaining Spice family descended on the wagon as soon as it arrived. James swept Anna off the wagon and John did the same with Janet. "I have a surprise for you Janet."

"No puppies from Wally McDaniel," she said suspiciously.

John laughed, "I wish."

As soon as Janet and Anna entered the kitchen, the delicious aromas that permeated the house revived them. Janet and Anna were famous hosts and just as famous for receiving hospitality with grace and appreciation. They were both tired, but were determined not to let it show as they were carefully seated at the dining room table.

The boys deposited the day's purchases in the pantry as Dad had instructed, and each found their seat at the table.

The moment they had all been waiting for—heaping portions of spaghetti and meatballs smothered in a sauce that would impress a king. A prayer was offered, and for the next twenty minutes the only sounds that were heard at the Spice dining room table were "oohs and aahs." Matthew had perfected the triple "mmm . . . mmm . . . mmm" and repeated it endlessly throughout the meal.

Marie beamed as she accepted praise and gratitude from the truly appreciative Spice family. It was a night to remember, and it was just getting started.

As the meal wound down and everyone sat wondering if they had ever been so full in their lives, Janet rose from the table and fetched the letter from the publisher addressed to John. She handed the letter to John, gave him a kiss, and said, "Keep trying sweet heart, your day will come."

John looked at the letter and read the return address, "The Gospel Lamplighter Publishing House." John rose from the table and slipped into his room and opened the letter, as he had done a hundred times before, expecting to read a nicely crafted rejection letter.

As John opened the letter and pulled it out of the envelope, a piece of paper drifted to the floor. John picked it up and gazed at it with shock and surprise. It was a money order made out to John Spice for twenty-five dollars. John sat on the bed, stunned, as his mind went swimming in the deep waters of wonder and amazement.

John read the letter and then composed himself. John, always the "drama king", put on his saddest face as he dropped his shoulders and slowly marched to the kitchen. He went around the corner that led into the kitchen and caught Janet's eye. "Sweetheart," he said sadly, "would you come here?" Janet was not used to her husband taking the news of rejection from a publisher so seriously. After all, he had hundreds of them in his desk drawer, and usually greeted the bad news with humor and levity.

Obviously this was different.

Janet excused herself and escorted her husband to the bedroom. "I think your stories are wonderful, John; don't get discouraged," she comforted.

John didn't say a word but just escorted his wife into the bedroom where he sat her down on the bed and handed her the letter and the check.

"You kidder," she said, obviously surprised that she had been taken in by his big act. Janet then jumped to her feet and grabbed her husband by the neck.

The rest of the dinner guests were not unaware of the drama taking place in the bedroom, although not quite sure what to make of it. But when the muffled shouts of "Praise the Lord" reached a crescendo, everyone was reassured that whatever the news was, it was good news.

John arrived back in the kitchen with Janet hanging on his shoulder, tears streaming down her delicate cheeks. "Do you have something you want to share with the rest of us?" asked Grandpa James.

"Yes, Dad, I do have an announcement," said John. "After ten years of submitting at least one story a month to publishers all over the country, I have finally sold my first short story."

Wally gave out a shout and started clapping. Everyone joined in, and for five minutes John went around the room taking bows and kissing the hands of his daughters. When Janet could not stand it anymore she stood up and said, "Obviously God has orchestrated this celebration, knowing exactly what was going to happen this day."

John and Janet immediately recognized God's fingerprints on the events and the opportunity it provided. They had also been looking for a way of presenting the gospel to Wally and Marie, and the opportunity had just been given to them on a silver platter.

"We would like you all," said John, "to retire to the living room where I am going to read the short story that was just accepted by Lamplighter's Publishing Company."

"Wally and Marie," said Janet, "we cannot tell you how much we have appreciated this dinner, and we would like you to stay and be with us for the rest of the evening."

Wally looked at Marie with a surprised smile. "Why sure, we would be honored." Wally then asked, "What is the name of this story?"

John answered, "The Hanging Judge!"

"That sounds like my kind of story," said Wally.

The Spice girls did the dishes and cleaned up the kitchen as the adults all retired to the living room. Janet took three apple pies out of the pantry and put a generous slice on each plate. Rosemary distributed the pie as everyone got settled. John went to his bedroom and pulled the story out of a large envelope tucked away in his roll top desk, and then went to the living room to read the story of The Hanging Judge.

Mark 16:15
And he said unto them, Go ye into all the world,
and preach the gospel to every creature.

Chapter 19

The Hanging Judge

J ames started a fire to add some warmth and cheer to the evening, as John pulled up a chair and allowed a couple more minutes for everyone to find a seat and get comfortable. John then began to read the story "The Hanging Judge."

Judge Herbert T. Bridgewater was known as the fairest and most kindhearted judge in the entire Missouri territory. He ruled with equity and justice, and sprinkled all his decisions with heaping shovels full of mercy. With his King James Bible in his right pocket and his gavel always held tightly in his left hand, he was the one judge in the territory every criminal and horse thief prayed out loud would be the one handing out justice if they ever were to get themselves caught. Of course, the criminal class in the untamed Missouri territory was only positive about one thing: that they would never be cornered, shackled and brought to justice. But if they ever were, they figured they had an ace in the hole—Judge H. T. Bridgewater.

The world changed for the criminal class on September 14, 1848, when Judge Herbert T. Bridgewater, nicknamed "Sweet Tea," announced that after nearly thirty years of service, he was retiring from the Judging business and going into the mercantile business.

A week later the sign over the newly opened Mercantile announced, "Good merchandise at a fair price - Judge H. T. Bridgewater, Proprietor."

Without a Judge on the bench, the Missouri territory, which was granted statehood in 1821, erupted with petty crimes and misdemeanors. The reports of horse thievery reached 50 in less than a month. This was a scandal in the minds of the law-abiding citizens of the newly formed state of Missouri. A new Judge was summoned.

Riding on a black horse with a slight limp rode a man that looked to be of an over exaggerated stature. He was well over six feet tall and rotund. He was dressed in all black with a satchel hung on the side of his poorly maintained western saddle. He was smoking a cigar and watching the smoke trail upwards when he heard a commotion from behind.

Two men with bandanas tightly tied to cover their faces advanced. The man in black was soon relieved of his horse, hog tied, and shoved over like a three-legged dog. As he landed on a patch of tumbleweeds, a diamond back rattled a warning. It slithered and coiled itself about three feet from the tall man in black who had just been pitched into the prairie.

"Kill the sidewinder," the tall man in black pleaded. One of the bushwhackers pulled out his colt single action army pistol, nicknamed "the peacemaker," and pointed it at the snake. "Shoot it you fool," commanded the tall hog-tied stranger.

"Naw, that critter ain't done nothin' to bother me, and I ain't wastin' my bullet," the horse thief said as he re-holstered his Colt.

Lying on his back, the stranger in black looked intently at the horse thief and noticed two things: the outlaw had a scar that started on the inside of his palm—right next to his thumb—and went all the way up his arm, and he smelled of boiled onions.

The following day around noon, the beleaguered stranger wandered into Jefferson City, Missouri on foot and reported to the Sherriff's office, where he was escorted to the finest hotel in town.

Two days later, Judge Melville Booster took his seat at the County Courthouse and began meeting out justice like a man on fire. His first week as the sitting judge in the territory, he faced off with five horse thieves, and they all swung by the neck until their boots were pulled off and given to Sister Amy who ran the county orphanage. Within a month, the tall man in black had earned himself the appellation, Judge Melville "Hang em High" Booster, the meanest Judge in Missouri.

Onion Thief

On the August 20, 1849, Judge Melville Booster looked up from his bench to view a strangely familiar face that he could not immediately place.

"What is he in for?" the Judge queried.

"The man who stands before you is Gustavo "Clem" Stein, and he was caught red handed 'stealing onions from widow McAllister's garden,'" the prosecuting attorney reported with a sweeping bow.

"Is that right?" asked the Judge.

"I was just borrowing a few onions to go into my rabbit stew." Clem protested. "Honest to God," he said as he raised his right hand in the air to swear an oath.

Judge Booster's eyes bulged and his eyebrows furled as he focused on the hand with the scar that started at the thumb and made its way like the Mississippi river up his arm.

The courtroom erupted as the Judge pronounced doom and gloom on the criminal and finally ordered him to be hung—without the complimentary steak and potatoes dinner or any other last requests. "If I could hang you twice, I would!" the Judge raged.

The two opposing attorneys were stunned. It was the prosecuting attorney that waited for things to cool down a little and then meekly asked the judge to reconsider his sentence. "After all Judge, we're only talking about a half-dozen onions."

The horse thief was strung up that very afternoon with onion on his breath and a "What did I do?" look on his sorry face.

Strange justice had been done that day, and the fear of God swept like a prairie wildfire through the entire town. Widow McAllister's onions, and all the rest of the homegrown vegetables in Jefferson, Missouri, were left unmolested from that moment forward.

Strange Justice

But this is not where the story ends.

That very afternoon, the highly exasperated Judge Melville "Hang em High" Booster went back to his plush hotel room and lay down for a nap. He was not seen for three days, and when he finally returned, he was a different man.

What happened was recorded in his daily journal and private diary. It was long after his death that the diary was finally investigated. The story it revealed went like this:

I was just about to nod off when two strangers showed up at my bedside. They were not from Missouri.

"What?" I began to ask as I was lifted up by both my elbows, by what appeared to be angels, and escorted out of the hotel through the roof without so much as disturbing a single cedar shingle. At first, I thought I must be dreaming, but I soon realized that was not the case.

Without a word, I was escorted to the most dreadful place I had ever seen, or dared to dream exists. I was in a deep cave that echoed with the far off pitiful anguished cries and moans. The sculptured cavern was lit by the flickering fire light that was coming from a huge pit, which was just on the very edges of my vision.

I was taken to a place I immediately recognized. There before me was the all too familiar bench that crowned the courtroom in Jefferson, Missouri. How it got there, I did not ask. The initials that had been carved into the side of the oak dock immediately caught my attention and alerted me to the fact that this was not a facsimile, it was my bench. Yes, the very bench I had sat at dispensing Missouri justice for half decade.

"Please have a seat, Melville."

I turned around to see who it was that was directing me to sit down, and there before me was a creature that towered over me; he looked like a man, but shone as if his skin was laced with brass and silver. I did as I was told.

It was then that a large book was produced and placed in front of me. "We will start with Bill Hardy, a new arrival from Jefferson City, Missouri."

The book was opened to a page simply titled "Bill Hardy.'

"Bill Hardy," I muttered under my breath. I knew Bill Hardy; he was my barber and one of my few friends. Bill was a friendly sort and loved by almost everyone. **A good fellow with no criminal record**, I thought to myself.

I looked up with amazement and consternation and asked, "Where am I?"

One of the angels who had escorted me, the one at my left elbow, leaned down to whisper into my ear, "You're in the hallway that leads to Hell, the place where the inmates are escorted to their final destination."

"Why am I here?"

The angel on my right elbow leaned down and whispered in my ear, "We have summoned you here for reasons you will discover in the future."

"What do you want me to do?"

"We want you to view the lives of twelve souls who have lived and just recently died in your lifetime and in your territory, and give us your legal opinion about the disposition of each one. The first case is a friend of yours who has just passed from earth to this dreadful place. His life is before you, and we await your opinion."

I poured through the documents titled "The life of Bill Hardy" piled up before me. It read like a horror story. "Who collected all this information, and how do I know it is all true?"

Un-intimidated by the question, the Shining One gently made his way to the front of the dock.

"Melville," he said calmly, but with great authority, "these records have been kept by the Almighty Creator Himself, who cannot lie or ever dissemble the truth. You can be assured that everything you read is accurate in every detail."

"But," I complained, "there are things in this document that no one could ever know; they are the secrets of his thought life and the musings of his heart."

"How very perceptive of you, Judge Booster", said the Shining One. "You're used to only judging the actions of a man—the Almighty judges the actions, the heart, and the mind of a man. Nothing is hidden; all is revealed."

With that explanation, I poured through the papers that chronicled the sinful, rebellious life of "good ol'" Bill Hardy. Every evil thought that entered into his mind —every secret slander, malicious wish that hid behind a silent smile, and every carnal indulgence that settled into his withered soul was recounted as if it had been acted out on a large stage.

I soon realized that these charges were true and could not be overlooked by the Almighty any more than I could overlook the scar that marked the criminal hand of Clem Stein.

"I have read enough," I complained.

"Begging your pardon," said the angel on my right side, "you must read all the charges against the accused."

For what seemed like an eternity, I read through stacks of documents, all reporting on the lives and times of 12 souls that had lived and died in Jefferson County, Missouri. It was all too much for me in the end.

I was a man who thought I had insight into the worst criminal minds that roamed the earth, but by the time I was finished reading all the documentary evidence, I was convinced that I could scarcely conceive of the depravity that afflicted my fellow citizens of Jefferson, Missouri.

After what seemed like days of research, I was convinced that if this was the standard of judgment, then all men were guilty of gross crimes and rebellion... including me. Who could ever survive this level of scrutiny? And yet, I had to admit, that in the interest of justice, there must be a penalty.

When the last page was read, the books were removed, and a piece of parchment with an ink pen was placed before me, the one they call Judge Melville "Hang em High" Booster.

"We have one last duty for you to perform before we leave this place," said the Shining One. "You are required to write down your verdict in one word."

I thought for a moment and the first word that came into my head was **guilty***. I pondered that response, and then finally took the pen in hand and carefully wrote the word "DESERVED".*

No sooner had I penned the word when it was suddenly carved with a blaze of white light by an unseen fiery finger, into the granite rock header that led to the fiery pit. DESERVED! I was immediately transported out of the dreary hallways that led to the pit of hell and into the heights of Heaven. It was from this vantage point that I could see a pleasant land beneath my feet.

Within just a few minutes, I found myself outside the gates that opened to a gleaming city so beautiful words could not describe it. As I gazed in wonder at the aspect of this wondrous place, I immediately found myself sitting at the same bench that had greeted me on my visit to the hallways to hell.

The same two angels escorted me and the same third Shining One soon arrived to give me instructions.

"Where is this place?" I asked.

"This is the Celestial City—the place you probably know as Heaven," the Shining One reported.

"I hear music," I said.
"It is a City that never sleeps, and where no darkness ever casts a shadow, and where songs never cease," the Shining One said.

Just then, a stack of documents was put in front of me. I didn't need to ask what they were. I opened the folder and read the name out loud. "Abigail Pennyworth. Only one document to read?" I asked.

"Only one resident of Jefferson, Missouri will be taking up residence in the Celestial City today," the Shining One said.

If I have just left the gates of Hell and these are the gates of Heaven, I thought, **then Abigail Pennyworth must be a saint.** Determined to discover what qualified Abigail Pennyworth to enter into the Celestial City, I took my time and carefully read the story of her life. Expecting to find a saint, I was surprised and horrified to discover that Abigail Pennyworth was no saint; she was in fact a notorious sinner.

"I think you have made a mistake," I announced as I lifted up the document. "I don't need to read anymore to know that this is not someone who deserves to enter into Heaven."

"Remember, Melville, you are to read the entire life story before you pronounce your opinion."

I kept reading, but the story did not get any better. Abigail Pennyworth was a malicious liar, an unfaithful wife, and a thief. She was cruel to both man and beast, and was continually a vexation to everyone around her. The story of her sordid life was every bit as bad or worse than any of the life stories I had read in the halls of hell. I could not find one good thing written in the ledger about Abigail Pennyworth.

As I was just about finished reading the document, I came to a page that was boldly stamped with a title that read "BORN AGAIN." I wondered what this was all about. I continued to read the life story of Abigail Pennyworth with great interest.

The rest of the story of Abigail Pennyworth changed abruptly. It was a life stained by tears of sorrow and graced with kindness and selfless living. But it was not a perfect life by any means; flaws in her character still crept out, and it seemed to me that she was a woman in a desperate struggle against evil. A struggle in which she did not always prevail.

On the whole, I could see that the last chapters of the life of her were absent of the evil malevolence that dripped off the pages of the former chapters. Something had happened to her that changed her for the better, but not to the point of perfection.

I was willing to admit that there had been a marked difference in her thought life, the treasury of her heart and her actions, but I could not be persuaded to consider her a Saint, worthy of the Celestial City. Her life was too wicked, her temperament too inconstant to ever merit such a merciful judgment, and yet, here she was being led up to the gates of the Celestial City.

When I turned the last page in the life story of Abigail Pennyworth I could not help but notice the crimson red seal at the bottom of the page. It said, "Paid in Full" and it was signed by the King of the Celestial City.

The book containing the record of the life of Abigail Pennyworth was removed and replaced with a pen and blank parchment.

"We await your opinion, Judge Melville." said the Shining One.

I certainly am not going to write DESERVED. If anyone was less deserving it was Abigail Pennyworth. She did nothing worthy of an acquittal, I thought to myself. There was nothing meritorious about her life.

I thought about writing UN-DESERVED on the parchment, but as I watched Abigail Pennyworth enter into the splendid Celestial City, I thought of a better response.

I did not think what I was about to write on the parchment was going to please my three hosts. They had told me to limit my comment to one word, and I was going to write two words. Incensed by the apparent lack of rhyme or reason to the whole qualification process—which sent people to hell that were not nearly as mean and ornery as Abigail Pennyworth—I finally stretched out my hand, grabbed hold of the ink pen, and wrote the following in big bold letters:

FREE GIFT

Instead of irritating my hosts, my answer seemed to please them greatly. "You are very astute, Judge Melville Booster," noted the Shining One, directing his attention to the newly displayed sign hanging over the gate that led to the Celestial City.

I strained my eyes and finally said, "Well, I'll be." The sign over the Celestial City read "The Free Gift."

With that, the two escorts each grabbed an elbow and the next thing I knew I was slipping through the roof of the hotel and gently placed face up in my bed.

The next day, Judge Melville "Hang em High" Booster went to visit Judge Herbert T. Bridgewater at his General Store. Judge Booster purchased a King James Bible and began reading it with great interest. He also developed a lifelong friendship with Judge Herbert, and the two only talked about one thing. I will let you guess what it is they discussed as both of them thumbed through their King James Bibles.

The change in Judge Booster was slow at first and then almost overnight his life changed forever.

Born Again

In his personal journal on May 14, 1853 the words BORN AGAIN were boldly printed at the top of his diary. Under the title it read, "Received the Free Gift today, and I can't wait to meet Abigail Pennyworth."

When Judge Melville finally died in 1884, his funeral was attended by everyone in town who, over the years, had come to love Judge Melville Booster. Shortly after his conversion in 1853, he had been given a new appellation.

Here lies Judge Melville "the preacher" Booster. A man who could never stop talking about the FREE GIFT.

John 4:10
Jesus answered and said unto her, If thou knewest the gift of God, and who it is that saith to thee, Give me to drink; thou wouldest have asked of him, and he would have given thee living water.

Romans 6:23
For the wages of sin is death; but the gift of God is eternal life through Jesus Christ our Lord.

Chapter 20

The Free Gift

hen the story was finished, the kids were all bundled up and put in bed. Grandpa carried Charlie up to the Eagle's Nest and placed him gently on the bed. "I am learning a lot about Heaven lately," said Charlie.

"Yes you are, Charlie," Grandpa paused. "And there is a lot more to learn."

"I want to know more about what I will be like after I receive my new body."

Grandpa smiled. "Tomorrow morning you and I are going to have a talk about the Super Blue Bicycle."

With that, Grandpa tucked Charlie into bed and headed back downstairs.

Wally and Marie had not left, and they seemed to want to stay and talk. Janet and Anna kept the coffee and pie coming while John and James did what they loved best—leading folks to the foot of the cross to meet Jesus.

Wally started the conversation by asking John what he had in mind when he wrote this short story.

John immediately began a soul searching conversation with Wally and Marie, who were listening with great interest. They knew they were missing something in their lives, but just couldn't put their finger on it. John's short story had struck a nerve, and they were in no hurry to leave until they had probed both John and James with questions that

HEAVEN'S PROMISE - THE SPICE FAMILY CHRONICLES

had eternal significance.

John explained to Wally that any serious consideration of this subject of who *"goes to Heaven"* will soon lead to two conclusions: it was a Free Gift to some, and it came at a price that nobody could pay.

Silver and Gold are worthless commodities when eternal life is the prize. Meritorious living could not begin to balance the scales. And all our prayers and tears are of no value.

So how do we "buy" this precious prize of eternal life?

Wally and Marie listened as John and James spelled out the redemptive plan of God for fallen and hopeless mankind.

Heaven cannot be purchased; it can only be freely received.

Receiving is not payment. We can add nothing and nothing will pay the debt except the blood of Jesus.

"Are we likely to receive such a marvelous gift?" asked James, who then gave the answer.

"The answer is that everything in our sinful nature rejects the free offer. We think so little of our great debt that we imagine all we need from the hand of God is a little forgiveness of the interest due on the debt, and if

234 | Chapter 20

a small portion of the principle is paid, we can make up the rest." This struck a nerve with both Wally and Marie, who had both assumed that they needed just a little Divine help to nudge them into the Pearly Gates. Now they were not so sure.

"So what is the Father and Son's response to this blindness?" asked John. "Do the Heavenly Father and His Only Begotten Son turn on their heels in disgust and leave us to perish in our miserable, ungrateful condition? No, they freely send the Holy Spirit to enable us to receive the gift that we cannot obtain by any other means."

Wally and Marie were having the blinders lifted off their eyes and were now able to begin to view Heaven with more clarity.

James gently prodded them to think biblically about the topic instead of just repeating the worthless traditions and stories of men.

"Heaven," said James, "is a possession that has been purchased by the Son of God. It is a gift that is freely given to those who were once His enemies, including me and what merit did he see in us to initiate this blessed gift? The answer cannot be found by looking at yourself but only as you gaze intently at the Savior. The answer is that he freely loved you when you were unlovely, wretched, diseased and despised. He clothed you in the brightness of His glory because He loved you."

Wally and Marie were beginning to tear up as they considered the "Free

Gift" that was being offered to them that very night. They began to understand, that in a strange way, they had been led by the Heavenly Father to a place where they would clearly hear him calling them by name into His kingdom.

"This kind of love is beyond our human reckoning," said John. "I can imagine loving the lovely, or even a child who has strayed—but to love an enemy that has lived a life of desperate and deliberate rebellion, slandering his Creator and treating all His gentle favors with hatred and disdain—God's love is uniquely God's. To say that His love is unfathomable, and then try and plumb its depths is blessed futility."

James continued, "Blood bought and freely given! This is what we possess in Heaven, and without it, there is no Heaven. It is a possession that possess us, and a Free Gift that never stops giving."

"So then," said John, "write DESERVED on the door that leads to hell, but on the door that leads to Heaven, write THE FREE GIFT."

Hours later, Wally and Marie received the Free Gift of salvation. The four prayed for what seemed like hours. Janet brought blankets into the living room and some sleeping bags and pillows. Wally and Marie spent the night—a blissful, peaceful sleep, and everybody knew it. Wally's snoring would wake the dead, and it certainly kept the living from getting any sleep in the Spice household that night. It was a wonderful time to be awakened, and John and Janet rejoiced as each sawed log fell to the ground and thundered.

It was three thirty in the morning, and Janet nudged John. "John, you still awake?" asked Janet.

"Of course," said John.

"You know the angels in Heaven are rejoicing over Wally and Marie Mc-Daniel tonight?"

"Yes, I know," said John.

"And," added Janet, "I think any angels that were hanging around here have gone up to join them."

"To get away from the noise?" asked John.

Janet replied, "You read my mind," as they both joyfully laughed.

Luke 15:10
Likewise, I say unto you, there is joy in the presence of the angels of God over one sinner that repenteth.

Chapter 21

Spaghetti for Breakfast

Any breakfast that began with spaghetti, meatballs, and scrambled eggs seasoned with exotic spices was a morning that was getting off to a most auspicious start. Marie stirred and seasoned the eggs as the aroma from the simmering, marinated spaghetti sauce wafted through the farmhouse eagerly awakening each member of the Spice family.

The first Spice into the kitchen was Janet. She immediately greeted Marie with a gentle pat on her delicate shoulders. "Good morning, Marie," said Janet.

Marie wiped her brow and said, "Leftover spaghetti and scrambled eggs, hope that's alright."

"Alright?" said Janet, "it's wonderful!"

Marie was going to get heaping portions of gratitude from the Spice family who regularly enjoyed their traditional—flapjacks, eggs easy over, fried up bacon, and honey on cornmeal cakes—but had never been treated to anything quite like the breakfast that they were about to enjoy. The scrumptious smells drew the Spice children into the kitchen like flies to honey.

Janet finished fixing a big pot of coffee, and placed it on the kitchen table, while Rosemary and Matthew set the table. John and Wally poured themselves a cup of coffee as they sat down at the kitchen table. "Ain't she a wonder!" Wally exclaimed.

John laughed and said, "Wally, we both got better than we deserved." "That's the truth," said Wally as he took a sip of his coffee and wiped his chin. "But ain't she a wonder!" he repeated.

"You're a very blessed man," said John.

Janet fixed a breakfast tray for Charlie and headed up the stairs. "Can I come too?" said Matthew. "I want to show Charlie my new rifle."

Janet smiled and said, "Oh, he would like that."

Matthew went to his room to retrieve his new rifle as Janet slipped up the stairs into the attic. "Good morning, Charlie," Janet exclaimed.

"Are Wally and Marie still here?" Charlie asked.

"Yes, as a matter of fact they are. Marie has made a special breakfast for you this morning." Charlie looked at the plate and then at his mom, who laughed. "It looks a little scary, but it is delicious," reported mom, as she helped Charlie sit up in his bed and gently placed the breakfast tray in front of him.

Charlie needed no coaxing and immediately began feasting on the most unusual breakfast he had ever had in his short life. "Pretty good?" asked mom.

"Mmmm, delicious," announced Charlie, who within three bites already had a spaghetti sauce mustache.

Just then, Matthew entered the Eagle's Nest with his new rifle. The next fifteen minutes of an hour was spent recounting the events of the previous day.

Charlie listened as Matthew told the story of the Turkey Shooting drama that ended with the gift of the prize rifle. Janet watched as her son Charlie listened with interest and enthusiasm to Matthew, who chronicled the adventures of the previous day.

Janet smiled inside as she thought about what she *didn't* hear pass between her two eldest sons. There was no jealousy and no competition between her two boys, only love and genuine interest.

"I bet dad will teach you to target shoot," said Charlie.

"Maybe mom will," Matthew smiled as he hugged his mom.

"No, that's a job between a father and son," said Janet. "Your dad is a crack shot, and I am sure he would love to teach you all the secrets he has learned from me." Janet laughed playfully.

Matthew heard his dad call for him up the stairs. "See you later, Charlie," said Matthew as he headed down the stairs.

"See you later," echoed Charlie.

Janet waited for Matthew to leave, and then she embraced her son Charlie and gave him a kiss on both cheeks.

"You know, Charlie," Mom said, "you have a gift that is better than any rifle."

"What do you mean, Mom?" Charlie asked.

"Well," said Mom, "every time you listen to someone else with genuine interest, you're giving them a gift. Every time you encourage someone else, you're giving them a gift, and every time you are really happy that someone else was blessed, you're giving them a gift."

"I was happy that you gave Matthew the rifle, Mom."

"I know you were Charlie. That is a gift you gave, and one you were given."

"Given?" asked Charlie.

"Oh yes!" said Mom. "You can't give away to others, unless that gift was first given to you." Charlie was soaking it all in but didn't really know what to say.

Janet leaned over and picked up Charlie's Bible and shuffled through the pages. "Ah, here are the verses I was looking for." Charlie listened carefully as mom read from the book of First John.

1 John 4:7-11

Beloved, let us love one another: for love is of God; and every one that loveth is born of God, and knoweth God. He that loveth not knoweth not God; for God is love. In this was manifested the love of God toward us, because that God sent his only begotten Son into the world, that we might live through him. Herein is love, not that we loved God, but that he loved us, and sent his Son to be the propitiation for our sins. Beloved, if God so loved us, we ought also to love one another.

Just then, they heard a commotion coming from the front porch.

Janet gave Charlie another kiss on the cheek as she headed down the stairs.

Charlie looked out the window. He could see that Mr. and Mrs. McDaniel were getting ready to head back to their farm. Charlie rapped on the window. Wally waved as he helped Marie up into the wagon, and then he disappeared back into the house. The next thing Charlie heard was the thundering footsteps of Mr. McDaniel as he clamored up the stairs and into the attic.

"I apologize, Charlie," said Mr. McDaniel. Charlie didn't know what Mr. McDaniel was apologizing for but thought he better not ask. Mr. McDaniel made his way to Charlie's bedside and stuck out his very large hand. Charlie stuck out his hand, hoping it wouldn't be squeezed too hard. Mr. McDaniel, knowing Charlie was weak, gave him a gentle handshake.

"I might have gone without saying goodbye to you, Charlie, and that would have been a dog-gone shame," the large man said. "Now, next time I come to visit, I am going to bring you something I think you will really enjoy."

Charlie's eyes lit up. "A puppy?" Charlie said hopefully.

Mr. McDaniel laughed. "Your Mom would have my hide if I saddled her with another mouth to feed," said Mr. McDaniel. "What I have in mind will let you see the world in a way you have never seen it before. Now you think about that between now and next Sunday," said Mr. McDaniel.

"You're coming back next Sunday?"

"Yep," Mr. McDaniel beamed with a radiance Charlie had never seen him display before. "Marie and I are going to start going to church with your family, starting this Sunday."

Charlie watched and waved out the window as Wally and Marie McDaniel's farm wagon, with Eager trailing behind, left the Spice family farm.

The Spice family had been treated to a feast of fellowship and food that would live on in the memories of every member of the Spice family. Wally and Marie had come to a crossroads in their lives, and by God's gracious providence, had entered a path that led directly to the Celestial City.

With company safely on the way home, John and Janet quickly began shepherding the family back into the normal routines that make a farm run smoothly. There was a time to feast and enjoy the company of others without the drudgery of daily chores hanging over your head, and there was a time to get busy, returning the Spice domain back into an orderly and well-managed household.

John and Janet were good at loosening the reigns when they felt a higher purpose was in the works. but at the core they were, a very disciplined couple that understood how important it was for children to have structure built on expectations that built character and teamwork.

Each child was personally encouraged to get busy and do their chores, starting with Matthew and ending with Ginger. Ginger was hoping that baking Gingerbread cookies was on her list of things to do—it wasn't.

After all the Spice "worker bees" were busy doing their chores, Janet and Grandma Anna began unpacking all the treasures they had purchased the previous day in Elkin. They carefully found a place for everything and put everything in its place.

"Anna," said Janet, "I know you were planning a special dinner tonight, but I was wondering…"

Anna interrupted the conversation. "I was thinking the same thing," said Anna. "Too many treats, too close together is never a good idea."

Janet gave Anna a hug as she thought to herself how fortunate she was to have a mother so wise and caring. "Better to let things drift back to normal, and then we can have that special Indian feast," said Anna. "And besides, said Anna, after Marie's Italian cooking, we need to let the taste buds stop celebrating if we want your kids to enjoy Indian fare."

"I think Marie is a wonderful cook, and I think you are a wonderful cook," said Janet. "And I think my kids are going to love Italy and India."

Anna grinned and said, "We will give it a week or two."

"Great minds think alike," said Janet, who was thinking the same thing.

Grandpa finished helping John Jr. carry his third small arm-full of firewood to the woodbin in the living room. Now go ask your mom what she wants you to do next, and give me a salute, sergeant," commanded Grandpa. "Now give me a salute sergeant," commanded Grandpa. John Jr. saluted smartly and then was dismissed to go find his mom for further orders.

Grandpa then went up the stairs to talk with Charlie.

"Hi Grandpa," Charlie saluted.

"Namastē Namastē," greeted Grandpa, as he seated himself next to Charlie and opened his Bible. "Charlie, I am going to read you a couple verses and then I am going to tell you a story." Charlie was all ears. "Charlie, do you know the longest story in the Bible?"

Charlie thought for a while and finally said, "Noah and the Ark?"

"Well, that is probably one of the most exciting stories in the Bible, but it is not the longest."

James Spice found the passage starting in Genesis 37 and began reading the story of Joseph.

Charlie's father had taught him the story of Joseph.

Grandpa was heartened and pleasantly surprised by the ease with which Charlie made the connections between the life of Joseph and the life of the Lord Jesus Christ. Charlie understood that Joseph was a *shadow type* of Jesus Christ. Grandpa had another lesson in mind.

When Grandpa finished reading the story, he paused and then began asking Charlie questions.

"Charlie, how many sons did Jacob have?"
Charlie answered without hesitation. "Twelve."

"And which son did Jacob love the most?"

Again, Charlie answered without hesitation. "Joseph."

"Was there anyone else in this story that really loved Joseph?" asked Grandpa.

Charlie thought for a minute and then said, "I don't know."

"Joseph was loved by his earthly father," then "Grandpa said, and then added, "and loved even more by his Heavenly Father."

Grandpa continued, "Charlie, I want to teach you something very important about how God worked things out with Joseph." Grandpa then leaned over and whispered in Charlie's ear. "And how He works things out with us."

Grandpa opened his Bible and read from Romans 8:28-31,

Romans 8:28-31

And we know that all things work together for good to them that love God, to them who are the called according to his purpose. For whom he did foreknow, he also did predestinate to be conformed to the image of his Son, that he might be the firstborn among many brethren. Moreover whom he did predestinate, them he also called: and whom he called, them he also justified: and whom he justified, them he also glorified. What shall we then say to these things?
If God be for us, who can be against us?

"Let's talk about all the horrible things that happened to Joseph," said Grandpa. "Can you help me remember them, Charlie?"

Charlie thought for a minute in order to get all the events organized in his mind. "He was clobbered by his brothers and thrown into a pit, and then he was sold into slavery and taken to Egypt where he was sold to a guy named Potiphar." said Charlie.

"What else?" inquired Grandpa.

"He went to work for Potiphar and was doing pretty good until Potiphar's wife told her husband that Joseph had done something really evil, which he didn't do."

"That is called slander, Charlie, and it is Satan's number one weapon against God's friends. So what happened next?"

Charlie thought for a minute. "Potiphar took Joseph and put him into prison. While he was in prison he met two of the servants from Pharaoh's court and interpreted their dreams. They said they would help Joseph, but they didn't."

"That must have been pretty disheartening," said Grandpa. "These are all horrible things that happened to Joseph over a long period of time. I bet there were times when Joseph got pretty discouraged and lonely."

Charlie nodded in agreement.

"Now, I want you to think about the next question carefully, Charlie," said Grandpa. "Why did all these evil things happen to Joseph?"

Charlie thought for a minute and finally said, "Because his brothers hated Joseph, and Satan hated Joseph."

Grandpa was stunned. "Charlie you are absolutely right. Any other reason you can think of?"

"I think it was because of sin, Grandpa."

Again, Grandpa was taken back. "Charlie you got it!" he exclaimed.

"Sin causes everyone trouble, and in this story, sin and Satan caused a lot of trouble for Joseph." Grandpa stroked his chin thoughtfully. "Charlie did you know that Joseph had a secret weapon against all the effects of sin. Do you know what it was?"

Charlie thought for a minute and finally said, "I am not sure."

"Charlie we talked about all the bad things that happened to Joseph because of sin and Satan, now let's look at how the story ends."

Charlie quickly rehearsed the end of the story. He told Grandpa about King Pharaoh's dream and how God told Joseph what it meant. Charlie recited how Joseph was chosen to be the Prince of all Egypt, and how he saved hundreds of thousands of people from starving to death by storing up grain for the time of drought and pestilence.

Grandpa listened with great interest as he thought to himself how his son John had faithfully and patiently invested the stories from the Bible into the life of his first-born son.

Charlie finished telling his grandfather the end of the marvelous story of Joseph.

Grandpa had just one thing to add. "Charlie," he said, "do you know what happened after Joseph's father, Jacob, died?"

Charlie shook his head.

"The eleven brothers of Joseph started feeling guilty about what they had done to their brother, and began to imagine that Joseph was as evil as they were. They were sure that as soon as their father, Jacob, died that Joseph would take revenge on them for all their wickedness."

"What did they do?" asked Charlie.

Grandpa opened his Bible up to Genesis 50:15-17 and read it out loud to Charlie.

Genesis 50:15-17

And when Joseph's brethren saw that their father was dead, they said, Joseph will peradventure hate us, and will certainly requite us all the evil which we did unto him. And they sent a messenger unto Joseph, saying, Thy father did command before he died, saying, So shall ye say unto Joseph, Forgive, I pray thee now, the trespass of thy brethren, and their sin; for they did unto thee evil: and now, we pray thee, forgive the trespass of the servants of the God of thy father. "And Joseph wept when they spake unto him.

"What did Joseph do?" asked Charlie.

Grandpa handed Charlie the Bible and pointed to verse 19. "Go ahead and read verses 19 and 20, Charlie."

Charlie took Grandpa's falling apart Bible and carefully began reading.

"*And Joseph said unto them, Fear not: for am I in the place of God? But as for you, ye thought evil against me; but God meant it unto good, to bring to pass, as it is this day, to save much people alive.*"

Grandpa reached for his Bible and found Romans 8:28 and read it out loud. "*And we know that all things work together for good to them that love God, to them who are the called according to his purpose.*"

And while you're thinking about that, I am going to go 'rustle us up', as Mr. McDaniel says, a cup of hot cocoa.

Acts 7:9-10
And the patriarchs, moved with envy, sold Joseph into Egypt:
but God was with him, And delivered him out of
all his afflictions, and gave him favour and wisdom in
the sight of Pharaoh king of Egypt; and he made
him governor over Egypt and all his house.

Chapter 22

Two Miracles

G randpa returned a couple minutes later with two cups of hot cocoa. Grandpa and Charlie sipped the delicious brew as Grandpa waited a minute for the promise God made in Romans 8 to sink in.

Finally, Grandpa said, "Charlie, we live in a sinful world. All sorts of bad things happen all the time because of sin. Disease and death are because of sin. People lie and steal because sin is in their hearts and souls. We are all sinners, Charlie, and we see the effects of it all around us."

Charlie nodded in agreement.

"Now let me ask you a question, Charlie."

Charlie's eyes brightened.

"What promise does God make to those that love him?"

Charlie smiled. "God says he will work it all out so that something good comes from it, just like with Joseph."

"Did you know that in the last couple of months God has worked out a miracle similar to the miracle he worked for Joseph?"

Charlie raised his eyebrows, "really?"

"That's right," said Grandpa. "Would you like me to tell you the story of the miracle of how God worked things out right under our noses?"

Charlie was eager to find out the "mystery of the miracles" as he put his hands under his chin and waited for his grandfather to reveal the story.

The Blue Ridge Mountains' Canine Kidnapper

There was a young man hunting up in the woods of the Blue Ridge Mountains. He set his traps in hopes of catching a rabbit so he could cook up some stew. He checked his traps that day and they were all empty.

In the distance, the man could hear the barking of a hunting dog. The barking just kept getting louder and louder. The hunting dog was headed in his direction. The young man hid himself behind some brush.

He watched as the hunting dog treed a big old raccoon. The dog barked and barked, and finally the dog's master, who was a very large man, huffed and puffed his way up the hill and into the small valley where his prize-hunting dog had cornered the raccoon.

The large man aimed his rifle and shot the raccoon that dropped dead to the ground. The hunting dog sniffed the dead raccoon as the large man stroked the dog and praised him for a job well done.

The man took the raccoon, put it in a potato sack and slung it over his shoulder as he headed back down the hill.

The man and his hunting dog were not alone. The young man followed from a distance, keeping the hunting dog in his sights.

The young man said to himself. "That is what I need, a good hunting dog." It was right then and there that the young man decided that he was going to get that hunting dog no matter what.

He followed the man and the dog to their farm, and then he just waited and watched as the sun went down and the moon went up.

It was a dark night with just a silvery crescent. At about three o'clock in the morning, the young man crept up to the front porch of the farmhouse where the dog was tied. He could hear the large man snoring.

The young man quietly untied the rope from the porch and led the dog away into the night and up into the mountains where he lived with his uncle.

He was now officially a dog thief. The thief kept the dog inside his shed for a couple of days, just in case the large man retraced his steps and came around looking for his lost dog.

After about a week, the thief began trying to work with the hunting dog, with no success. The dog would not obey the man; he became angry at the dog and began beating him over and over again.

Instead of trying to train the hunting dog with care and respect, the man began treating the dog with cruelty and abuse. He kept the dog barely alive and on a short leash.

After weeks of abuse, the hunting dog was desperate to escape. One night he gnawed his way through the rope. The dog ran for its life, down the mountain, and down the road that led home. Exhausted and half dead, the dog found a place of shelter behind a big maple tree about two miles from his owner's farm.

Early that morning, an old man wandered down the lane to find his secret praying spot under the very tree the dog had hidden behind as it licked it wounds.

The next thing the old man knew, the dog was licking his hand, hoping for help. The old man examined the dog and realized that it had been terribly mistreated, so he decided to take it home to receive some much needed care.

Charlie piped up, "You're talking about Eager, aren't you Grandpa?"

"That's right," said Grandpa. "And you can tell me what happened next."

Charlie paused for a second and then began telling the story, as he understood it. "The dog thief came riding up on a horse and told you to give him his dog back or he would horse whip you. He pulled out a bullwhip and was going to give you a lashing when you took the bullwhip away from him and gave him a licking. The dog thief then went chasing after his horse back up into the mountains and has not been seen since. You brought Eager back to the farm where Rosemary and Ginger cleaned him up and gave him something to eat. Then Dad, Matthew and Mark took Eager back to Mr. McDaniel's farm. Mr. McDaniel was so happy to get his dog back, he doubled the reward from two dollars and fifty cents to five dollars."

Grandpa smiled, "That is pretty close to what happened," he said.

"Is that the miracle, Grandpa?"

"No," said Grandpa, as he looked at Charlie who was obviously puzzled.

"Charlie, let me tie all the threads together for you. Now, we both understand that stealing another man's dog is a wicked thing to do. Beating and mistreating a dog is also something that is sinful, agreed?"

"Agreed," said Charlie.

"So, Charlie, is God responsible for Mr. McDaniel having his best hunting dog stolen and then beaten and mistreated by a dog thief?"

"No," said Charlie.

"Well if God is not responsible then who is?" asked Grandpa.

"The Devil?" replied Charlie.

"Yes, in a way you're right. The answer is that the sin in the heart of man is responsible. And where did that sinful nature come from?"

Charlie thought for a moment. "Satan tempted Adam and Eve, and they sinned."

"That's right," said Grandpa. "We all have a sin nature because Adam first sinned in the garden."

Grandpa let Charlie think about it for a while and then asked his grandson a question. "So, Charlie, how do you think things end up that start out with sin?"

"Pretty bad," said Charlie.

Grandpa nodded his head and added, "The end result is death and separation from God, and that is pretty bad."

"Now for the good news," said Grandpa. "Because God was not willing to see us perish in our sins, He sent His Son to pay the penalty for our sin so we could be with Him in His home in Heaven." Charlie smiled. "But Charlie, that does not erase all the sin in this world, so God made a special promise to those that love His Son and love Him. And do you know what that special promise is?"

"I know what it is Grandpa," Charlie beamed. "God promised that if we love Him that He will make ALL things turn out for good."

"Does that mean everything?" asked Grandpa.

"Yes, *all* means everything."

"So now let's take a look at the bad thing that happened to Mr. McDaniel, and see how many ways God made it turn out for good."

"I can think of some ways," said Charlie. "Dad got a five dollar reward."

Grandpa chuckled. "Yes, and because of the five dollar reward, your mom was able to pay the one dollar fee to enter the Turkey Shoot. And because of the Turkey Shoot, Matthew got a rifle for his birthday and your mom and dad were four dollars richer. Not exactly what I had in mind, but I do see your point."

"I can think of another way it worked out for good, Grandpa."

"Please tell me." Grandpa replied as Charlie continued.

"Ginger had been praying every night that God would keep Eager from harm and return him home to Mr. McDaniel."

"Is that right?"

"Yep," said Charlie.

"So think about that for a minute, Charlie. Ginger has now had her faith increased. She knows that God hears and answers her prayers. We need people who pray, and it looks like God is preparing Ginger to be one of His special prayer warriors." Grandpa paused for a moment and then asked, "what else?" asked Grandpa.

"I know," said Charlie, "Mr. McDaniel was so happy you rescued his dog that he and Mrs. McDaniel came over and made a spaghetti dinner and breakfast for our whole family."

Grandpa laughed. "Can you think of anything else?" said Grandpa.

"No," said Charlie.

"Well, Charlie, all the things you mentioned are true and important in their own way, but there is one big miracle that happened that makes all the things you mentioned seem small by comparison." Grandpa continued, "The miracle happened last night in the Spice family living room."

Charlie didn't know what Grandpa was talking about since he had been taken back to his bed in the attic immediately after his dad read the story "The Hanging Judge."

"The miracle happened after you went to bed, Charlie. The story your dad got published, that just happened to show up that very night the McDaniels showed up for dinner, touched the souls of Mr. and Mrs. McDaniel.

"That night, Charlie, they both became very concerned about where they were going to spend eternity. Well, your Dad and I had the great privilege of leading Wally and Marie, I mean Mr. and Mrs. McDaniel, to the cross of Jesus Christ. They received the *free gift* of salvation offered by our Savior."

"Charlie, you look a little puzzled," said Grandpa. "Let me see if I can help you understand the ways of our God. You might think that nothing good could come out of someone stealing and mistreating your dog. But what that dog thief meant for evil, God turned into something good."

Charlie listened carefully as Grandfather explained, "If Eager had not been stolen, then I would never have been able to rescue him. And if I had not rescued him, then they would never have come to our farm to thank me and make a meal for our family. And if they had not come over for dinner, they would never have heard your dad read the story "The Hanging Judge." It was that simple story about the hanging judge that made them think about where they were going to spend eternity. And if they had not been concerned about their souls, then your dad and I would never have had the opportunity to tell them about the Savior, Jesus. If we had never told them about Jesus, then they might never have trusted in Him. And if they had not trusted in him, they would not be joining us in Heaven one day." Charlie had never thought about life the way Grandpa explained it. Charlie took a couple minutes to absorb it all and then said, "Grandpa, you mean that God takes the bad things, caused by sin and Satan, and works them out so people go to Heaven?"

Grandpa smiled. "He does it all the time, Charlie. Do you think maybe that is what he did with me?" said Charlie, looking down at his crippled legs.

"I think that is very possible," said Grandpa.

"It is pretty hard to get upset with God when all He wants is for you to be in Heaven with Him." said Charlie. "Pretty hard for us not to love Him, huh, Charlie?"

Charlie grinned and nodded.

Romans 8:28
And we know that all things work together for good to them that love God, to them who are the called according to his purpose.

Chapter 23

THE RAT

"hat in the world is that racket?" said Janet. "John, wake up, something is going on."

John stirred and finally awoke, "What is it, Honey?"

"I don't know, but it sounds like it is coming from the attic."

John stumbled around and was finally able to light the kerosene lantern that was on the small table next to his desk. "I will go investigate."

John put on his bathrobe and headed into the hallway. Janet followed close behind. "Definitely coming from the attic," said John. Just then, there was a crash. In the dark, Janet made a beeline for the attic with John following behind.

Charlie was throwing books and yelling his head off. "Charlie what on earth is the matter?" Janet said. They approached Charlie, who was white as a sheep.

"Son, you look like you have just seen a ghost," said Dad.

"Not a ghost Dad, a giant rat."

Janet cringed.

It was three o'clock in the morning, and there was nothing that could be done except to comfort Charlie and stay by his bedside until the morning sunrise lit up the attic.

There was no keeping a secret in the Spice family, and by the time everyone had eaten breakfast, the story of the rat in the attic had grown to biblical proportions. "I heard it was as big as a pole cat," Matthew teased John Jr.

"How big is a pole cat?" asked Luke. "Are there man eating rats?" Luke wondered out loud.

Mom finally said, "You eat your breakfast, and forget about the rats."

Matthew nudged Rosemary and said, "I told you there was more than one; there was a whole herd of rats." Rosemary responded back, "Rats don't travel in herds, they travel in flocks like ducks."

Luke piped up, "you're both wrong, rats travel in packs like dogs."

"No more rat talk!" announced Mom in her most commanding voice.

Just then, Grandpa and Grandma showed up for breakfast. "What was that commotion about last night?"

As if conducted by the baton of an orchestra leader, everyone chimed in at the same time to raise a rousing chorus of "RATS!"

Everyone had an opinion about how to deal with the very unwelcome intruder. John listened to Janet and Anna conspire together to concoct a homemade rat poison, while Mark and Luke were busy drawing up plans for a rat trap.

Finally, John, as the head of the household, announced his solution. "Tonight," proclaimed John, "Scruffy is going to sleep in the attic." Everyone agreed that this was a wonderful idea. Matthew was the first to point out that Scruffy was a Retriever and not a Rat Terrier. John was quick to point out that Scruffy had dealt with raccoons, snakes, possums, wild cats and even a porcupine. "Scruffy will make short work of a scrawny rat," Dad declared, feeling a tinge of pride as he lifted up the reputation of the dog that had come from a line that went back to a famous canine hero of the Civil War.

When Charlie heard that Scruffy was going to be sleeping by his bed-side, he was cheered and comforted. It seemed that the rat problem was well in hand.

The day passed, and just before nightfall Scruffy was brought into the house and led up the stairs to the attic. Once there, she was coaxed and bribed into settling into a pile of old blankets that were carefully placed next to Charlie's bed.

Everyone went to bed that night convinced that the rat terror was about to come to an unhappy end. Any rodent who dared to trespass on the domain of Scruffy—the celebrated ancestor of the first famous Scruffy, who was the most decorated dog in the Civil War—was doomed.

Of course, the Civil War stories about Scruffy's great, great, great grand-mother were highly exaggerated at best, and probably whopping untruths at worst.

Stories like the tall tales of Scruffy were the stuff of great family legends. Since the stories were never to be printed in the pages of any historical documents, but only held gently in the collective oral history of the Spice family, who would ever dispute it?

Nightfall came and the Spice household drifted off into slumber that lasted about four hours.

A clatter arose from the Spice family attic. Every member of the Spice family was roused out of their sleep. Converging in the hallway with candles and lanterns, they were all heading up the stairs to the Eagle's Nest.

Janet was wielding a frying pan, Anna a broom, John a had baseball bat, and Grandpa had grabbed his bullwhip. Matthew was heading up the stairs with his unloaded, new 22 caliber rifle, Luke was armed with a crusty fly swatter, Mark had pulled a wooden plank out from under his bed, and Rosemary was wielding a rolling pin. Ginger and Cinnamon were both

clutching their apple head dolls and John Jr. was marching up the stairs with his bow and arrows with the rubber suction cups.

This rat was in serious trouble!

Just then, Scruffy let out a yelp that would raise the dead and went tearing down the stairs knocking everything over in her path, including John Jr., Ginger and Cinnamon. Scruffy was yelping like a puppy that just put her nose in a wasp nest.

Undeterred, the family continued up the stairs. Charlie was yelling his head off and throwing anything he could get his hands on at the illusive phantom rat.

The room lit up with all the candles and kerosene lanterns.

Janet and Anna got everyone settled down as John went down the stairs to check on Scruffy, who was nowhere to be found. John heard her whimpering and finally found her hiding under the kitchen table. "Come here, girl," he commanded. Scruffy dutifully arrived to put her big head in John's gentle hands. "What happened to you?" he said as he carefully examined the dog under the dim kerosene light. "Oh, I see," said John, "that rat took a bite out of your tender nose."

Just then Janet entered the kitchen.

"Grandma is tucking all the children back into bed."

"I will sit up with Charlie," said John. "You need to get some sleep."

"We both need to get some sleep," announced Janet. "Grandpa has volunteered to sit up with Charlie."

Janet nursed Scruffy and let him outside where they both figured she would be safe.

It took about a half an hour for things to quiet down and get back to the sleep that had eluded them all for the past two nights.

The next morning was filled with nothing but rat talk. The Spice family had all descended into a murderous conspiracy to kill the rat. Everyone had an idea of just how to dispose of the rodent.

The next plan was employed by Janet and Anna who did their best to remember all the ingredients that went into Great Grandma's toxic rat remedy. Great Grandma, as they all clearly remembered, had come up with a recipe so potent that once the rat took a single bite out of the poison cookie, he would fall over dead on the spot. One big batch of the deadly rat cookies was made and carefully baked in the oven.

John made the announcement, "No children are to go into the attic for any reason until the rat is dead." John and Janet were not concerned about a rat attack, but were concerned that one of the smaller children would think they had found a cookie and poison themselves. Charlie was told that only adults were to enter into his Eagle's Nest until they had poisoned the rat.

The rat cookies were strategically and carefully placed. "That's ten," said Janet.

"Ten is right," Anna confirmed.

Janet decided that she would sit up with Charlie that night.

Janet put her trusty frying pan on Charlie's nightstand and reached for one of his books. "When is the last time you read Daniel Defoe's *Robinson Crusoe*?" asked Mom.

"Dad and I have been reading it together," said Charlie.

"Tell me about the story." Janet said who had started reading the book as a young girl but had never finished it.

"It is about a man that is shipwrecked on an island." said Charlie.

"Would it be all right if I read it with you?" asked Janet as she opened to the place where the red ribbon marked the next chapter. Janet opened the book and began reading at Chapter four.

Janet looked up from the book as she heard the soft breathing of her son. Charlie had drifted into a peaceful slumber. She bookmarked the previous page, not quite sure when Charlie had nodded off. Janet slipped the book back into the space it had just vacated and left it sticking out for easy retrieval.

There were a lot of things that Charlie could *not* do, but the one thing he *could* do was embark on great adventures by reading books—a pleasure he had learned to treasure.

Janet made herself as comfortable as she could in the overstuffed chair John had slid over by the side of Charlie's bed. She put her feet up on the embroidered stool, covered herself with blankets and fluffed the pillow. Just before she went to sleep, she reached over and grabbed her frying pan and placed it on top of the covers, and turned off the lantern.

Charlie and Mom spent the next several hours in restful sleep. It was approximately three in the morning when Janet felt Charlie tugging on her sleeve. "Mom, Mom," Charlie whispered. Janet opened her eyes and rubbed them and said, "What?" Charlie continued to whisper, "Mom the rat is eating your poison cookies." Janet reached over and found the matches and quietly lit the lantern. Janet scanned the attic and although it was dimly lit, she could see the rat in the corner by the table with the checker board munching greedily on one of her cookies.

"He will drop dead before you can count to three," said Janet confidently.

"One... two... three," Charlie counted slowly. "Mom, he's moving!"

Charlie and his mom watched as the large rodent sniffed his way to the location of the next cookie. "One bite should have done him in," said Janet, still whispering.

"He ate the whole cookie, I think he likes them," said Charlie.

"I am going to give him something he won't like," said Janet as she grabbed the handle of her cast iron frying pan. She then leapt from the chair and headed in the direction of the rat, tripping as she knocked over the checker table and one of the chairs. She lifted the frying pan and aimed it in the direction of the rat, which was on the move. She missed the rat but did manage to put a huge hole in the wallboard.

Charlie grabbed the lantern, rolled over to the side of his bed, and shone the lantern on the floor to help his mom locate the rat. "There it is," yelled Charlie, "next to the clock with the angels." Janet picked herself up off the floor and quickly made her way to the bookshelf with the porcelain clock. The rat had found another cookie and seemed more interested in eating it than escaping. Janet took careful aim and swung the iron skillet with all her might. The antique clock broke into a hundred pieces and the two gold angels went flying into the middle of the attic where they landed in a dozen pieces. The rat dashed safely out of range and out of sight.

Charlie moved the lantern around to see if he could locate the rodent. "He is over by the toy chest!" shouted Charlie. In a blind rage, Janet headed for the toy chest and began pummeling everything in sight, and swinging her frying pan with deadly force. "He ran under the floor," reported Charlie.

By this time, half the family was on their way up into the attic—armed with lanterns, bats, bullwhips, and a big kitchen knife.

As the room was lit up with the additional two lanterns, the extent of the carnage became visible.

John viewed the destruction with amazement but thought better of actually saying what he was thinking. Instead, John comforted his wife who was in no mood to have a conversation with anyone. She had worked herself into an emotional state and had begun to cry. "It won't seem so bad in the morning," said John as he escorted his wife to her bed. It wasn't true.

Psalm 27:1
The LORD is my light and my salvation;
whom shall I fear?
the LORD is the strength of my life;
of whom shall I be afraid?

Chapter 24

The Contraption

T he next morning, everyone except Janet made a beeline for the Eagle's Nest. Grandpa had taken up sentry duty after the "Battle of Rat Hill," which was the name given to the fiasco. It was a name that would conjure up the most delicious escapades in the memories of the Spice family for generations to come.

Grandpa fell asleep in the big stuffed chair next to Charlie's bed. He was happy to be gently awakened the next morning by his wife, who had brought him a piping hot cup of very strong coffee. "Thank you, Love," Grandpa whispered, not wanting to wake up Charlie.

Grandpa James and Grandma Anna surveyed the damage in the attic with amazement. "Looks like the Battle of Bull Run," said Grandpa.

Grandma spearheaded a cleanup operation that was designed to get the place in order before Janet came up and viewed the damage. Everyone got busy putting things back in place and sweeping up the broken clock and a couple other collectibles that were damaged beyond repair.

"Well, except for that hole in the wall, and the two missing pictures, some broken brick-a-brack, and the clock, everything looks normal," said Grandpa.

"I will bring your breakfast up in a couple minutes Charlie," said Dad. "OK, everybody scoot downstairs and help your mom get breakfast ready."

The usual din that accompanied breakfast was absent that morning— all except for Mark and Luke who were obviously up to something.

"Hey Dad," said Mark, "can we show you something we made in the barn?"

"As soon as you have finished your breakfast," said Dad.

As soon as breakfast was done, Mark and Luke grabbed their dad's hand and eagerly escorted him into the barn. "What have you boys been up to?" Dad asked. Mark and Luke just smiled as they headed for the small workshop that was tucked into the corner of the barn.

"Wow!" said Dad. "What in the world is that?"

"It is our latest invention."

"What does it do?" asked Dad.

"It kills rats," said Mark proudly.

John gazed in disbelief. "Ah, kills rats?"

"Yep," said Luke.

Mark and Luke had salvaged a large tin washing tub. "Let me show you how it works," said Mark. "You see this see-saw?"

"Hmmm," acknowledged Dad.

It took about five minutes for Mark and Luke to explain how the contraption worked. Basically, it was a tub with a metal rod that was fastened between the two handles on the top of the washtub. Mark and Luke had fashioned what looked like a teeter-totter; it was hinged to the metal rod.

One end of the wooden plank that was acting as a teeter-totter overlapped one end of the tub. The other end of the teeter-totter was about six inches short of reaching the other end of the top of the tub. On the outside of the tub they had built a make shift ladder that led up to the teeter-totter.

"Let me show you how it works, Dad," said Mark as he picked up a small dirt clod. "OK. Let's pretend this dirt clod is the rat bait."

"OK," said Dad, who was still not completely sure what it was he was looking at, and how it was ever going to catch or kill a rat.

Mark carefully placed the small dirt clod on the end of the teeter-totter, suspended by the rod that went through the handles of the washtub. Mark explained, "Now, imagine that the tub is filled with water, but not to the top. Imagine that we smear bacon grease along the inside of the tub above the water line."

"OK," said Luke, "pretend I am the rat." Dad watched as Luke walked with his index and middle finger up the makeshift ladder onto the teeter-totter. He then made his way down the teeter-totter to where the dirt clod was. Then Luke pushed the teeter totter down, spilling the dirt clod into the bottom of that washtub. "Oh, I am drowning," said Luke in a high squeaky voice. "I am drowning and I can't climb out of this washtub because the sides are too slippery from bacon grease."

Just then, Grandpa, who was on the trail of this adventure, entered the workshop.

"Look at this," said John with a broad smile, "a rat killing machine."

Grandpa looked it over and immediately understood the concept. "It just might work," said Grandpa, "and it is certainly worth a try."

John stroked his chin. "Better keep this our secret weapon and not let Janet see us carrying this thing up into the attic," said Dad.

"Agreed," said Grandpa.

The four conspirators waited until Janet was outdoor hanging up the wash. With great stealth, they carefully carried the rat contraption up the stairs and into the attic.

They decided to set up the rat contraption in the middle of the Eagle's Nest. "We need to fill it with water," said Grandpa.

"The buckets are in the pantry," announced Dad.

"Don't forget the bacon grease," added Mark.

After fifteen minutes, and many trips up and down the stairs, the "rat water death trap" was filled and ready for action.

There was only one small, but very important, missing ingredient. "What are we going to use for bait?" asked Mark.

"Good question," replied Grandpa.

John smiled, as he headed downstairs and fished one of the rat cookies out of the trash. Upon his quick return, the rat bait was placed at the end of the teeter-totter. The two grown men and two small boys gathered around the water tub and just stared at it for a couple of minutes.

They found themselves in a brotherhood that knew no age limit, forged together with high purpose and secrecy. It was the stuff of legends and gave each of them a connection with the other that was hard to explain but would last a lifetime.

The four conspirators quietly slipped down the stairs without bringing any attention to themselves—each secretly praying that the plan would work.

Later on that afternoon, Janet, still traumatized by the events of the night before, asked John if it would be all right if they ate in the dining room instead of the Eagle's Nest. "Would you mind bringing Charlie down tonight for dinner?" Mom asked.

"I think that is a great idea," said John, who was not eager to hear Janet's opinion about the water trap that was now the centerpiece of the Spice family attic.

Dinnertime arrived as the sun was about to go down. Grandpa went upstairs to fetch Charlie, and on the way down he told Charlie not to mention the "rat water trap". "If it doesn't work, we will never hear the end of it," said Grandpa, who was always one to promote peace in the family, which sometimes meant waiting for something to actually work out before declaring authoritatively that it would.

Grandpa and his son both had their doubts about the efficacy of Mark and Luke's invention, but figured, "nothing ventured, nothing gained." Mark and Luke had no doubts. They could hardly wait for the sun to go down and the rat to come out and finally meet his match.

Dinner went smoothly without a word about what was on everyone's minds—rats.

Grandpa finished before everyone else and went back up into the attic to retrieve *Pilgrim's Progress*.

"Where were we?" asked Grandpa as he turned the pages of the old book.

"Let me see, where did we leave Christian?"

"He just fell into the Slough of Despond," said Rosemary.

"Oh yes, here we are," said Grandpa, and began reading.

Now I saw in my dream, just as they had finished talking, that they came near to a very miry swamp that was in the middle of the valley. Then suddenly, both Christian and Pliable, who were not paying attention to where they were walking, fell into the swamp. The name of the swamp was the Slough of Despond. Both wallowed there until they were both completely covered with mud. Christian, weighed down by the burden on his back, began to sink into the slime.

Matthew nudged Luke, who was seated next to him. "The Rat Slough of Despond", whispered Matthew.

Luke snickered, which brought a quick rebuke from their dad. "You boys pay attention and stop giggling."

"Yes, Dad," both boys chimed.

Grandpa finished reading the passage from *Pilgrim's Progress*, which was always followed by questions and answers.

"Let's make an early night of it," announced Mom.

Rosemary had taken the family temperature and decided that getting Mom to bed was going to be the best medicine for a mother who obviously needed some sleep and solace. "I will take care of all the dishes and clean up," announced Rosemary, who immediately began clearing the table.

John immediately got out of his chair and walked behind Janet's chair, leaned over and gave her a kiss on the neck. He then pulled her chair out and escorted her to the bedroom where he kissed her again, fluffed her pillow and bid her sweet dreams. "I will be back in a minute," said John. Janet responded with a mumble as she immediately went to sleep.

The rest of the family tried to stay quiet as they did their bedtime chores, cleaned up the kitchen, and went to bed. John said, "goodnight," and slipped into the bedroom, careful not to wake his wife.

Grandpa and Charlie were the last ones up. "Do you want to sleep down here tonight?" Grandpa asked.

"Oh no," said Charlie, "I want to be in the attic when the rat gets baptized."

Grandpa laughed out loud. "Charlie you say the funniest things sometimes."

"That's what Dad says all the time."

"He does?"

"Yep, he says there are some sinners in town he would like to baptize until the bubbles stop coming up."

Grandpa laughed again.

Charlie was carried up the stairs and tucked into his bed.

The Spice family house was silent from the bottom to the top. Four hours of uninterrupted sleep became five, and then six, and then seven, and then "KERSPLASH!"

Charlie was up in his bed in a flash. He lit his lantern and looked at his clock. It was four thirty in the morning. He wanted to wait until the family rose at sunrise, but that was two hours away. Finally, he gave into the most tremendous urge he had ever experienced, grabbed the knot on the rope that hung above his bed, and began ringing the bell.

The clanging was deafening. Everyone was immediately awakened and after fully coming to their senses, began streaming up the stairs and into the attic.

John was the first one to arrive, with Grandpa James on his heels. They did not need to ask Charlie why he was ringing the bell, as they immediately headed toward the washtub. "Did we get em?" yelled Charlie, who was obviously excited.

Grandpa looked at John and then turned to Charlie and exclaimed, "Got em!" Charlie started bouncing on his bed with glee.

The next three up the stairs were Matthew, Mark and Luke. Mark and Luke shook hands with each other and received their congratulatory praise from everyone present.

The next one up the stairs was Ginger, followed by Cinnamon and Grandma.

Soon everyone arrived, except Janet. As they all stood around the "Rat Slough of Despond," Janet finally arrived.

"What in the world?" she said.

"Come here darling," said John. Janet approached to view the very large floating dead rat. "You know what did him in?" said John.

"What?" said Janet.

"That rat walked the plank for your cookies," John jokingly replied. Janet laughed, for the first time in days.

There is really no way to explain it—since normally viewing a dead rat floating in a washtub would not be humorous—but for the Spice family, in the wee hours of a cold October morning, the sight of a floating dead rat was the funniest thing in the entire world.

Psalm 40:1-2

*I waited patiently for the Lord; and he inclined unto me,
and heard my cry. He brought me up also out of an horrible pit,
out of the miry clay, and set my feet upon a rock,
and established my goings.*

Chapter 25

Work

Bert Henderson considered John Spice a good friend. He also considered him his best employee, even if he only worked part time. Bert had taken over the mill from his father who had ambitions of building a business, manufacturing dressers and washboards. Those plans never seemed to materialize, and after several failed attempts, Bert Henderson had settled into milling hardwood for other manufacturers.

Bert was a man that was slow to make changes. This caution kept him solvent for many years while some of his competitors boomed and then went bust.

In the end Bert's, milling operation was simply too old fashioned to keep up the competition. Since most of his customers were located a hundred miles or more from Elkin, the cost of transporting his lumber, even with the introduction of the railroad, was cutting his margins so low that he could simply not compete.

Bert had a decision to make. He could take all his savings and reinvest in new machinery with hopes of catching up with his competition, or he could close up his mill, sell the land and retire. Bert was nearly seventy years old and decided not to risk his remaining capital on restarting his business. His one son had left Elkin years ago, and had gone on to work for a furniture manufacturer in Drexel, North Carolina. *The most sensible thing to do*, thought Bert, *was to put a "FOR SALE" sign in front of the mill, suspend all operations and retire.* And that is exactly what he did.

John was aware that things weren't going well for Bert, but when he was brought into his office, he was surprised, Bert sat him down and handed him a leather bag that contained seventy-five silver dollars and a letter of thanks for all his faithful service.

John had been like a second son to Bert, and so it was not surprising that a tear trickled down his cheek as he reached over the table to shake John's hand. "Sorry, John, wish things had turned out different."

John shook Bert's hand and asked, "Are you going to be alright?"

Bert smiled, "I am going to be fine. I have one more load of maple and walnut going to Drexel and that's the final order."

"What are you going to do with the rest of this lumber?" asked John. Bert paused and smiled at John.

"The question, John Spice," said Bert, suddenly energized by the inquiry, "is what are *you* going to do with all this lumber?"

John was stunned, "You're joking."

"John Spice, when have you ever known me to joke about anything?" asked Bert. John was at a loss for words. He stood up and went around the table and gave the old man a bear hug.

John spent the rest of the week making trips to and from the mill, loading and unloading a thousand dollars or more worth of hardwood lumber.

By the middle of the week, John had made six trips back and forth from the farm to the mill and had collected about half the lumber. Wally McDaniel got wind of what John was doing and showed up with his wagon the following morning. By the end of the week, the two men had the job completed.

"I don't know how to thank you, Wally," said John.

"I do," said Wally. "Let me have a couple of those walnut slabs so I can build a table for my big family."

"Your big family?"

"That's right," said Wally. "Marie is cooking up a batch of youngsters as we speak." "You mean Marie is pregnant?" exclaimed John.

"That is one way of looking at it," said Wally.

John beamed with excitement, "That is wonderful, Wally, congratulations! Take anything you need."

Wally pointed to the two walnut slabs that were still in his wagon smiled, and said, "They're already loaded," Wally.

Wally waved to John as he headed home with his two slabs of walnut and his visions of a growing family. Just then, Janet came into the barn to see what she could do to help. "What in the world!" she exclaimed.

"I know what you mean," said John. "We will never lack for wood again."

Janet smiled, "Looks like the Lord has plans for you," she said with a wry smile.

"Looks like," said John, who had been thinking the same thing.

It would take John another week to organize and grade all the varieties of hardwood. And another week to strategically locate it for long-term storage.

Bert Henderson's gift would keep on giving for years to come. Which, of course, was the very thought he had in mind when he decided to bless John Spice with a couple thousand board feet of premium hardwoods. It was a gift that would give pleasure to the Spice family for years to come. John was a skilled carpenter and loved making furniture. And as it turned out, there were plenty of folks that loved the furniture John made. A cottage industry, with a large profit margin already built into it, was unloaded in the Spice family barn that week.

Charlie and Grandpa could see the last load of hardwood being slowly pulled to the barn by Stubborn, who was clearly moving a lot slower than normal. This was the hardest work Stubborn had ever done, and he was going to need a lot of alfalfa hay, a good rubdown, some sweet-talking and some down time to recover some of his optimism for pulling the Spice Farm wagon.

Grandpa yelled a greeting out the window as Charlie waved at Mr. McDaniel, who was heading home with a wagon filled with two giant walnut slabs. Wally took his cowboy hat off and waved it over his head. He then shouted "Yee-haw, giddy-up," as his two horses picked up their pace and quickly trotted off the Spice farm.

Proverbs 3:9-10

Honour the Lord with thy substance, and with the firstfruits of all thine increase: So shall thy barns be filled with plenty, and thy presses shall burst out with new wine.

Chapter 26

The Mystery of the Black Wall

randpa closed the window and helped Charlie sit up in the bed. "You ready to learn more about Heaven?" asked Grandpa.

"Yes, sir," said Charlie, who couldn't think of anything he was more interested in than learning about the Celestial City where he was going to spend eternity.

Grandpa James had asked John if it was all right if he read through some of his unpublished stories. As he sorted through them, he found one that caught his eye. It was titled *A Particular Place for A Particular People*.

"OK, Charlie, are you ready for Heaven's quiz before I read you this story your dad wrote?"

"Ready," said Charlie, as he focused in preparation for the first question.

"Why are you going to Heaven in the first place?" Grandpa asked.

"Because Jesus has a soft spot in His heart for sinners," announced Charlie.

Grandpa smiled at Charlie and shook his head. "Charlie it's not just that Jesus has a soft spot in His heart for sinners."

Grandpa thought for a minute and then said. "OK, Charlie. Jesus had five other 'soft spots,' do you know where they were?"

Charlie scratched his head and finally gave up. "I don't know, Grandpa."

Grandpa lifted up his right hand and pointed to it with his left index finger. Charlie looked puzzled. Grandpa then pointed to his other hand. Grandpa then stood up and pointed to his side. And finally, Charlie leaned over the side of his bed to watch as Grandpa pointed to his feet.

Grandpa sat back down and took Charlie's hand and pressed his index finger gently into the soft spot between his wrist and his palm.

"One nail went right there, Charlie."

Grandpa took Charlie's other hand and lifted it gently up in the air. "And another nail went right there," said Grandpa, as he pressed gently into the same spot on the other hand.

Grandpa slowly lifted the blanket from Charlie's bed and pressed his hand against his side. "And right there is where a Roman soldier pierced Jesus with a spear," Grandpa said. "And where are the other two soft spots, Charlie?"

"Where they nailed the feet of Jesus to the cross," said Charlie.

"So we might say that Jesus had a soft spot in His heart for sinners and five wounds to prove it.

"Next Question," said "Grandpa. "Heaven is a lot of things, but first and foremost, what is Heaven?"

Charlie quickly answered, "It is a gift."

"So, Charlie, it didn't cost you anything?"

"Nothing," said Charlie, "Heaven is a free gift."

"That is quite a gift don't you think?"

"I think it is the best gift ever," said Charlie.

"Are you sure it didn't cost anything?" asked Grandpa again.

Charlie stopped to think. "Well it didn't cost *me* anything," answered Charlie.

"But it did cost something," Grandpa inquired again.

"Yes, it cost Jesus a lot," said Charlie. "It cost Him His life and a lot of suffering on the cross."

Grandpa opened up his Bible to 1 Peter 1 and read the following verses, *"Forasmuch as ye know that ye were not redeemed with corruptible things, as silver and gold, from your vain conversation received by tradition from your fathers; But with the precious blood of Christ, as of a lamb without blemish and without spot:*

Charlie watched with interest as Grandpa carefully fished the handwritten manuscript out of the large envelope. He shuffled the pages and put his glasses on and began to read one of the stories Charlie's dad had written.

"Your dad has written a very interesting story, Charlie," Grandpa said, as he adjusted his glasses and began to read.

A Particular Place for a Particular People

Double Trouble

Ethan and his wife, Anna watched their twin boys playing tag together in the lush meadow that gently curled around their modest home. "If Jacob and Esau struggled with each other in Rebekah's womb, then Amos and Benjamin were giggling inside yours." Ethan said with a smile.

It must have been true because there were never two people in the world that enjoyed each other's company more than these two 11-year-old boys. They were two peas in a pod from all appearances. But appearances can be deceiving.

Amos and Benjamin were the mirror images of each other, but their personalities were as different as day and night. Amos was the adventurer, and Benjamin was the thinker. Amos was impetuous, and Benjamin was cautious and careful.

When Amos and Benjamin were not romping together, they were scheming together. The two boys had developed a curiosity about life that was always landing them into the middle of somebody else's business.

To put it plainly, they were snoops who were always looking for some mystery to solve. They considered themselves quite the duo when it came to getting to the bottom of anything that seemed out of order.

The secret to solving mysteries, they had discovered, was gathering information and following the trail of clues wherever it leads. And these two tykes were just the right size to go un-noticed as they lurked and spied around the bustling town that they called home.

It was the twins who discovered the identity of the thief that stole their Aunt Deborah's missing pendant. Not only did they uncover the feathered culprit, but they followed him until they found his nest. There, they retrieved the jewelry, along with some other trinkets, and secreted away in a hidden hole covered by a special rock scratched with the initials A for Amos and B for Benjamin.

It was the twins that figured out why the bread their Uncle Ezra baked always went missing every Saturday before sundown. And it was the twins who followed the stray dog into the small wooded patch next to the meadow and found four puppies in need of care and feeding.

One of those puppies had grown into a handsome mutt that followed the twins wherever they went. The twins adopted him and gave him the name *Sniffer* because he always had his nose to the ground following the scent of one thing or another.

The Mystery of the Black Wall

"Amos, look," yelled Benjamin, "it's Uncle Ezra."

Amos and Benjamin watched their Uncle Ezra running to greet Mom and dad. Something was wrong. Ezra was an old man and he never ran anywhere.

"C'mon," Amos yelled at Benjamin, "something is going on."

Amos and Benjamin made their way to the side of the house where they crept to the outside corner to hear what was being said without being seen. Sniffer followed behind with his nose to the ground.

Uncle Ezra stopped to catch his breath as Ethan and Anna rushed to meet him. "What's wrong, Uncle?" said Anna. Ezra lifted his hand, but said nothing, as he inhaled and exhaled to catch his breath. Finally, he lifted his head and began to speak.

Amos and Benjamin where too far away to hear very clearly, but they did make out the gist of what Uncle Ezra was aerated about.

Benjamin was the best listener of the two and reported the conversation as best he could to Amos.

"Uncle Ezra says something terrible is happening, a great wall has surrounded our city," said Benjamin. He thought for a minute and then turned to Amos and said, "We better find out what is happening." Amos agreed, and the boys made their way back down into the meadow and into the little woods where they hid themselves for a couple of minutes, until they figured it was safe to travel. They knew that if anything strange was going on that their mom was going to lock them in their rooms. There was a mystery to solve, a big mystery—and Amos and Benjamin were going to solve it.

The two boys quietly and quickly made their way through the little wooded patch and into the green valley with its rolling hills and farms. Amos pointed across the valley to a familiar spot that suddenly looked eerily unfamiliar, "That's where we need to go," pointed Amos.

It was a sunny day; the wildflowers were in bloom and the birds and the bees were all doing what they always do on a beautiful spring day. As the boys pressed forward, they became aware that something was different; something was wrong.

The two boys traveled quickly with no stops or delays. As they approached their destination they began to see the signs of something they had never seen before; something ominous was just ahead, towering above them.

They slowed their pace as they approached the wall their Uncle Ezra had described to Mom and Dad.

As the boys drew closer, their eyes were drawn upward. "This wall goes all the way up into the sky," said Amos.

"I can't see the top of it," replied Benjamin.

The Night Terror

As they approached the wall, they began to be afraid. "Let's go home," Benjamin insisted.

"No," said Amos, "I am going to touch the wall and then we can go home."

Amos approached the giant, black wall with Benjamin and Sniffer a pace or two behind. Whatever this was, Sniffer didn't want anything to do with it. He stopped in his tracks and just sat there watching and whining.

Amos cautiously crept forward. Finally, within a foot of the wall, Amos carefully reached out to touch it. He reached further and further but could not feel the wall. Benjamin, who was watching the drama intently, said, "Amos, your hand just went into the wall."

The two boys looked at each other and wondered what to do next. "This is no ordinary wall," said Benjamin, as Amos plunged his arm in and out of the wall, watching his forearm disappear and reappear.

"I am going in," said Amos.

"No, you're not," protested Benjamin.

"Yes, I am," said Amos, stubbornly.

"OK. If you're going in, then I am going to hold on to you."

Amos positioned himself to walk into the black barrier while Benjamin held onto his left hand. Slowly, Amos inched into the wall; first his feet disappeared and then his legs and shoulder. Finally, Amos tucked his head in the pitch-black darkness and completely disappeared, except for his left hand.

Suddenly, Amos let out a bone-chilling shriek. "Help me!" Amos yelled, as Benjamin pulled Amos back into the daylight.

"What did you see?" asked Benjamin frantically.

Amos kept ahold of Benjamin's hand and pulled him well away from the black wall. Now safely away from the straight up, vertical, black-as-pitch wall of darkness, Amos caught his breath and said, "I think it's alive."
"What do you mean?" asked Benjamin.

"I can't explain it exactly, but it, felt like it was going to eat me."

306 | Chapter 26

"What did you see?" Benjamin pressed.

"You can't see anything except blackness," said Amos.

"Like the night?"

"Nothing like the night," said Amos. "It is a blackness you can feel."

Amos, who was usually the one who lingered, was anxious to get home as quickly as possible. Whatever this was, he wanted nothing more to do with it. All of a sudden, seemed home like a wonderful idea.

Amos was quiet for most of the way home, but as they approached the crest of the rolling hill that gave them a view of their home, he said, "The sun sure does feel good." Although Benjamin had not experienced the terror of the black night, he had ventured close enough to feel its horror and understood exactly what his brother meant.

When they arrived home, they were greeted by a flurry of hugs and kisses. "Where have you two been?" asked Mom.

"We went to see the black wall," said Benjamin.

The Mystery is Solved!

Just then, a new visitor burst into the house—it was Aunt Deborah, and she was in a state of elevated excitement. It must be something important because she didn't even notice Amos or Benjamin, who were her favorite nephews, and the recipients of an unmerciful wave of hugging and kissing every time she showed up.

"Aaron has brought us news of the night terror," she reported. "Moses has given the King another sign from YHVH. Egypt is completely enveloped in a black horror. God has spared us and shines His light on us while Egypt trembles in the black darkness."

Grandpa finished the story, neatened the pages, and put them back into the large envelope.

"Do you recognize the story, Charlie?"

"Yes," said Charlie, "it is the story of one of the plagues that God brought upon Egypt."

"So let me ask you a question, Charlie. If God had not sent the darkness to Egypt, would it have made any difference to the children of Israel?"

Charlie mused and shrugged his shoulders.

Grandpa continued, "The day would be no brighter for them than any other day."

"So, it wouldn't make any difference?"

Grandpa smiled, "Do you think God wanted it to make a difference? When Egypt went into darkness, the children of Israel were to understand their privilege of living in the light. The darkness would have made them appreciate something they had taken for granted."

Grandpa continued, "Charlie, when if you were in the light and your neighbors were trapped in thick darkness, what would you think?" Charlie smiled, "I would think that God sure loved me a lot." Grandpa continued, "That's right, Charlie. You would not take the light for granted anymore; it would increase your understanding of God's grace and His favor."

"The people in the darkness must have been very afraid."

"Yes, and for good reason. Their wicked king was defying God by not letting his children go free." "Do you know what they called the land that the Hebrews were living in?"

"It was called the land of Goshen," said Charlie, who had obviously read this story many times.

"Do you understand that the land of Goshen was a particular place for a particular people, and only for those special people?" asked Grandpa. Charlie shook his head, yes. "OK, Charlie. So the lesson is that Heaven is a special, and very particular place, for those who have been redeemed by the blood of Jesus. Heaven is not for everyone. It is only for those who have received God's freely offered gift of His Son, and for none others."

"So let me ask you a real serious question, Charlie," Grandpa said, as he leaned over closer to his grandson. "Would Heaven still be Heaven if there were no hell?"

Charlie thought for a moment and said, "I suppose so."

Grandpa smiled, "You're right, but it is hell that sharpens our spiritual wits to the realities of eternal life. It is hell, like the night terror that enveloped Egypt, that is meant to remind us that Heaven is a Particular Place for those who have put their trust in the Lord Jesus, and it is not for anyone else. Do you know what I call that?" Charlie shook his head no, "I call it God's distinguishing Mercy!"

Charlie then asked, "Can anyone find mercy—no matter who they are or what they have done?"

Grandpa smiled and answered, "The first thing you need to understand about mercy, Charlie, is that God is not required, and God is under no obligation, to offer it to anyone. Against all odds, God has shown mercy to those who call upon His name with repentant and believing hearts. Others, who are enslaved by their lusts and happy in their darkness, will not seek mercy."

"They won't?" Charlie asked, clearly puzzled.

"No, they won't because they think themselves above it and in no need of it. So the answer to your question is *yes!* No one is excluded from coming to the cross of Jesus and trusting in Him in order to find mercy and grace. Anyone that comes God's way will find mercy; He has never turned anyone away.

"Charlie do you know what you are saved from?"

Charlie thought for a moment and answered, "From sin?"

Grandpa smiled, "It is true that Jesus took all our sin upon himself on the cross, but that is not what we are saved from."

"What are we saved from, Grandpa?"

"Charlie, you and I have been saved from the wrath of God, and it should make us rejoice and sing. That is one of the reasons that Heaven will be so wonderful. Heaven is a City of Refuge for the redeemed!"

Grandpa went over to the table with the checker board, picked it up and carefully put the board on Charlie's lap. They both tucked and smoothed the blankets until the board was level, and then they set up all the pieces. "Think you can beat me at checkers?" Grandpa said with a sly smile.

"Every day of the week, and twice on Sunday," said Charlie, who had played more games of checkers than any child on earth. Grandpa soon learned that Charlie was not kidding. After four games, Grandpa was convinced that in the checkers department, he was no match for Charlie Spice.

Psalm 86:4-5

*Rejoice the soul of thy servant: for unto thee, O Lord,
do I lift up my soul. For thou, Lord, art good,
and ready to forgive; and plenteous in mercy
unto all them that call upon thee.*

Chapter 27

Typewriters

hile Grandpa and Charlie were reading Dad's story and playing checkers, John and Janet were in the barn trying to figure out the path forward for the Spice family.

Janet produced a hot cup of coffee. John pulled down a bale of hay and sat on it as he beckoned his wife to join him.

John had not yet shared the news that he had lost his job at the mill. Janet knew that something was up when the wagon loads of wood started arriving on the farm. She also knew that John would let her know what was happening in his own time. Janet had learned that John took a while to sort things out in his mind and that it was not a good idea to press him too early when it came to changes.

John placed his cup of coffee in Janet's hand as he rose and went to get something out of the wagon. He returned with a leather pouch full of silver dollars. "Seventy-Five dollars," said John.

"From Bert?" asked Janet, having already guessed that whatever was going on had something to do with Bert and the mill.

"He closed the mill yesterday," John said.

Janet smiled. "So I will be seeing a lot more of you," she said, grabbing John's arm spilling hot coffee in his lap.

John and Janet sat on the bale of hay for over an hour as they discussed the future of the Spice family. Without a job, even a part-time job, life was going to change. Janet did some quick calculating and announced, "We have almost $200 saved up, and that is ten times more than we have ever had on hand at one time."

John smiled, "Yes, the Lord has been getting us ready for a new adventure."

This revelation from John was not bad news to Janet. She had a grateful and attentive heart, and was used to seeing the guiding hand of God in her life and the life of her family.

John bowed his head and began praying and thanking God for His gracious provisions. Janet prayed that God would give John wisdom as he led his household forward into an uncertain future.

The two kissed and walked hand in hand to the welcome warmth of the kitchen. Janet began heating up a pot of coffee.

The kids were all doing their inside chores as Anna came into the kitchen to join John and Janet. She listened carefully as they continued to discuss what the future was going to look like without a steady source of income.

James slipped down the stairs a few minutes later and also listened carefully to all the plans that were being discussed. James would not speak until he was asked for his opinion, which always provoked a lot of questions. He was not a man to offer advice until he understood what was going on. So it was not surprising when James was finally asked for his opinion that he began the conversation with a question. At first, it seemed like a question that was strangely out of place.

"So, what do you think, Dad?" asked John.

"I was wondering," said James, "what was different about the last story you sent to the publisher—the one that paid you $25 to print?"

"I don't understand what you mean, Dad." responded John.

"I guess what I am asking is this, was there anything different about that particular story? I have been reading your stories, Son, and they are all wonderful. So, I am asking, why was that story accepted and the other 50 or more stories you have been sending for the past three or four years, not?"

John thought for a moment. "Dad, there was nothing different about that story."

There was silence, and then Janet cleared her throat. "Well actually, John, there was one thing different about your story."

John looked puzzled. "I don't know what you mean, Janet." Janet grabbed a cup of coffee for herself and sat up straight in her chair. All eyes were now on Janet, as she obviously had a piece to the puzzle that was apparently a mystery to John and everyone else.

"Remember when we went to town three months ago to shop at the grocery store and mail in your latest story?"

"Yes, I remember," said John. I handed you the manuscript and you took it to the Post Office while the boys and I went to the Mercantile to buy some supplies," recounted John.

"Well," said Janet, "I didn't go to the Post Office with your manuscript, I went to the Elkin Times."

John listened intently as Janet continued telling her story.

"I had made the arrangements with Mr. Cartwright weeks earlier," she said.

"What arrangements?" asked John.

"Well, John, he agreed to have one of his reporters type out your handwritten manuscript and then mail it out in exchange for ten jars of apple jam."

Grandpa James knew nothing about this when he asked the question, but as it turned out, it was a question that would forever change the fortunes of the Spice family.

"So let me understand this," interjected James. "All the manuscripts except this one were sent out to publishers in long hand?"

"That's right," said Janet. "And I figured no one was reading them, so I decided to see what would happen if we sent one out that was typewritten."

John was stunned. He had never considered that his stories would be passed over because they were not typewritten.

Janet turned to John. "John, I knew your stories were wonderful, and I knew there must be some reason they were all being returned. So about a year ago, I started putting a dab of honey to stick some of the inside pages together. When they were returned, I began to check and see if the pages were still stuck together, and they were. So I knew no one was reading your stories."

John began to laugh. "You are the most clever, wonderful woman in the world." John beamed. James and Anna agreed as they all considered the door of opportunity that had just been opened.

Once things settled down, John became serious and said, "I really don't think we can afford to buy a typewriter right now. They cost about fifty dollars and that is just too much to spend on a pipe dream."

"I agree," said Janet. "Fifty dollars is way too much to spend right now, so we will only spend two dollars," Janet announced with a big grin. All eyes were on Janet again. "OK," she began, as everyone was looking to her for an explanation.

"Once I figured out that John's stories were not being read, I went in to talk to Mr. Cartwright at the Elkin Times. He agreed that publishers were probably getting hundreds of stories a week sent to them and just automatically sent back anything that was handwritten."

John, who was now on the trail of his wife's adventure, interrupted with, "I can't believe that Edgar Cartwright is going to sell you a typewriter for two dollars. Except for Elmer Horatio Smyth, Thaddeus E. Cartwright is the most tight-fisted man this side of Charlotte."

Janet looked at John, "You're right. He told me that they were going to be buying the latest typewriters in the fall and I could have my pick of the six Underwood typewriters they were replacing. He wanted twenty-five dollars for each one, but I whittled him down to ten dollars and 24 jars of apple jelly. I delivered the final jar of apple jelly to his wife last week and have been sending him a dollar a month from the egg money since January. I talked to him last time we were in town, and he said the new shipment of typewriters had arrived last week, and that I could pick up the Underwood typewriter as soon as I made the final payment of two dollars. He's also going to throw in a box of a dozen new ink ribbons." Janet concluded.

Anna, who had been quiet the entire time, asked if she might add something to the conversation. "Sure Mom," encouraged John, knowing that

Mom was not one for idle chatter and if she had something to say, it was always thoughtful and well timed.

"The last couple years in Bombay," said Anna, "I worked part time at the British Port Authority in order to help supplement the dwindling support we were receiving from our friends in England. To be fair, many of the old saints that were supporting us had gone to be with the Lord."

Anna continued, "To make a long story short, I was finally hired as a secretary for the British Port Authority. It turned out that I had a talent for keeping my typewriter working, while others were always having difficulty—bending the keys and keeping the ribbons fresh. It wasn't long before I was given the job of maintaining all the typewriters in the office. I also learned how to type quickly since the pay scale for secretaries was based on your secretarial skills, including how many words per minute you could type."

James interrupted, "Tell John and Janet how many words you can type a minute."

Anna smiled, "It took me a couple months of practice, but the last time I was tested I typed over thirty words a minutes on a well-oiled typewriter—which is the fastest you can type without bending the keys on a William's typewriter. Now, I have never used an Underwood typewriter, but I have heard you can type up to fifty words a minute on them without jamming the keys."

Anna continued, "John, I can help you pick out the best typewriter, and I would love to re-type all your stories so we can send them off to be published."

John did not know what to say and just sat there thinking about what had just happened. God had opened a door that a week before he thought was shut and bolted. James sensed the moment was right for prayer and led the family in a tearful melody of praise and thanksgiving to their Heavenly Father, who was so gently and kindly shepherding the path ahead.

Matthew 6:31-34
Therefore take no thought, saying, What shall we eat?
or, What shall we drink? or, Wherewithal shall we be clothed?
(For after all these things do the Gentiles seek:) for your
heavenly Father knoweth that ye have need of all these things.
But seek ye first the kingdom of God, and his righteousness;
and all these things shall be added unto you. Take therefore
no thought for the morrow: for the morrow shall take
thought for the things of itself. Sufficient unto
the day is the evil thereof.

Chapter 28

Goats

"Now let's talk about goats," announced Janet.

"Goats?" exclaimed John, who was still camped on the idea of earning his living as a Christian writer.

"Goats!" repeated Janet.

"When I was in town," Janet continued, "I had a conversation with Dick Grier, who agreed to buy all the goat cheese and milk I could produce, as long as it was fresh and clean."

"That's a lot of trips into town, and we only have one goat," said John.

Janet proceeded, "Judge William, goes into town every day, and his office is just three buildings and one flight of stairs up from Grier's Grocery. His wife loves my apple preserves, so I told him I would give him a jar of preserves and a half-dozen eggs for each trip he made into town with our goat's milk and cheese. He agreed as long as he did not have to load and unload the milk and cheese. So I talked to Dick Grier, who said he would unload the milk and cheese and supply the glass bottles and caps for the return trip."

John was amazed was as things seemed to be moving pretty fast under his feet. "But Love, we only have one goat," John repeated.

Janet's smile was the first clue that John's world was not as he had imagined it just moments before.

"You know Widow Benson's small goat dairy farm?" asked Janet.

"Yes," said John, half expecting to hear exactly what he did hear.

"Well, John, Widow Benson, as you know, is almost seventy years old. Her helper moved back to Charlotte, and she is unable to keep up with all the chores of the dairy. She decided last spring that she was going to live with her sister in Elkin, the one who just lost her husband. Widow Benson's biggest concern was what to do with her eighteen milking goats and Buster the billy goat."

John was an expert at only three things, writing, woodworking and goats. He had grown up in India and had managed his parent's small goat herd since he was old enough to milk. James and Anna were also very familiar with managing goats and listened carefully as Janet laid out her plan.

"Remind me again, Janet, what breed of dairy goat is Widow Benson milking?" asked John.

"Well," said Janet, "right now she is only milking one goat, and all the others have dried up. Four are pregnant, and the other thirteen are just eating up the profits."

Janet continued, "I am not sure about the breed of goat. About five years ago, she introduced a pure white buck and six white nannies."
"So Buster the billy goat is white?" asked John.

"Yep," replied Janet.

John had always had a strong interest in goats since he was a boy living in India, where goats were a way of life. "I think that white goat is called a Saanen. It's from Switzerland, or Austria, I am not sure which. Anyway, it is supposed to be a very good milker," said John.

"So how many white goats in her herd?" inquired John.

"I think I counted six," responded Janet. "The rest are just good old American milk goats, except for two others she just introduced to the herd."

"What do they look like?"

Janet thought for a minute. "They were larger than the other goats— chocolate brown with white ears and two white stripes down their face, and their legs were white."

John smiled, "That sounds like a Toggenburg; I have been reading about them. They are supposed to be a terrific milk goat, much better than the American milk goat."

"One more question, Janet," said John, "do you remember which goats were pregnant?"

"Oh, that's easy, all the white ones."

"That's perfect," said John.

"How much does she want for her dairy goats?" asked Grandpa James.

"She was asking $250 for the entire herd and all the equipment, including a year's supply of alfalfa hay and twenty-five bags of grain."

John's heart sunk. "Janet we don't have $250, and if we did, we wouldn't gamble it on a dairy business with only one goat to milk.

"Yes, I know that," said Janet.

John smiled at his dad as they both waited for the next shoe to drop. "So I suppose you 'negotiated' something with Widow Benson."

"Well," said Janet, "I did make a suggestion that she agreed to. But I did tell her that I would need to make sure you agreed also."

"So, what is it exactly that I need to agree to?" asked John.

There was a long pause as Janet took a deep breath. "I told her that we would move her to town."

John thought for a minute and said, "That's it?"

"Well," said Janet, "I also told her we would clean up the place for her so

the land agent could get top price for the property."

"And?" said John, knowing there was more.

"I told her we would paint her house next summer if it hadn't sold, but she has to buy the paint."

"Is that all?" John said as he leaned forward.

"Not exactly," said Janet. "I told her that we would give her one pound of goat cheese per month for the next year—and that is all," Janet proudly announced.

"Are you sure that's it?" John asked.

"Yep," said Janet with a big smile.

John thought about it for a minute and then said, "I think we are both getting a great deal. When does Widow Benson want to move?"

Janet clenched her teeth and said, "Immediately!"

"That's perfect," said John, without the slightest hesitation. "We will get this all done before winter."

"I can see you have a plan," said Grandpa James.

John stroked his chin and continued, "We get all the doe's pregnant right away so they have their kids in March and early April. We then sell all of the goats except the Saanen and Toggenburg. That's eleven milk goats we can sell off next summer. Last I checked, a good milk goat fetched about fifteen dollars and the female kids sell for about five dollars each. So, based on the law of averages, we end up with twenty kids, and let's guess that ten are female. We could make as much as $215. We keep all the Billie's until they are about nine months old, and then we butcher them for meat. We keep all the Saanen and Toggenburg kids to build up the herd. That would give us eight goats to milk the first year, and we could double that number every other year.

"I read that the Saanens can produce about a gallon of milk a day," continued John, "eight gallons a day is over 240 gallons a month. Goat's milk sells for about forty cents a half gallon, and goat cheese sells for eighty-five cents a pound. So if we find our own customers, that is about $200 a month before our expenses. It could be as much as $150 a month profit, but that's if nothing goes wrong, and we both know that never happens."

"So what's the rule I taught you since you were a kid?" asked Grandpa.

John didn't need to think about the rule that had been drilled into him as a young entrepreneur. "Make your best guess and cut it in half," said John as he smiled.

"So, this whole enterprise is going to cost all of us a couple weeks of hard labor, if we all pitch in. You might make $100 selling the goats you don't want to keep and maybe $75 a month selling milk and cheese, and maybe more as you go forward." Grandpa paused, "Have I left anything out?"

"That is pretty much it," said John.

"How much were you making working at Bert's?" Grandpa asked.

"When all was said and done, I brought home about eight dollars a week John responded, and then added, and, it was a lot of time traveling back and forth."

Grandpa paused and then said, "It sounds like a lot of work at the front end, but once that is done you will make about three times what you were making in about half the time," said James.

"Not really, Dad," said John with a big smile. "Every hour I was away from the family, I wished I was here working on the farm. Remember what you taught me? You don't count hours when you're working with your family." John smiled broadly, and announced, "This is a dream come true!"

Grandpa James smiled, "I was about to point out the very same thing."

Psalm 1:1-3

*Blessed is the man that walketh not in the counsel of
the ungodly, nor standeth in the way of sinners, nor sitteth in the
seat of the scornful. But his delight is in the law of
the LORD; and in his law doth he meditate day and night.
And he shall be like a tree planted by the rivers of water,
that bringeth forth his fruit in his season; his leaf also
shall not wither; and whatsoever he doeth shall prosper.*

Chapter 29

Getting Ready for Something

T he following morning was the beginning of an adventure that would leave the Spice family joyfully exhausted. When the last member of the Spice family showed up at the breakfast table, Dad made the announcement. "Today your bedroom chores are suspended," said Dad. This of course brought a smile to everyone's face as they imagined an entire day free from the drudgery of those everyday monotonous chores.

"Yippee" yelled Mark, who was already planning his own holiday.

"We have a big job to do and I need everyone to do, their part," continued John.

John went on to explain that as soon as breakfast was over he was going to hitch up the wagon and they were all—except for Grandma, Charlie, Cori, Ginger, and John Jr.—going to take a trip to Widow Benson's farm and begin moving her furniture to her sister's house in town.

After the announcement was made, Janet began barking out orders. "Rosemary, you get going and milk the goat and cow and make sure they are all fed. Matthew, you go help your father hitch up Stubborn. Mark, you go get all the blankets out of the attic and put them in the wagon. Luke, you go fetch the eggs from the hen house and bring them into the kitchen, carefully. Cinnamon, you go feed Scruffy and tie him up, I don't want him tagging along."

Grandma and the youngsters waved as the "Spice Family Furniture Moving Crew" made their way out to the dirt road that led to Widow Benson's farm, about two miles away.

They arrived at the Benson dairy at about 8 a.m., just in time to see the land agent put the for sale sign on the fence outside the farm. He tipped his hat and went on his way without as much as a "how do you do?" The widow had signed the sales agreement and the agent was briskly on his way to another appointment in town. John took it all in and just shook his head. "Too busy to care about anything but your next dollar," said John.

Grandpa smiled and added, "God knows how to slow people down when He wants to get their attention."

"I think we just preached a sermon, Dad," said John. James laughed.

Widow Benson was already up and offering everyone hot chocolate before anyone had done a lick of work. Three hours later, the first load going into town was ready to depart. They all unpacked the basket that Mom had prepared and took a thirty-minute lunch break.

Janet decided to stay at the Widow Benson's house with Cinnamon and Luke and get it ready for the next load while John, Widow Benson, Matthew, Rosemary and Mark drove the wagon into town and unloaded it into the widow's sister's home.

John drove the wagon slowly so that Stubborn did not get too winded carrying the heavy load. It was late afternoon when they arrived at Clare Hopkin's home, Widow Benson's younger sister.

Widow Benson was a mild mannered, quiet, hardworking, no nonsense lady. Her sister had grown up in town and lived the life of a rich man's wife. She had a cook and a maid and a spotless, well-ordered, small home.

It didn't take too long before the two sisters were engaged in a "discussion" that continued for several days. The bone of contention was pretty simple to figure out. Clara, Widow Benson's sister, put it pretty succinctly, "What were you thinking, Constance? Where in the world are we going to put all this furniture?"

John decided that unloading Widow Benson's furniture into her sister's house was probably not a good idea. There needed to be some compromise and common sense applied, but until the two sisters said their piece and cooled down, compromise and common sense was not going to be found.

John leaned over to his dad and said, "This looks like a job for you, Dad."

James nodded his head and responded, "Give it a little more time."

Finally, James politely addressed Widow Benson's sister Clara and asked if he could have a word with her. She agreed, and the two went off into the corner and sat down for a chat. A minute later he was following Clara up the stairs and into a large vacant room.

"This is going to be my sister's room," said Clara. James paced off the room to get some idea of the size. He then followed Clara back down the stairs and went to find Widow Benson, who was sulking out by the wagon.

"Constance, may I have a word with you?" he asked calmly.

"Certainly, James," said Widow Benson.

"Could you come with me?" James led her up the stairs to the large bedroom. "From what I can tell, this is the nicest and largest bedroom in the house," said James. "Clara has cleared it out and cleaned it up for you."

Constance soon realized that she had only two options. She could either find another place to live, or she could reconcile herself to moving only the furniture that would fit into her new bedroom. After a little fussing and fuming, and wishing she hadn't signed that agreement to sell her farm, she decided to move into the bedroom that her sister had so graciously provided. With a little more coaching, she even managed to sit down with her sister and have a civil conversation over a cup of tea.

Most of the furniture stayed on the wagon, and only a few pieces were fished out and put into the bedroom. Widow Benson's bed had not been loaded onto the wagon. This turned out to be a fortunate decision.

As the wagon, still half loaded with furniture, made its way back to Widow Benson's farm, Constance began forming a new plan. She began bouncing ideas off James and John, who were more than happy to listen attentively and offer suggestions.

"You could auction off all the furniture you aren't going to move," suggested John.

"Oh I could never do that," retorted Widow Benson. "I don't want strangers taking furniture out of my house." John and James had run out of ideas when Widow Benson made her own suggestion.

"I have an idea," the widow announced. ""Tomorrow morning, we will load up my bed and the rest of the furniture I can fit into my new bedroom. The rest of the furniture we will leave in the house for whoever buys the farm. That might even help me get it sold sooner," she announced.

John and James looked at each other, and they both shook their heads, "That is a wonderful idea, Constance," said James.

While John was driving the wagon back to the widow's farm, Grandma Anna was putting the youngsters down for a late nap. She needed a rest, and the only way she was going to get it was to put the kids down for a nap.

An afternoon nap was a new concept for the young Spice children. They were eager to try it out, but only after making sure that they would be awakened in time for dinner and still get a bedtime story. With those promises firmly in place, the Spice Farm became strangely quiet.

Anna made herself a cup of green tea and headed up the stairs to have a visit with Charlie.

Colossians 3:23-24
And whatsoever ye do, do it heartily, as to the Lord, and not unto men; Knowing that of the Lord ye shall receive the reward of the inheritance: for ye serve the Lord Christ.

Chapter 30

Angels

i, Grandma," Charlie said with a smile, happy to have some company.

"Namastē Namastē," greeted Grandma.

Charlie let Grandma beat him at a game of checkers, as the two began to talk about important things.

"Grandpa tells me that the two of you are talking about Heaven," said Grandma.

"That's right," said Charlie.

"Tell me what you have learned."

Grandma listened carefully as Charlie talked about all the things that he and Grandpa had discussed.

When he was all through, Grandma thought for a minute and asked, "Did Grandpa tell you about the 'Immortals'?"

"The what?" asked Charlie.

"The Immortals," replied Grandma.

Charlie had never heard of the *Immortals* and was anxious for Grandma to share something about Heaven that he had never heard of.

"The Immortals," said Grandma, "are creatures that God made to never die. That's why they are called Immortals."

"What do they look like?" asked Charlie.

Grandma patted Charlie on the shoulder as she said, "You will be very surprised Charlie."

"As long as they don't look like rats," said Charlie.

Grandma laughed. "There are no rats in Heaven, but there are some pretty strange looking creatures, from our point of view," she said.

"Will I see them when I get to Heaven?" asked Charlie.

"Yes, you will, Charlie, and since you're going to spend eternity in Heaven, you might want to get prepared for some of the amazing creatures you're going to see when you get there."

Charlie was at full attention. He had no idea his Grandma knew things about Heaven that he had never heard before.

"The first Immortals we read about in the Bible are called Cherubim. They have a head that has four faces."

"Really?" asked Charlie in surprise.

Grandma continued, "One face is the face of a Lion, another is the face of an Ox, one face is the face of an Eagle and the fourth face is the face of a Man."

Charlie's mouth dropped open. "Are you sure, Grandma; is that in the Bible?"

"Everything I am going to tell you is in the Bible, or I wouldn't bother mentioning it," said Grandma reassuringly, as she reached for Charlie's Bible and turned to Ezekiel 10:14 and read, *And every one had four faces: the first face was the face of a cherub, and the second face was the face of a man, and the third the face of a lion, and the fourth the face of an eagle.*

 "You can also read about the Cherubim in Genesis 3:24, said Grandma as she turned the pages to find the passage, "so *he drove out the man; and he placed at the east of the Garden of Eden Cherubims, and a flaming sword which turned every way, to keep the way of the tree of life.*"

"Are the Cherubim angels?" asked Charlie.

"No, they are not angels," said Grandma. "Angel means *messenger*, and the Cherubim are never called angels."

"Do all the Cherubim have four faces?" asked Charlie.

"Interesting that you should ask that question, Charlie." Grandma began thumbing through the scriptures. "There *is* one place in the Bible where it talks about four Cherubim, each having just one face. One Cherubim had the face of a lion, one had the face of a calf, one had the face of an Eagle and one had the face of a man." Grandma found the passage in Revelation 4:7. "Now, Charlie, you need to understand that when the Bible says 'beast', it is talking about a creature, an immortal Cherubim.

"And the first beast was like a lion, and the second beast like a calf, and the third beast had a face as a man, and the fourth beast was like a flying eagle."

Grandma kept thumbing through the Bible as she continued talking to Charlie. "There is another place in the Bible where it talks about the Cherubim having just two faces.

"Here it is," said Grandma as she read from Ezekiel 41:18-19. *"And it was made with cherubim's and palm trees, so that a palm tree was between a cherub and a cherub; and every cherub had two faces; so that the face of a man was toward the palm tree on the one side, and the face of a young lion toward the palm tree on the other side: it was made through all the house round about.*

"So to answer your question, Charlie, it seems like they do not all have four faces."

"Do they have wings?" asked Charlie.

"Yes, the Bible says they have wings. God told Moses to make the likeness of two Cherubs out of gold to be the covering on top of the Ark of the Covenant. It is called the Mercy Seat.

"The Bible tells us about them in Exodus 37:9. *And the cherubims spread-out their wings on high, and covered with their wings over the mercy seat...*

"The Bible also tells us about another Immortal," said Grandma.

"What are they called?" asked Charlie.

"They are called Seraphim."

Grandma opened Charlie's Bible to Isaiah 6:1-3 and said, "Let me read what the Bible says about these creatures.

"*In the year that king Uzziah died I saw also the Lord sitting upon a throne, high and lifted up, and his train filled the temple. Above it stood the Seraphims: each one had six wings; with twain he covered his face, and with twain he covered his feet, and with twain he did fly. And one cried unto another, and said, Holy, holy, holy, is the Lord of hosts: the whole earth is full of his glory.*"

"Six wings?" asked Charlie.

"That's right, Charlie—two to lift them up as they hover around the throne of God, two to cover their feet and two to cover their eyes."

"What about the angels, Grandma, aren't there angels in Heaven?"

Grandma paused for a moment to consider the question, then replied, "Charlie, what does the word *angel* mean?"

Charlie thought for a minute. "I don't remember, Grandma."

"An angel," said Grandma, "is the job title given to immortal creatures that are messengers."

"Will they be in Heaven with me?" Charlie asked.

"Oh, yes!" said Grandma. "They will be in Heaven with you."

"Do the messenger angels have wings?" asked Charlie.

"Charlie, the Bible *does* mention that His messengers, the angels, fly. So, angels may indeed have wings. But, since the Bible never mentions angels having wings, we cannot be sure. Many mysteries like this one will be answered when we get to heaven. We will just have to wait and see."

"What do they look like?" Charlie asked.

Grandma paused. "Well, Charlie, it seems that they can take on many forms, but when we see them, they usually look like handsome young men."

"Have you ever met an angel, Grandma?"

"Yes, Charlie, I have 'entertained' an angel just like the Bible says in Hebrews 13:2." Grandma found the passage and read it to Charlie, "*Be not forgetful to entertain strangers: for thereby some have entertained angels unawares.*"

Charlie was intrigued and began asking questions. Grandma shared the story of the night the angel came and ate their very last meal and left a gift. This story excited Charlie's imagination.

Grandma expanded on the theme of angels "providing" physical needs. She reminded Charlie about the story of Hagar and how God provided her with water in the desert and promised to preserve her life and the life of her son Ishmael. She then turned in her Bible and found the story of Elijah in 1 Kings 19:6. And finally, she reminded Charlie about the angels that showed up to provide comfort to Jesus after His temptation in the wilderness.

"Charlie, help me think about all the ways that God has allowed His angels to help His people."

Charlie thought for a moment. "I know they are messengers. Gabriel told Mary that she was going to have a baby boy named Jesus who would be the Messiah."

"That's right," said Grandma. "Did you know that God uses angels to protect us?"

"Like *Daniel in the Lion's Den.*" said Charlie.

"And what about the fiery furnace?" asked Grandma.

"Let me see," Grandma said thoughtfully, as she put her index finger up to her bottom lip. "God also uses angels to deliver his people sometimes. Can you think of an example Charlie?" Charlie thought and shook his head. Grandma turned to Acts chapter five and read the story of how God sent angels to help the Apostles escape from prison.

"God also uses angels to answer prayer," said Grandma. "Do you remember the time that Daniel prayed and God sent him an angel to answer his prayer?"

"I sort of remember," said Charlie.

Grandma turned the pages of the Bible and found the book of Daniel chapter nine, where she read the story. She also turned to the book of Acts chapter twelve, in the New Testament, and read about how God answered the prayers of His Church and delivered the Apostle Peter from prison.

Finally, Grandma read Luke 16:22 where the Scriptures tell the story of the angels carrying the spirit of Lazarus to "Abraham's bosom" when he died.

"Maybe someday I will see an angel," announced Charlie.

Grandma tried hard to hold back her tears. Finally, she said, "I would not be a bit surprised if you see an angel someday in this life."

Charlie smiled, "Grandpa says that I will see them in Heaven."

"That's right," said Grandma, "angels are going to be among your companions in Heaven."

As Charlie was thinking about what it would be like to be among the angels in Heaven, he heard the hoof beats of Stubborn as he pulled the Spice family back home.

Revelation 5:11-13
*And I beheld, and I heard the voice of many
angels round about the throne and the
beasts and the elders: and the number of
them was ten thousand times ten thousand,
and thousands of thousands; Saying with
a loud voice, Worthy is the Lamb that
was slain to receive power, and riches, and*

wisdom, and strength, and honour, and glory, and blessing. And every creature which is in heaven, and on the earth, and under the earth, and such as are in the sea, and all that are in them, heard I saying, Blessing, and honour, and glory, and power, be unto him that sitteth upon the throne, and unto the Lamb for ever and ever.

Chapter 31

The Dairy

Breakfast came early the following morning. John and Janet hoped to get an early start on all the projects that needed attending at Widow Bensons. "Everybody ready to go?" Mom asked. The family took the cue and started filing out of the kitchen, through the front door, and into the awaiting wagon. Janet took a minute to give a kiss and word of encouragement to her little ones that were staying behind. Parting was eased with the help of Grandma, who was doing her best to spoil all her grandchildren with the one thing she had lots of, love. The small Spice children were delighted to be in the tender care of Grandma.

Stubborn, happy to only be hauling a three quarter load of Spices, arrived at Widow Benson's farm just before seven in the morning. Widow Benson was ready for them and had made all her moving decisions. The bed was the first large piece of furniture loaded. John and James made short work of loading the rest of the treasured pieces that Widow Benson had decided she could not live without.

The farm wagon was fully loaded. Janet and Constance were fussing about where to put the remaining furniture for the best effect on anyone considering the purchase of the farm. This was fine with John and James, who quietly headed for the pasture.

Before going out the back kitchen door John asked, "Constance, have you milked your goat yet today?"

"Oh dear," said Widow Benson as she put her hand up to her mouth, "in all the hustle and bustle, I forgot all about Snowflake."

"I will milk her," said John.

"Well," said Widow Benson, "she belongs to you now, so I guess she might as well get used to you milking her." John smiled. Widow Benson went to the pantry and pulled out the freshly sterilized milk bucket. "Here you go, John," she said as she handed him the bucket.

John and James went to the barn and found the open bag of oats and scooped a handful into the feed trough that was attached to the milking stanchion. James went out and retrieved Snowflake, who was uncomfortably bloated and anxious to be milked.

John put Snowflake in the stanchion and began milking. About ten minutes later, he had over a half gallon of milk. "Would you look at that Dad?"

James came over and nodded his head. "I have never seen so much milk come out of one goat before," he remarked.

"Dad, she didn't try and kick me once. I have never milked a goat with such ease."

"How does she compare to Six-Pints?" asked James.

"Well I haven't milked our goat in over a year. The last time I milked Six-Pints, before I gave the job to Rosemary, I remember that she was fine until she ran out of grain. After that, it was everything I could do to keep her back legs out of the milk bucket."

"How much milk does Six-Pints produce a day?"

John laughed. "Well, Dad, let me put it this way, if I had to name her again today, I would name her Three-Pints, not six."

"So she produces less than a half gallon of milk a day," calculated James.

"That's about right," said John. "Snowflake, here, just produced nearly five pints in one milking."

John pulled out a bale of hay and moved it to where they could sit and watch the goat herd. The two men had a lot of experience with goats and they knew what they were looking for. "Those Saanen goats are the future in dairy goats," said John.

"I can't disagree," said James.

"Did you notice how they interacted with the rest of the herd?" asked John.

"Yes, I noticed that they are very tranquil and they don't like to waste energy fussing and fighting with the other goats." John shook his head.

"Dad," said John, "I think we should get rid of all the goats, except the five pregnant Saanens and Snowflake. This breed of goat will cut our work in half and double our milk production."

"John," Janet shouted from the back door, "we are ready to go."

John and James went back in the house. They were both given a cup of coffee and led around the house to admire all the decisions that had been made regarding the remaining furniture.

Janet and the girls stayed behind to continue cleaning up the house while John, James and the rest of the boys found their places on the wagon and began the trip to town.

"I think I am going to stay in town," said Widow Benson. "Janet knows what to do with the house, and we can talk about the dairy on the way."

John listened as the widow explained all the ins and outs of her herd. There really wasn't much for John to learn, but he listened politely since it seemed important to Widow Benson. *This is her way of letting it go,* thought John, as he listened carefully.

When Widow Benson was through, John made a suggestion. He wasn't real sure how Widow Benson was going to take to his idea, but, wanted to get it all out in the open so there was no misunderstanding.

John told the widow that he wanted to keep the six Saanen and Buster, and sell the rest of the goats. John said that since they didn't end up moving all the furniture, as they had agreed, he thought it only fair that he give the widow all the money from the sale of the other eleven goats.

Widow Benson wouldn't hear of it, and after some negotiating, John agreed to accept half of the revenue from the sale of the goats. John then asked Widow Benson if he could keep all but the six Saanen on the widow's pasture next to her barn. John figured it would take him about ten minutes to ride over to the widow's farm on his horse and take care of the remaining goats while they were being offered for sale. This daily chore would take an hour out of John's day, but compared to the time and energy it would take to accommodate sixteen goats and a Billy, it was a good trade off.

The widow agreed to all John's suggestions, and it was clear that she wanted a fresh start without the burden of taking care of, or even thinking about, the daily grind of caring for eighteen goats. It was also clear that until Widow Benson's farm sold, John Spice was in charge of keeping it in tip top shape.

Fitting all the new animals and equipment into the Spice family farm puzzle was not that easy. Some of the turmoil caused by the new dairy enterprise was temporary and some of it was permanent.

Preparing a place for a growing herd of milk goats was made much easier by reducing the size of the herd from eighteen to seven. Selling eleven goats in the middle of October was a job that was only made a little easier when Wally McDaniel immediately purchased the two Toggenburgs for thirty dollars each. This left nine American milk goats.

The following morning, John and all the older children were dropped off at Widow Benson's farm where they continued all of the outdoor chores and cleanup. James was left to take care of Charlie and the smaller children.

After dropping everyone off at Widow Benson's, Janet and Anna headed for town. Two hours later, Janet arrived at the Elkin Times with Anna.

"Hello Janet," said Edgar, "here to pay for your typewriter?"

"This is my mother, Anna," Janet said.

Edgar Cartwright shook Anna's hand.

"Mr. Cartwright, would you mind if we tested all the typewriters before making our choice?" Janet asked.

Edgar scratched his chin and disappeared for a few seconds, reappearing with a couple pieces of white paper. "I suppose you will be needing this?" he said as he handed Anna two sheets of typewriter paper.

"Yes, thank you very much," Anna replied.

"Just follow me," said Edgar, as he led Janet and Anna into the dimly lit storeroom where the old typewriters were all piled up on a half-dozen turned over crates.

One by one, Anna carefully examined and tested each Underwood typewriter. After testing about eight of them, she proudly announced, "I have found John's typewriter."

Janet looked at the typewriter carefully and said, "Looks like someone has scratched their name on this one with a penknife." They both looked carefully, and finally, Janet said, "Do you know who Sally Potts is?"

Janet picked up the typewriter and headed for the main office of the Elkin Times. She plunked down two silver dollars on the counter top and said. "We found the typewriter we want." She plunked down two silver dollars on the counter top.

"Thank you, Janet," said Edgar as he headed to a closet where he fetched a box of new typewriter ribbons.

"How much for 1000 sheets of typewriter paper?" asked Janet.

"Hmmm," muttered Edgar. "They cost me thirty-two cents for a thousand sheets. So, what do you say we call it forty-five cents?

"Sounds fair enough," said Janet as she fished through her pockets and finally produced a half dollar. "You owe me five cents," Janet said. "You can put it on my account," she smiled, having finally put Edgar Cartwright in her debt—even if it was only for five cents. "I will put it on your account," Edgar smiled, half getting the joke himself.

"By the way Edgar," said Janet as she picked up her typewriter, and Anna scooped up the box with all the ribbons and paper, "who is Sally Potts?"

Edgar looked at Janet and then began to laugh. "You picked out Sally Potts' typewriter, didn't you?"

"Well, actually, we only discovered her name etched on the typewriter after we picked it out," said Janet.

"Sally Potts is my brother's 'no account' daughter that he foisted on me last summer. I gave her a six-month trial, which she failed miserably."

Janet was beginning to feel sorry she had asked.

"And," added Edgar, "if you have her typewriter, I can guarantee you it is like new; she never did a lick of work on it."

"Sorry to hear that," said Anna sympathetically. "Thank you, Lord," mumbled Janet under her breath, feeling blessed that God had worked it out so she ended up with a brand new typewriter for a fraction of its true value.

Getting a square deal from Edgar Cartwright was not something that happened every day, as he was known as one of the sharpest businessmen in the town. It seems that Edgar Cartwright was no match for the good plans that God had for the Spice family.

On the way out of town, Janet stopped at a run-down farmhouse. "I will be right back," she reassured Anna as she picked up a box full of fruit from the back of the wagon. Janet went to the door and was greeted by Sally Simpson and a couple of her small children. Janet and Sally exchanged pleasantries, and then Janet handed her the box full of fruit and assorted vegetables from the Spice garden.

Janet and Anna headed toward the Widow Benson farm. They would arrive in the middle of the afternoon with plenty of time to clean all the windows and sashes inside Widow Benson's farmhouse.

When Janet and Anna arrived, they were surprised to see how much clean-up had been done. A neat pile of stanchions, pails, bags of oats, and several bales of hay were waiting to be loaded into the wagon.

It was going to take several trips back and forth to move all the dairy equipment and feed. John left most of the hay in the barn, not knowing how long it was going to take him to sell the remaining nine American milk goats. John decided that the last thing they would move over were the six Saanen milk goats and Buster, the billy goat.

After Janet and all the girls finished cleaning the windows of Widow Benson's farm, they all got together on the large front porch. Janet had planned ahead, and within a few minutes, everyone had a mug of hot cider.

This brief respite gave John a chance to share with Janet his plans for the dairy. Janet was relieved to know that the dairy business was going to be starting out slowly with prize, high-producing milk goats. Janet had listened to John's previous plan, and although she voiced no objections, she was very aware that it was going to be very labor intensive. This new plan sounded like something she could manage.

"Janet, I am going to need you to help me sell all these goats."

Janet thought for a minute, and replied, "I have a plan."

"That is good enough for me," said John, "I will stop worrying about it."

Janet had a gift for commerce and knew how to get a fair price for whatever it was she was selling. This was a gift that was very much appreciated by John, who had a gift for giving things away. That was a talent not required at this juncture in the new Spice family dairy business. It was going to be a year before they were milking more than two goats, and the extra income from the goat sales would really help keep them afloat in the meantime.

"John, I want to show you something," said Anna, as she grabbed her son's hand, lifted him off the front porch, and led him to the wagon. Anna carefully unwrapped the typewriter. John's eyes got big as he gathered his mother up in his arms and gave her a hug and a kiss. "I thought you would be pleased."

"Pleased?" said John. "I am amazed!"

John and Anna walked back to the porch where he sat next to Janet and gave her a big hug as he tearfully thanked her for helping him make his dream of becoming a Christian author come true.

James 1:27
Pure religion and undefiled before God and the Father is this, To visit the fatherless and widows in their affliction, and to keep himself unspotted from the world.

Chapter 32

The Indian Feast

B ack at the Spice Farm, Grandpa was having the time of his life taking care of his small grandchildren. He had finally worn them out and put them all down for a long nap. He spent the next couple of hours preparing his favorite meal, Indian *Butter Chicken*. James learned to cook in India and had developed over the years a half-dozen recipes that he had become quite an expert at preparing.

The simmering spices filled the house with an exotic mist that transported him far away from the Blue Ridge Mountains. James could close his eyes and imagine himself back in Bombay, India, where he had spent most of his life. He missed India once in a while, and the fragrant perfume of his marinating meal provided just enough atmosphere to allow his imagination to lite, for just a moment, on the fair memories of a place far away and as different from North Carolina as hunting dogs and elephants.

Grandpa James had prepared a small exotic snack for Charlie, who had been neglected for most of the day. Grandpa prepared a sample plate of Indian delicacies and headed up the stairs.

"Did you think I had forgotten about you, Charlie?" asked Grandpa.

"You would never do that Grandpa," smiled Charlie, who was very happy for the company.

Grandpa presented Charlie with the snack plate, and watched with interest as his grandson savored every morsel. Charlie had been well trained not to ask for more of anything, but on this occasion, he was sorely tempted to inquire if there was more where this came from.

Grandpa anticipated the response and comforted Charlie with the delectable news that he had prepared an Indian feast for a king, and as soon as all the Spice family members were together again, they would eat until they burst. Charlie was excited to hear it. The samples that disappeared quickly had only increased his appetite.

"Waiting for something good reminds me of Heaven," said Grandpa. Charlie perked up; there was no subject as interesting to him as the subject of Heaven. Grandpa was obviously relishing the thought of going to heaven, and Charlie was eager to understand all the reasons why.

Grandpa picked up Charlie's empty plate. "Did you enjoy the exotic snack, Charlie?"

"Yes," said Charlie "I liked it a lot."

Grandpa paused for a minute sensing an opportunity to share a truth about Heaven. "Charlie, all the things that you enjoyed eating in this small snack came from somewhere." Charlie looked puzzled. "Can you help me think of all the places this small meal came from?"

"You cooked it Grandpa; it came from you," said Charlie.

"Yes I did have my small part to play, but without all the ingredients, all my cooking wouldn't amount to anything."

"It came from the chicken," Charlie said.

"That's right, Charlie, without that chicken it would not have been a very savory meal."

Grandpa paused, "Charlie, this little meal you enjoyed so much came from the all over the earth," said Grandpa.

"It did?" asked Charlie with a puzzled look.

Grandpa began listing off all the ingredients that went into the meal, including all the spices, herbs, and even the silverware and the plate that Charlie had licked clean.

"Did you know that there are farmers in India that cultivated and harvested some of the spices that went into making that meal so delicious? Did you know that the plate you ate the food on was made in China? Did you know that the silverware you used was brought over from England? And did you know that I came all the way from Bombay, India to fix this meal for you?"

Charlie had never considered all the people, and plants, and animals that went into making just one small meal.

"You know, Charlie, without the sun and rain, your meal would not have been possible. And if I did not have Christ in my heart, I probably would not be here to prepare it for you."

"What about the angels, Grandpa?" Grandpa laughed.

"Let me think about that for a minute." Grandpa had not intended to include angels in his lesson. "Angels are ministering spirits that are active in the lives of all Christians, including you and me. So, while I did not see an angel in the kitchen helping me cook this meal, I am certain that without the assistance of angels I would not be here in the first place. Therefore we can certainly include angels in this illustration.

"Think about this for a moment, Charlie. All the momentary joy you got from eating that small, tasty meal came second and third hand from God. It came from men whom God made and, it came from God's earth, where a farmer planted a seed and harvested the plant that grew from the seed. Then a merchant transported the plant and put it in a package, another man sold the package, and so on.

"Think about the joy you have by simply being born into this family. Where does it come from? It comes from God's Spirit, working love and goodness into the hearts of your mom and dad, who pass it along to you.

"And we cannot forget the angels that God sends to minister, help, and protect His people. We may not see what they do, but without them, we would have all probably perished years ago.

"Consider God's word—His revelation comes to us through a book. This all means that receiving joy is a result of second and third hand receiving of God's grace. And it is all very wonderful. Wouldn't you agree, Charlie?"

Charlie's eyes were open wide as he considered everything his grandfather was sharing with him. "Yes," said Charlie. "It is wonderful!"

"Now consider this," continued Grandpa, "none of these things come immediately from God." Charlie looked perplexed. "Let me explain it this way, Charlie. God is using His earth, His people, His angels, and His Word to minister to you. He is not doing it directly Himself. His Spirit lives in you and one day will change you into someone that He can have face to face fellowship with. But that cannot happen now because you and I are still sinful creatures."

Charlie was taking it all in and sorting it all out.

"What about Heaven?" Charlie finally asked.

"Glad you asked, Charlie. What I want you to understand is that there is joy in receiving all the blessings and bounty that come indirectly from God, into our lives.

"Like a letter from a friend that contains a gift—it is wonderful, and without it our lives on this earth would end in despair and hopelessness.

"In Heaven, will receive all our joy and hope directly from God; we will be in His presence, and everything we receive will come directly from Him."

"We won't need the sun anymore to light the day, or the moon to light the night. There will only be day, and God will light it without the moon or sun. The Glory of God and the Lamb is the Light. We will understand things, then, without the aid of Scripture, and we will be governed without the aid of a written law.

"God is going to change our hearts so that we can be taught by Him without a preacher, teacher or prophet. Our joy will be immediate and everlasting. Our peace will be instant and never ending. On the earth, if you have needs, they are supplied by other means and usually through God's creature, man.

"In Heaven, all our necessities are supplied by God, without the need for man's feeble supplies or services. In Heaven, we will be living in a place where there are no un-met needs. He not only supplies all our needs, He is the fountainhead of all our desires. That is what Heaven is like for you and me, Charlie."

Just then, Charlie heard the Spice Farm wagon approaching. "Grandpa," said Charlie, "I think everybody is coming home."

Grandpa peered out the window. "I think you're right."

"So let me ask you something, Charlie. What did we learn about *heaven* this afternoon?"

Charlie smiled and said, "We learned that in Heaven God takes care of us without anybody needing to be in between."

Grandpa smiled. "That is a pretty good summary, Charlie. Now I need to go and get dinner organized for all the hungry Spicelings."

Grandpa slipped down the stairs and went outside to greet the incoming Spices. He had a private word with Anna to let her know that he had *Indian Butter Chicken* cooking. "I will let you finish off the preparations for dinner, Love, while I help John get all the dairy equipment and feed put into the barn."

"You cooked *Butter Chicken*?" she smiled approvingly.

"Yep," answered James as he went to the back of the wagon to help unload.

Janet made a beeline for the kitchen, imagining that dinner needed to be prepared. She didn't even get into the kitchen before she turned on her heels and headed for James, who was pulling a bale of hay out of the wagon. Janet tackled James who dropped the hay as he received a kiss on the neck. "James, you have no idea how tired I am—and to have dinner ready for us—well, all I can say is that I love you, and thank you."

James smiled, "I love you too, and it was my pleasure."

Just then, the kitchen door opened and the little Spicelings started pouring out of the house to say hello and to tell anyone who would listen about all the adventures they had with Grandpa.

"Grandpa taught us an Indian word," announced Ginger.

"What word would that be?" inquired John.

"Don Yada," said Ginger.

John started to laugh. "I think you mean Dhan'yavāda," said John.

Matthew, who was listening to the conversation, asked, "Dad what does Dhan'yavāda mean?"

"It means "Thank you", in Hindi," replied John.

Matthew, who loved learning new Hindi Indian words, began chanting "Dhan'yavāda" until everyone joined in.

Grandpa laughed as he whispered to John, "And to think, I could have taught them the first word *you* learned to say in Hindi."

"And what was that, Dad?"

"Asvīkāra," said Grandpa, with a wry smile.

John chuckled.

Asvīkāra is the Hindi word for "no".

"What did you do to make Janet so happy?" John finally asked.

"Mākhana Cikana," whispered James.

"*Butter Chicken,*" said John, who instantly hastened his pace.

The *Butter Chicken* along with a number of other exotic Indian dishes, drinks and desserts were carefully carried up to the Eagle's Nest. The delicious smells lifted everyone's spirits and breathed new life into the thoroughly tired Spice Family.

Grandpa had made a double portion so that no one would leave hungry. The bountiful table, combined with exhaustion and a tinge of hunger, made this meal the most slowly eaten and finger licking delicious meal the Spice family had ever experienced.

Although no one ever could have guessed it, that evening, the culinary skills of Grandpa were elevated beyond the Marie McDaniel's level. And that is saying something.

The evening ended as Grandpa read a passage from *Pilgrim's Progress*.

Everyone went to bed and slept through the night without a peep. Everyone, except Charlie. Charlie could not stop imagining what it would be like to have a father/son relationship with God. Grandpa had planted a seed that would grow and grow in Charlie's heart, producing a harvest of hope that would encourage and enliven the faith of every single member of the Spice family. Grandpa was getting Charlie ready for his journey to Heaven, and Charlie knew it and was embracing it, with childlike wonder and faith.

James 1:17
Every good gift and every perfect gift is from above,
and cometh down from the Father of lights,
with whom is no variableness, neither shadow of turning.

Chapter 33

Target Practice

he weeks passed as the job of cleaning up Widow Benson's farm finally came to a conclusion.

Breakfast was served early because the Spice family wanted to get an early start on all the projects that needed to be completed. It was the last workday at Widow Benson's.

Janet rubbed her eyes and poured John a cup of coffee. "Today we pick up the goats," said John.

Janet smiled, "We did it John. We did it."

John smiled, "Of course we did it, was there ever a doubt?"

"Last week, when Rosemary accidently left the pasture gate open, and I spent the afternoon chasing nine goats all over Yadkin Valley, I did have my doubts."

"Rosemary will never do that again, and we learned something," said John.

"What was that?" asked Janet.

"Rosemary is still a kid, and the six Saanen goats stayed in the pasture."

Janet smiled.

"The decision to just go with the Saanen breed is going to be the best dairy decision we ever made," added John.

"Hi, Grandma," said Cinnamon, who was using her index finger to scrape the last bit of raspberry jam out of the jar.

"Hi, Darling," said Grandma.

"Who is going to stay home with the kids today?" asked John.

"I will be staying home with the children," responded Grandma Anna.

"Thanks, Mom," said Janet, who saddled up to her, handing her a hot cup of coffee.

"Have a seat, Anna." Janet pulled the chair out and seated Anna while Rosemary sprinkled cinnamon on a hot piece of toast that she presented to Grandma on a fancy desert plate.

"Oh my," said Grandma, "doesn't that look delicious. Thank you, Rosemary." Rosemary did a deep curtsy and sat back down at the table.

Matthew could not resist responding to Rosemary's affectations. He got up and dumped John Jr. out of his chair and did a curtsy.

"Mom," yelled John Jr. as he scrambled around on the kitchen floor.

Janet gave Matthew her famous "stare," and without a further word, Matthew scooped John Jr. off the floor, tickled him and set him back in his seat and then did a deep bow. "Your highness," he said.

Matthew got a laugh whenever he imitated Rosemary's dramatic play-acting. Mom drew the line at any antics that she saw as disrespectful. Matthew had clearly crossed the line and was going to pay the price.

"Matthew," said Mom as she made a little curtsy, "you may go outside and get Stubborn hitched up."

"But Mom, I haven't finished my breakfast."

"Well, sir Matthew," Mom responded with another bow that had all the rest of the family giggling, "that is where you are wrong. Your breakfast ended when you poured your little brother onto the floor and mocked your sister."

Matthew hung his head. "Sorry John Jr., sorry Rosemary, sorry Mom," he said as he headed out the door hungry and hoping that lunch would come early that day.

"Janet," said John, "I want you to drop us off at the Widow's farm and then go into town and pick up Constance and bring her back to the farm. I would like her to see first-hand the work that has been done."

"That is a good idea, John," nodded Janet.

John continued, "The land agent has a reputation for talking behind the backs of his customers, and I don't want false tales of what the farm looks like getting back to Widow Benson. She needs to see that we did what we said we would do. She needs to be satisfied that we completed our part of the bargain."

James laughed, "That is wise Son, but a little sad that we have to think the worst of the land agent."

"Well," said John, "from what I have heard, I am being very generous in my appraisal; the tales I have heard make me very cautious."

"Enough said," reported James.

"Agreed," said John.

The Spice work crew all loaded into the wagon. "Matthew," said Dad, "I want you to get your new 22 rifle." Matthew's mood immediately changed from gloomy to sunny as he hopped out of the wagon and headed toward his bedroom to retrieve his new rifle that had never been used.

After grabbing his rifle, he found his Mom in the kitchen and asked her for a box of 22 shells. Janet smiled as she disappeared into the pantry closet and fished the shells out of her secret hiding place. "Here you go

Matthew," said Mom, as she lured him within reach, with the prized box of 22-caliber ammo.

As Matthew stepped forward, she grabbed him and gave him a hug. "Sorry about this morning," Matthew said. "I thought I was being funny."

Janet looked Matthew, in the eyes and said, "Matthew you were very funny, but we never want to be funny at someone else's expense."

Mom gave Matthew a big kiss on the cheek as she handed him the box of shells. "I love you, Son," said Mom. "Dad told me he was going to teach you how to shoot straight and safe, so you pay attention."

"I will Mom," smiled Matthew, as he exited the farm house a much better boy than when he had entered it just a few minutes earlier.

"Come sit up here between your grandpa and me," yelled John. Matthew handed his dad the gun and ammo and waited for him to put it in the gun box he had built next to the wagon seat. Safely put away, Dad grabbed Matthew's hand and pulled him up into the wagon where he was seated and given a shoulder squeeze from Grandpa.

John waited patiently as Janet led the rest of the Spice family into the farm wagon.

"Giddy-up Stubborn," said John as he leaned over to speak to Matthew.

"Did I ever tell you the story of Nigel 'Nine Toes' Thompson?" asked John. Grandpa leaned over and smiled at John.

Matthew looked at his dad and said, "Nine Toes Thompson?"

"That's right, Nigel 'Nine Toes.'"

"No, I have never heard of him," said Matthew.

As Stubborn trotted down the road toward Widow Benson's farm, John began to spin the tale of Nigel "Nine Toes" Thompson—a cautionary tale that was told to every young man that grew up in the shadow of the Blue Ridge Mountains. A tale that was always saved for the moment when a young lad was initiated into man's world of firearms.

John had just gotten to the final dramatic ending of the "Nine Toes " tale when Widow Benson's farm came into view.

John added drama as he sped toward the end of the story—

"No, Dad, my rifle isn't loaded," declared Nigel.

"Are you sure, Son?" asked Nigel's father.

"Sure as shooting!" said Nigel, as he pulled the trigger on his rifle."

John raised his voice and let out a blood-curdling howl.

"Yih Yih Yih," shouted Nigel, grabbing his foot and hopping around the yard, like a toad on a hot skillet.

"Blood was spurting out the hole in Nigel's boot," added John.

By this time, Matthew was on the edge of his seat with eyes wide as a pie plate. "He shot himself in the foot?" asked Matthew.

"Blew a hole in his boots and shot his big toe clean off," concluded Dad.

It was a story that Matthew would never forget, which of course was the general idea.

"All the rifles and pistols that come into the Spice house are unloaded and put in a safe place. The ammo is stored in a secret place known only to your Mom and me, and Grandpa, of course," said Dad. "All except for 'Old Betsy,'" he added. Matthew knew that "Old Betsy" was a name borrowed from the wilderness tales of Daniel Boone and referred to the bear rifle that hung high above the fireplace mantle.

"Old Betsy is always loaded; do you know why?"

Matthew shook his head no.

"Because Son, an unloaded gun is not going to help you a bit in an emergency."

Matthew looked puzzled.

"If you have an intruder, like a bear or a desperado, you don't want to be spending your time fiddling around trying to find your ammo and loading your rifle," Grandpa added.

"That's right," agreed John, "an unloaded gun is no good to anyone if you only have a few seconds to protect yourself and your family."

"So what have we learned?" asked Dad.

"Treat your gun like it is loaded, even if you think it isn't," said Matthew.

"That's right. And that means you never, ever point your gun at anyone, unless you are intending to shoot them dead." Matthew bristled at that idea of shooting anyone dead. "What else?" asked Dad.

"All the ammo is stored by you and Mom."

"That's right," said Dad.

"Do you know the next most important thing about a rifle?" asked Dad. "How to shoot it?" replied Matthew.

Dad laughed. "We will get to the shooting part pretty soon. No, the next most important thing, besides gun safety, is keeping your gun clean and well oiled." "I didn't know you oiled a gun," said Matthew.

"When we get back to the farm, I will show you how to clean and oil your rifle," said Dad, "now what's the next thing we need to learn about your rifle?"

Matthew smiled and said, "Shooting!"

"That's right, Matthew."

The wagon was unloaded and the outdoor chores were started as Janet headed into town to pick up Widow Benson. "See you in a couple hours," said John as he blew a kiss from the front porch of the farm.

"Come with me, Matthew," said John. Matthew had carefully unloaded his rifle and was carrying a box of 22 ammo with a hopeful grin on his face.

John and his son headed for the barn. "Over here," said Dad. John leaned over and picked up a large old rusty wash bucket. He held it up by the one remaining handle and noticed a half-dozen rusted holes through which the sun was streaming. "This will do nicely," said John.

Matthew followed as Dad led him out behind the barn. John immediately paced off twenty-five yards. He set the tin bucket on its side and propped it up with a couple rocks.

John spent the next thirty minutes showing Matthew shooting stances and teaching him how to load and unload his new rifle. They both counted the eight holes in the rusty bucket.

"OK, Matthew, I will buy you five more bullets for every bullet you shoot in the bucket," Dad said. Matthew got down on one knee and cradled his rifle to take his first shot. Matthew squinted and pulled the trigger. He missed the bucket by a couple yards. Dad watched his son as he took the next half-dozen shots, all falling short of the intended target.

"Son, let me take a shot," said John. John squeezed the trigger and hit the edge of the bucket. "I see the problem," said John, "I need to adjust your sites."

John took another half-dozen shots, adjusting the site with each shot. "Let me show you how to site your target." Matthew was eager to learn and watched with interest and carefully followed his dad's instructions.

"Now try it," said Dad. Matthew took his time and squeezed off a shot. It was wide off the mark but did manage to hit the bucket. This was all the encouragement Matthew needed.

John said goodbye with the final instructions: if he saw man or beast anywhere near his target that he was to unload his rifle and wait for the target area to clear.

Over the next couple of hours, Matthew made steady progress. He went from happy to hit the bucket to disappointed if he didn't shoot a hole in the center of the bucket. Matthew was a natural rifleman.

John milked Snowflake, impressed again by the production and ease of milking the Saanen breed. Rosemary fed the rest of the stock and made sure they were watered and brushed. Grandpa, Mark and Luke weeded and cleaned up the debris that had accumulated around the barn.

Everyone pitched in and worked steady for about four hours. Everyone except Matthew, who had been given the special job of learning how to shoot his rifle with confidence and accuracy.

Proverbs 13:4
The soul of the sluggard desireth, and hath nothing:
but the soul of the diligent shall be made fat.

Chapter 34

Goat Wrangler

The Widow Benson was anxious to see all the work that had been done by the Spice family on her farm. She had not milked a goat in a week, and thought she would miss it, but she didn't. Widow Benson was adjusting to life in the small town of Elkin with ease, and enjoying the comforts of a well heated home with lots of diversions.

Only one last detail troubled her mind, and that was getting a fair price for the farm she had lived in for all her adult life. Constance was married when she was sixteen years old to Walter Benson, a kind, hard working farmer who had treated his wife with love and respect. Life on the farm was hard work. Walter Benson was a man that did not believe in frivolities, and that included vacations or creature comforts. He had died with a plow in his hand and most thought he just plain worked himself to death. He saved all he earned and left his widow with a small fortune by the standards of the day.

Widow Benson started the goat dairy business as a way of trying to keep her only son on the farm. Bud Benson was a bright lad and had seen what farm work had done to his dad, and wanted nothing to do with it. As soon as he was of an independent age, he enrolled himself in a trade school with the goal of becoming a master ship builder. Bud had achieved his goal and only visited his mother a couple times a year. He was married but had no children.

Widow Benson was ready for a change—ready for the pampered life with her sister, when her sister's husband had died, he left her the house, the servants, and a large interest in a furniture making company, she was living the life of a Southern Belle.

It did not take much coaxing to convince Constance Benson that this was also the life for her. The only thing she retained from her former humble beginning was her common sense and a love for all her previous country neighbors. In all other respects, she was changing, and changing fast.

Mark was the first to announce the news that Mom and Widow Benson could be seen coming down the road. Everyone stopped what they were doing to greet them. Everyone, except Matthew, whose eagerness to become a sharp shooter cocooned him from all other distractions. It almost made him forget he had not eaten anything since yesterday evening.

Dad came around the corner as Matthew put a bullet through the middle of the three-inch hole he had created with multiple bull's eyes.

"Now that is what I call shooting," said John proudly.

"Dad, I can shoot the center of the bucket almost every time."

"That's great, Matthew. Now, I want you to unload your rifle and come for lunch; your Mom is almost here."

Janet arrived with Widow Benson. A quick tour was all it took. "What a wonderful job you have all done here," she gushed. "Everything looks just so wonderful and clean. Now Janet, let's cook these folks up some lunch." Janet went to the wagon and pulled out a grocery bag full of food that Widow Benson had purchased for the Spice family at Dick Grier's Grocery, just a couple hours earlier.

John put his arm around Matthew and said, "Looks like you've forgotten all about not having anything for breakfast." Matthew smiled.

Baked pork & beans, corn muffins with honey, blackberry yogurt, chocolate milk, and apple pie topped off with hot chocolate sprinkled with cinnamon—it was a feast that everyone enjoyed, especially Matthew. "Nothing improves your appetite and appreciation for good cooking like a tinge of hunger," said Janet, as she scooped another ladle full of baked beans with the rich brown sugar syrup and generous portions of smoked pork.

They were just about done when—who should they see coming up the road? Edwin Featherstone from the Blue Ridge Mountains Real Estate Company, that's who and with a customer in tow.

"Didn't realize you were having a convention here," Edwin said sarcastically. "Oh, hello Mrs. Benson, I didn't see you over there." Widow Benson was not pleased with Edwin's condescending ways, but nodded politely anyway.

Janet came and saddled up next to John as the Widow Benson, Edwin and the customer went in to inspect the house.

"Well this is an answer to prayer," said Janet.

"Two birds with one stone," said John.

"Two birds, I only count one bird?" said Janet, who was puzzled.

"Well," said John, "Edwin can see the place is in great shape so, we won't be hearing rumors in town about how us 'country folk' live in barefoot squalor with our dirty pigs and rusty spoons."

"That's right," said Janet. "So what is the second bird?" she whispered. "You can't guess?" said John.

"I don't have any idea what you're thinking, Love," said Janet, as she snuggled close and gave him a gentle poke in the ribs.

"Edwin can take Widow Benson home and save you four and a half hours of bumpy traveling."

Janet straightened up, "That's right," she said in a low whisper, "and save me listening to the widow complain about her younger sister in the bargain. Those two are precious when they are apart, but put them together and it's like putting two banty roosters together in a potato sack."

John smiled as he stood up. "I will go make the arrangements."

John waited until he found Widow Benson and Edwin together, knowing that was the sure fire way of hearing the answer he wanted to hear.

"Widow Benson," said John, "I was wondering if it might not be convenient for you to return to Elkin with Edwin, who I am sure would love to have your company, and perhaps his customer has some questions for you about the farm."

"Well, of course, Mrs. Benson, I would love to take you back into town," responded Edwin in his syrupy best mannered voice. Edwin then looked out the kitchen window to see his customer examining the barn. "I better see how he is doing," said Edwin, as he quickly went out the kitchen door and headed toward the barn.

The Widow Benson huffed, "I would much rather spend two hours with Janet than Edwin, but it will save you an extra trip and precious time, so I am happy to do it," said Widow Benson.

"I knew you would understand," said John as he gave her a hug.

John found James outside doing some last minute weeding and raking.

"Dad, as soon as Edwin leaves with his customer and Widow Benson, I think we need to round up the six Saanens and head home."

"What about Buster?"

"Who's Buster?"

James laughed. "The billy goat, Son."

"Oh, we will leave him here and fetch him in a couple weeks."

Edwin Featherstone's customer seemed genuinely interested in the farm and it looked like they were not going to be leaving for a while. While Rosemary cleaned up after lunch, Janet and Matthew went behind the barn to do a little target practice. Matthew was proud of how he had blown the entire center out of the tin washtub.

"Nice work," said Janet.

Janet went back into the barn and emerged with a rope and a couple twigs. "What are you doing, Mom?" asked Matthew.

"Well it looks like you're not going to learn anymore shooting up the washtub from this distance, so let's make this a little more challenging."

Janet and Matthew walked to the maple tree that was about twenty-five paces away. Janet tied the rope to the one remaining handle on the washtub. She then measured the twigs and broke them off and pressed them into the three-inch hole that Matthew had spent twenty bullets shooting up and through. The twigs made an X inside the hole in the washtub. Janet then threw the rope over the lowest limb and tied it off on the washtub handle. The tub spun in the gentle breeze.

The two walked back to the spot behind the barn. "OK, Matthew, show me what you can do."

"But, Mom, it's moving," complained Matthew.

"Matthew, what are you thinking? Do you think a rabbit is going to just stand there and let you shoot it? No, it is going to run for its life. You will never be a hunter if you can't learn to shoot a moving target."

Matthew stood up straight and tried to get a bead on the moving target. He squeezed off a shot that was wide of the mark. He tried again, and after about three shots, he was timing the movement of the washboard and hitting it almost every other time.

"You're getting better, Son, you just need to practice. When I come back, I expect you to have shot the twigs out from the bull's eye."

Matthew looked at his mom in disbelief. "Mom, I could never do that."

"Never, did a dog gone thing in his entire life, and we kicked him out of our family years ago. I do not want you bringing up his sorry name ever again."

Matthew smiled and then laughed. Janet had a no nonsense personality that was mixed with pure love. Matthew loved how his mom encouraged him.

"OK, Mom. I will do my best."

Janet returned to the house to see what she could do to move things along.

Edwin Featherstone was still jawboning his customer. John, James and Rosemary were trying to gather up the goats. It was not as easy as they thought it would be. The normally compliant and mild mannered goat had never been on a rope.

It didn't help that Rosemary had been reading *Cowgirls of the American West* and decided to lasso them like steers, complete with hoots and hollers.

"She has those goats absolutely terrified," remarked Grandpa.

John laughed as he yelled at Rosemary to huddle up for a pow-wow. "Rosemary I want you to quietly go up to the Saanen's and gently put a rope around their necks, and bring them here one at a time," John instructed.

"No problem, Dad," said Rosemary, who had no idea what a problem it was going to become.

Rosemary quietly walked up to the closest Saanen, but as she approached, Snowflake made a dash to get away.

Rosemary was apparently Goat-non-grata in the eyes of the herd. They wanted nothing to do with Rosemary or her rope. Rosemary finally cornered Snowflake and started to put the rope around her neck. Snowflake was having none of it and let out an SOS goat bleat that must have triggered some sort of primitive killer instinct in Buster.

Buster was on a full run to protect Snowflake, and Rosemary soon found herself running as fast as she could for the fence. Buster was a lot faster than Rosemary and she was finally given a head butt that lifted her off the ground and sent her sailing into the soft wet pasture grass.

By this time, the goat drama had attracted a crowd.

Mark and Luke, safely behind the fence, were shouting at Rosemary not to let that goat get the best of her.

Rosemary was tough, but Buster was tougher and with his head down, was ready to prove it.

"Should we help her out?" asked James.

"Not on your life," said John. "Rosemary has been ruling the roost with an iron hand way too long without a serious challenge, and this will be a great lesson for her."

Now Rosemary was no push-over and decided that running away from Buster was not the best tactic. So instead of running away, she ran straight at Buster, side stepped him, grabbed his two horns, and held on for dear life. Buster had a fit and tried to throw her off, but Rosemary had a grip like a blacksmith and would not let go.

The tide of battle went back and forth with the two determined combatants locked horns to hand.

John and Janet were laughing so hard that they were in tears. Edwin, Widow Benson and the customer came out of the farm house and got into the wagon and left. Only Widow Benson waved goodbye, unaware of the goat wrangling drama that was taking place in her pasture.

Finally, after about twenty minutes, knowing that Rosemary would never give up, and was starting to get the worst of it, John and James decided to intervene.

James had grabbed a shovel and was prepared to give the Billy a good whack to get his attention. This was a plan that turned out to be unnecessary.

The sound of the harmonica echoed over the pasture, and in an instant, Buster settled down as all the goats made their way toward the melodic sound of Matthew and his harmonica.

Matthew had discovered a couple days earlier that the goats loved his harmonica music and would follow him around the pasture as he played any tune that came into his head.

"Well, I never in my life!" said Janet. Grandpa returned the shovel to the barn as John carefully let the six Saanen's out of the pasture. As long as Matthew played the harmonica, the Saanen's followed him wherever he went, bleating out goat applause as far as anyone could tell. It was the most astounding thing any of them had ever seen.

"OK, Matthew, you keep playing and start walking home. We will catch up with you in a little bit."

"Dad, my rifle is leaning up against the back of the barn."

"Is it loaded, Nine Toes?" asked Dad.

"It isn't, but you should treat it like it is," Matthew responded.

John laughed.

Matthew played his harmonica as he marched the two miles home. The five goats followed close behind. John and Janet watched in wonder. "The Pied Piper of Goat-Dom," said John, as the repeating chorus of "Old Suzanna" drifted into "My Old Kentucky Home."

"Have you ever seen anything like it?" said James, as he put his arm around his son, John.

"Purely hilarious!" said John.

"That would make a nice segment for one of your stories," James said.

"If they were sheep, it would," responded John.

"My sheep hear my voice and they follow me," said James, "has a flip side."

"And what is that?" asked John.

"The goats hear any old thing, and off they go." "Hmmmm," said John,

"I think you might have something there."

Janet yelled instructions for all the children to get loaded into the farm wagon. John went off to get Matthew's rifle. He found it leaning up against the barn and unloaded. The shells were nowhere in sight, so John figured that either Matthew had fired over 500 rounds, or the remaining ammo was in his jacket pocket.

Just then, Janet showed up. "Come here. I want to show you something," said Janet, who went to the maple tree to inspect the spinning washtub target. "Will you look at that," said Janet.

"Look at what?" asked John. "All I see is a big hole in the middle of this washtub," he concluded.

"Exactly," said Janet, explaining that she had secured two twigs in the center of that big hole earlier in the day.

"You're not telling me that Matthew shot out the center of this washtub as it swung in the breeze twenty-five paces away," said John.

"That is exactly what I am telling you," said Janet. "I knew he favored my side of the family," she said, laughing.

"Wild Bill Hickok and Annie Oakley, what is this family coming to?" laughed John, as he swept his wife into his arms and off her feet, giving her a kiss right on the lips.

"As you can see," said John, as he put Janet back on the ground, "my aim isn't too bad either."

As they walked back to the wagon, to load up and head home, the two chuckled and about all the funny adventures the day had served up.

Grandpa had gotten all the kids and supplies into the wagon, including all the milk buckets and stanchions. "Ready to head home, Dad?" asked John.

"Everything has been taken care of here," reported Grandpa.

"By the way," he continued, "Constance says you can have all her chickens. She has two roosters and fourteen laying hens."

"The two roosters will go into the pot," said Janet. "We already have one too many roosters, but I sure could use the extra eggs."

"I will pick them up on my next visit," said John. "We will wait until they are all roosting, then bag 'em up and bring them home," John concluded.

Matthew got a special delight out of leading a small herd of bleating goats, all intent in getting as close to the source of his harmonic melodies as possible.

From the window of the Spice Farm, Charlie could hear the sound of harmonica music. As he looked out the window, he laughed to see his brother Matthew dancing his way into the farm, playing "Goober Peas" on his harmonica with six goats following along like they were in a parade.

John 10:27-29
My sheep hear my voice, and I know them, and they follow me:
And I give unto them eternal life; and they shall never perish,
neither shall any man pluck them out of my hand.
My Father, which gave them me, is greater than all;
and no man is able to pluck them out
of my Father's hand.

Chapter 35

The Perfect Place

M atthew arrived on the farm with six goats and not a clue as to what to do with them. So, he just settled on the front porch swing and played his harmonica. The goats listened intently as they munched his mother's silky dogwood plants that she had so carefully planted around the house. Fortunately for Matthew and the goats, Stubborn safely pulled the rest of the Spice family home in the early afternoon of that brisk November day. As soon as John drove the wagon into the farm there was a flurry of activity.

The first order of business was to pasture the goats far away from Mom's prized sweet ferns, Carolina roses and snowhill hydrangea.

Everyone pitched to help. By the time the sun went down and Mom rang the dinner bell, all the six new goats were safely pastured, the new dairy equipment was set up and put in place, the animals were all fed and watered, and everyone was exhausted.

Even though it was extra work, Janet insisted they eat their late sunset dinner in the Eagle's Nest. She had not spent much time with Charlie over the past couple of weeks and was determined to make up for lost time.

The dining table in the attic was set, and the wonderful dinner, prepared by Anna, was a comfort to everyone at the table. Charlie listened as everyone told the story of that action packed day from their own point of view.

Charlie especially loved hearing about the billy goat wrangling experience of Rosemary. To hear her tell it, if Matthew had not interrupted with his harmonica, Buster the blly goat was on the verge of total defeat and surrender.

Charlie wanted to hear that story over and over again from everyone's point of view. Everyone enjoyed retelling the legendary goat showdown from their perspective. It was a *Buster the Billy Goat meets The Goat Slayer Rosemary* legend that grew by miles over the years, and without Buster to tell his side of the story, no one doubted it. Or at least if they did, they were too polite to mention it.

The last morsels of Grandma's delicious meal found its way to the licked clean plates and then quickly disappeared.

It was time for Grandpa to read from *Pilgrim's Progress.*

In the story, Christian had made it to the House Beautiful and was just about to view the Delectable Mountains in the distance from the vantage point of the House Beautiful, which was a picture of the church. Grandpa read the story and then explained the allegorical meaning to the Spice family.

"We don't think about Heaven enough," Grandpa declared. "This passage in *Pilgrim's Progress* is a reminder to us that this world is not our home and we are not citizens of this world. Our inheritance is in Heaven."

"What is an 'in-hair-tunce?'" asked Ginger. Everyone laughed and then immediately re-fixed their gaze on Grandpa, who they knew from experience was going to give them an answer. As it turned out, it was an answer they would probably never forget.

Grandpa stroked his chin. John recognized the sign and knew that an interesting story was about to be spun.

"The year was 1851," began Grandpa. "It had been a very cold winter in Elkin, North Carolina. Most of the family thought that it was the bitter chill that finally ended the life of their beloved grandfather.

"Amos, who had immigrated to North Carolina as a young man, had lived a long and productive life. Once he settled in the Yadkin Valley, he never traveled more than fifty miles from his farm, and the truth be told, he never really wanted to.

"Amos was a man of simple habits, and unexaggerated expectation. Everyone loved him, and in his lifetime he made it a special point to love everyone God put in his path. He would be greatly missed.

"No one was going to miss him more than his grandson, Jay.

"Grandpa Amos had latched onto Jay when he was just a tyke, and made no secret about his special affection for his last born grandson. It was clear to everyone that something of Grandpa had been deposited into Jay over the years. Jay had adopted many of Grandpa Amos' dated sayings and was always turning heads and getting a chuckle when he polished off a sentence with one of Grandpa Amos' famous Spoonerisms.

"His favorite was a perennial dinnertime classic."

"When Mom entered the room with the last plate from the kitchen, Jay would rise, do a deep bow as he scooted out her chair and say, 'May I sew you to your sheet?' Everyone always laughed as Mom chided, 'There you go again, Jay, sounding like Grandpa Amos.' Jay took that as a high praise and always responded with 'Thank you, one and all.'

"Grandpa Amos had made an indelible imprint on Jay and his family, and now he was gone. The tears flowed endlessly, and every time there was a brief respite from the sorrow, some little remembrance would dart into their minds and the tears would begin to flow again.

"The reading of the will had been postponed for over a month, but the day finally arrived for the family to gather one last time, in memory of the dearest soul any of them had ever known.

"Dad took charge with Mother at his side. Dad did the reading and Mom did the distributing.

"Grandpa Amos was always quoting the Bible verse about "numbering your days" and had obviously taken it to heart.

"A letter and a gift had been carefully prepared for each member of the family. But before any of that took place, Grandpa had prepared a letter that was to be read out loud to his entire family.

"It was a cheerful letter addressed to all of them. The letter was written as if he had just packed up and gone on a journey to a far country filled with endless delights. The middle of the letter was an admonition to trek through this world with care, always keeping their hearts and minds focused on the Savior. It ended with the promise that he would see them all very soon.

"They all sat in silence as they considered the last cheerful and hopeful words of Grandpa Amos.

"'Time to read the will,' Dad reported with a twinkle in his eye and buoyancy that had been missing from the family for many weeks.

"Dad cleared his throat and began reading the last will and testament of Grandpa Amos."

"'To Ranger, I give the following instructions: Keep the family safe and keep those foxes and weasels away from the henhouse.' With that, Dad produced a gunnysack full of bones. Ranger sat at full attention as he licked his chops. 'This will last you a lifetime, Ranger,' Dad said as he pulled one of the bones from the sack and carefully placed it in Ranger's salivating mouth.

"'Only Grandpa Amos would remember the family dog in his last will and testament,' Mom said proudly, as they all chuckled.

"The next person on the list was Jay's older brother Robert. His letter was read and a small box was delivered. The box contained eight gold sovereigns from England that had belonged to his Grandfather. Each was stamped with the date 1801, the year he emigrated from England. It also contained a collection of war metals that Grandpa Amos had earned as a soldier before he sailed to America from England.

"All the grandchildren were read a special letter and all were given a special gift.

"'Jay you're next on the list,' said Dad.

"*Finally, it was my turn,* thought Jay. The letter was read and then a large box was slid from behind the old upright piano and slid in Jay's direction. In the box was Grandpa's sandstone grinding wheel with a foot pedal, a small oil can, Grandpa's favorite axe with the hickory handle, his dog-eared and well used King James Bible, and his favorite book, *Pilgrim's Progress.*

"Jay recognized all these gifts. Grandpa had taught him how to sharpen everything—from knives to spades and disc plow blades—on the treadle driven grinding wheel."

"The letter simply said, 'Jay, I want you to keep the axe sharp, and the oil fresh. I have given you my Bible so you can read the parts I loved the most. Keep reading *Pilgrim's Progress* and I will see you in the Celestial City. Love Grandpa.'

"Jay would often reflect on the events of this sad but joyous occasion, many years later, and remember every detail as if it occurred yesterday."

"I will, be right back," said Mark as he sailed out to of the room without so much as a howdy do. John and Janet just figured Mark was headed for the outhouse and didn't give it another thought.

"Please go on with your story, Dad," insisted John.

"Well Jay was only nine years old and did not fully understand the prize he had been given. Grandpa had read *Pilgrim's Progress* to him many times. Jay figured he knew exactly where the Celestial City was, and made up his mind right then and there that he would make it his destination in life.

"As the years passed, the meaning of the inheritance became clearer and clearer. Jay, as he was instructed, kept the axe sharp, the oil fresh, the Bible well read, and always had his eye focused on the Celestial City.

"In time, the inheritance finally accomplished what Grandpa Amos had prayed it would. It became the metaphor that defined Jay's pilgrimage on this earth."

Just then, Mark re-entered the room carrying an axe.

"Is this the axe, Grandpa?" asked Mark as he held up the axe with the hickory handle and the clean silvery sharpened edge.

Grandpa smiled, "Mark I always said you were the deep thinker in the family. Quiet, still waters run deep."

Grandpa held up his tattered King James Version of the Bible. "And this is the Bible I was given by my Grandfather Amos."

Charlie reached for *Pilgrim's Progress* and lifted it in the air. "Is this the copy of *Pilgrim's Progress* your Grandpa gave you?"

"Yes it is, Charlie."

"What about the old sandstone grinding wheel in the barn, Grandpa?" asked Rosemary.

"Yep, the very one," Grandpa confirmed.

Luke was a little slower at unraveling the mystery, and asked, "Who is Jay?"

Grandpa laughed. "*Jay* stands for *James*," Grandpa replied.

"Ohhhh, I understand now," said Luke, as he began to put the pieces of the puzzle together.

Grandpa continued, "I have looked forward to telling you my story. I have lived out my three score and ten years, and now is the time to have a heart to heart with my family.

"I have shared my simple story because it may help you understand another story that happened almost 2000 years ago," continued Grandpa. Although my story is pretty unimportant, it does illustrate a life changing truth that marks out for our consideration the most important event that ever took place in all of human history."

Grandpa paused and caught his breath. "Now," he continued, "I want to ask all of you two important questions. Are you ready?" Everyone nodded, yes. "OK, I want you to ask yourself these two questions."

"What is my inheritance?"

"And how have I treated it?"

Grandpa continued, "For hundreds of years, there have been headlines and human-interest stories printed in newspapers and books about the scores of heirs to great estates who have squandered their inheritance."

"Vast fortunes have been lost through neglect by people who had little or no regard for the one who gave them the inheritance in the first place. Some have lost their inheritance through riotous living and debauchery, and others have watched their inheritance disappear in an hour at the gambling tables.

"These are sad stories that stand in contrast to the inheritance I was given—an inheritance worth less than fifty dollars, but I wouldn't trade it for the whole world."

"So, children," asked Grandpa, "what is the difference between the inheritances I received and the inheritance countless others have received—inheritances a thousand times more valuable than my inheritance, which were received with little or no consideration for either the inheritance or the one who gave it?

"Can anyone tell me the answer?" Grandpa paused for a response.

Rosemary raised her hand, "I think I know, Grandpa."

"OK, Rosemary. What do you think is the answer?"

"Is the answer *love*?" queried Rosemary.

John and Janet smiled at each other as Grandpa nodded his head and said, "Rosemary, that is exactly the right answer, and I am so glad that you understand."

Grandpa continued, as he fished a piece of string out of his pocket. He tied one end of the string around Charlie's wrist and the other end around his own.

"Love is the connecting cord that ties the one who gave the inheritance with the one who receives it. Just like this string connects me to Charlie."

Grandpa then removed the string from his wrist. "You see, where love exists, there is a cord of love that ties the one who receives the inheritance with the one who gives the inheritance. And if there is no cord of love that ties the two together, then the inheritance has lost its power and has no purpose. When there is no cord of love that binds, there is no obligation to the memory of the one who gave the gift."

Ginger piped up, "Aunt Ida went to Heaven and left us our dining room table."

Grandpa laughed. "That is interesting, Ginger. It is true that often when someone dies they leave you a gift that once belonged to them." Of course, Ginger had this story all mixed up in her mind, but this was not the time to explain to Ginger that Aunt Ida was still among the living.

Grandpa continued. "Heaven is our inheritance; it is our possession because Jesus died on a cross and gave us Heaven as a possession. It is an inheritance that the Son of God purchased for each of us."

Everyone was silent and thoughtful as Grandpa allowed a few moments to pass, in order that the smaller children could absorb the message.

"Let me give you an example," said Grandpa, thoughtfully.

"Let's say your Mom goes to the mercantile to buy three big fur coats for Rosemary, Cinnamon and Ginger. But when Mom arrives at Smyth's Mercantile, she discovers that they are all sold out of fur coats. What would Mr. Elmer Smyth give your Mom instead of three fur coats?"

Charlie added, "You mean after Mom pays for coats?"

"That's right, Charlie," said Grandpa. "After your Mom pays for the three fur coats in advance."

Rosemary spoke up first, "Mr. Smyth gives Mom a piece of paper."

"That's right," said Grandpa. "That piece of paper is called a receipt. It says that the fur coats have been paid for, but not yet delivered.

"Can the receipt keep you warm in the snow?" asked Grandpa. "The answer is no; it just proves that Mom payed for the three fur coats and can pick them up when they finally arrive in the store.

"Now let me ask you an important question," continued Grandpa. "How do you know you're going to inherit Heaven? How do you know Heaven is your future possession?"

After a minute of silence, John spoke up. "Children, the answer is something you all know." And then he added, "Why are you going to Heaven in the first place?"

Mark answered, "Because Jesus died and paid our sin debt so we could go to Heaven."

Matthew added, "Jesus shed His blood on the cross so we could go to Heaven."

Grandpa grinned from ear to ear and said, "So, you understand that the payment of the debt for your sin happened at the cross. And where do you read about this happening?"

"In the Bible," said Matthew.

"The promise written in the Bible is your receipt that proves you're going to Heaven," Grandpa said.

"Now let me ask you another question. How do you know that Elmer Smyth is going to give your mother the three fur coats she paid for? All she has is a piece of paper."

"Because Mr. Smyth is in the business of selling things, and if he didn't give Mom what she bought, then word would get around and Mr. Smyth would lose his business," Rosemary piped up. And then added. "And Dad would show up with his gun."

"Well," said Grandpa, who was not quite expecting that precise answer, "could we say that your Mom trusts Elmer Smyth to keep his word and deliver the goods?"

"Yes," everyone agreed.

"OK. Let's see if we have this figured out," Grandpa grinned. "We have Heaven as an inheritance because of the payment Jesus made on the cross. His very blood is the proof of the purchase. He died on a cross so we could live in Heaven." Grandpa paused. "So, how do we know that Jesus can keep the promise that is recorded in His Word? How do we know He will take us all to Heaven to live with Him?" Grandpa asked.

Grandpa opened up his King James Bible while they were pondering the answer to the question. Finally, Grandpa read.

1 Corinthians 15:1-4

Moreover, brethren, I declare unto you the gospel which
I preached unto you, which also ye have received, and wherein
ye stand; By which also ye are saved, if ye keep in memory
what I preached unto you, unless ye have believed in vain.
For I delivered unto you first of all that which I also received,
how that Christ died for our sins according to the scriptures;
And that he was buried, and that he rose again the third day
according to the scriptures:

Grandpa closed his Bible and asked, "So, what is the 'Good News', Spice family?"

Charlie, who had memorized this verse a couple of years earlier, gave the answer. "The Good News, is that Jesus died for our sins, was buried and rose from the dead after three days."

Grandpa nodded. "So what is the guarantee that we will finally receive the inheritance that He promised to all those that trust Him?"

Rosemary raised her hand, "I know, Grandpa. The receipt is the blood of Jesus and the guarantee is that he rose from the dead."

Grandpa smiled and so did Heaven!

1 John 5:11-15

And this is the record, that God hath given to us eternal life,
and this life is in his Son. He that hath the Son hath life;
and he that hath not the Son of God hath not life. These things
have I written unto you that believe on the name of the
Son of God; that ye may know that ye have eternal life,
and that ye may believe on the name of the Son of God.
And this is the confidence that we have in him, that,
if we ask any thing according to his will, he heareth us:
And if we know that he hear us, whatsoever we ask,
we know that we have the petitions
that we desired of him.

Chapter 36

Dogs

T he Spice family was used to getting up with the sun. Janet was usually the first one awakened by the new day's rays that streamed through the partially opened window and danced to the rhythm of the gentle breeze through the lace curtain.

John was usually awakened by the smell of fresh coffee brewing on the stove. The children were always in the kitchen within fifteen minutes of Janet's rising, eager to eat breakfast, having made the direct connection between tardiness and hunger. Cinnamon was the exception to the rule. Rosemary made it her business to make sure Cinnamon arrived in time for breakfast.

This morning was different.

"John," whispered Janet, "someone is banging on our front door." John leaped out of bed and went to the living room and took his rifle off the rack above the mantle. The banging on the door was menacing and John was taking no chances. From the living room window, John peeked to see who was at the door. It was still dark, but John clearly made out the figure of Wally McDaniel. John put the rifle back over the fireplace and went to the front door and opened it.

"Wally, what is wrong?" asked John.

"Plenty, partner," said Wally with a scowl.

"Well, come in and let's talk about it," said John.

"First, I want to show you something," said Wally, as he beckoned John to come outside and take a look at what he had in the back of his wagon.

The sun was just beginning to peek over the Blue Ridge Mountains as morning was beginning to announce a new day.

Wally took John to the back of the wagon and pulled back a small tarp. "Oh my," he said, as he took a quick step back. Just then, John heard a yelp. "Sorry," said John as he went down on one knee to comfort Wally's hunting dog, Eager, who was licking his front paw. John stood back up and gazed at the half-eaten, bloody lamb carcass.

"That critter is half eaten," said Wally. "They gorged themselves, which is a bad sign," he continued.

"Wolves?" asked John.

"Worse than that," said Wally, "wild dogs—three of them."

John and Wally returned to the house as Janet was just lighting the stove to heat up a fresh pot of coffee. John and Wally sat down at the kitchen table.

"Wally, did you see the dogs?" John asked.

"Yep," said Wally, tapping his spoon on the table. "Marie got up to make herself a cup of tea about an hour ago. She came running into the bedroom and woke me up, said she heard a big ruckus out in the east pasture." Wally paused, and then continued, "By the time I got dressed, those three dogs were headed up the Blue Ridge toward Toad's Hollar."

"Toad's Hollar?" asked John.

"Oh," smiled Wally, "that's what I called it as a boy; it's about a mile and a half straight up from the Franklin's place."

"You mean 'Muddy Creek,'" said John.

Janet, who had been listening to the conversation, added, "I think you mean 'Lucy's Lagoon.'" The three laughed as they realized they had all named the same place something different, and none of them had any idea what it was actually called.

Janet put a mug of hot coffee in front of Wally, "Black, no sugar, and no cream," Janet said reassuringly to Wally, who had strong opinions about anyone "poisoning" his coffee.

Wally had been sent to spend the summer with his Uncle Clem, who was a cattle rancher in Texas, when he was thirteen years old. Wally loved the West and had picked up the lingo and the lifestyle of a cowboy.

He always wore a holstered Colt 45 by his side and claimed that it brought civilization everywhere it went.

Wally was a giant of a man who stood about six, feet two inches in his cowboy boots and weighed a hefty 325 pounds of pure muscle.

He didn't return home to North Carolina until his dad died in 1908. Wally was a "Son of the South" as a fourth generation North Carolinian, but you would never know it to look at him. And when he opened his mouth, what came out was El Paso, Texas. Of course, this just added to Wally's celebrity status in the Spice home—a home littered with dime novels telling the legendary stories of the Wild West.

It was no surprise when Rosemary seated herself right next to Mr. McDaniel. She carefully listened as the two men planned their response to the present danger.

A dog is a man's best friend; a wild, hungry dog is a rancher's worst nightmare. A wolf has a fear of man; a domesticated dog that has gone feral, due to abandonment, does not have a natural fear of man and will invade man's domain without giving it a second thought.

Rosemary tapped Mr. McDaniel on the arm to get his attention. "Yes, Little Lady," said Mr. McDaniel, "you have a question?"

"Well," said Rosemary, "couldn't we trap the dogs and then retrain them?"

"Sugar Pie," said Mr. McDaniel, "that is not possible; although, it has been tried many times. Once a dog gets a taste for blood, and has killed a domesticated animal, like a calf or a lamb, there is no way to train that out of them. They are killers from that moment on, and they must be destroyed."

John noticed Rosemary wince at the answer she received from Wally. "Rosemary, Honey," said John, "once those wild dogs get hungry again, they will come after our goats. And if Scruffy stands up to them, they will kill her. They would even go after Stubborn if they could corner him. How would you feel about that?"

Rosemary thought about it and said, "Dad, you and Mr. McDaniel need to find those dogs and kill them before they hurt us."

"Exactly my thoughts," said John.

Rosemary was not the only one listening intently to the conversation. Matthew was taking in every word. "Dad," said Matthew, "I am a good shot, and I want to come with you."

John looked at Janet for permission to give Matthew the answer he wanted to hear. Janet thought about it for a couple seconds and then nodded her head yes. Her natural concern for the safety of her 12-year-old son was outweighed by the knowledge that he would be in the tender care of two experienced hunters.

John looked at Matthew and said, "Better get your gun, put on your warmest clothes, and put that new box of 22 shells in your knapsack." Matthew raced out of the room, the most excited he had ever been in his life. An adventure of a lifetime was about to commence.

"John," said Wally, "I have all the gear we need in the wagon, including a tent and enough dried meat to last us a month."

Janet, hearing this, got busy in the pantry, pulling out four large cans of pork and beans and some other sundries.

"When would you like to leave?" asked John.

"As soon as you're ready," responded Wally.

The next hour was spent making sure that John and Matthew would be warm and well-fed for the three or four days Mr. McDaniel estimated it would take to find and kill the wild dogs.

John packed two rifles and a box of ammunition, matches, rain gear, a couple of extra blankets, and his "traveling KJV Bible."

Mom hugged and kissed both her boys.

"Janet," said Wally, "would you mind going to pick up Marie later this afternoon and bring her back to your farm until this is all over? My field hand, Hank, can take care of the ranch while I am gone, but I don't want to leave my wife alone in her delicate condition."

"Of course," said Janet. "I will pick Marie up after lunch."

As soon as Mark and Luke realized that Marie was coming to visit, they looked at each other and both blurted out what was on their minds, "Spaghetti!" they trumpeted in unison. Everyone had a good laugh.

"I will be right back," said Wally as he got up and went out the front door, heading for his wagon. A moment later he returned with something wrapped in old newspaper. Wally sat back down and put the package in front of him.

"What is that?" said Mark, bursting with curiosity.

Mr. McDaniel slid it over to Mark. "This is something I promised Charlie. You go ahead and open it, Mark." Mark carefully unwrapped the newspaper to reveal a brown leather case. "Go ahead and open it up," Mr. McDaniel prompted.

Mark opened it up and stared. "It's a telescope," said Mathew.

"Well, that is close, Matthew, but actually, it is a Deroy & Forestier pair of binoculars from Paris, France."

"Where is Paris, France?" asked Rosemary.

"Far away across the ocean," answered Mr. McDaniel. "I bet your Grandpa has been there and can show you where it is on a map."

Grandpa nodded and added, "After breakfast, I will find your Dad's atlas and show you where it is."

Janet and Anna began serving breakfast, with a double portion for John, Wally and Matthew.

Before breakfast was over, Wally excused himself and lumbered up the stairs to the attic, carrying Charlie's breakfast tray and the binoculars.

"Hey, partner, how are you doing?" greeted Mr. McDaniel. Charlie had just woken up and was busy rubbing his eyes.

"I have something for those eyes of yours," said Mr. McDaniel as he helped Charlie sit up, placing his breakfast tray on his lap and the leather case containing the binoculars by his side.

Charlie was too excited about the present to eat and immediately opened the leather case to discover the binoculars. Charlie had read about binoculars and seen them advertised in magazines, but had never actually held a pair in his own hands.

Mr. McDaniel spent the next fifteen minutes showing Charlie how to use them, warning him not to look directly at the sun through them, but encouraged him to look at the moon that evening. This new lens would magnify and brighten Charlie's world from that point forward.

Charlie was beside himself with excitement and was busy focusing on every bit of real estate outside his window. "Not only are things bigger, but I can see things in the distance I've never seen before!" Charlie exclaimed.

Mr. McDaniel basked in the high praise and appreciation as he secretly dreamed of the day when he would be treating his own children to the wonders of life.

Finally, and with great fanfare from Charlie, Mr. McDaniel went back downstairs and sat down at the kitchen table, wiping a tear from his eyes.

Mr. McDaniel could not imagine that he would be as happy and content as Charlie at fourteen years old, a cripple with heart disease. He knew it was not normal and that it had much to do with the Master of the Spice family household, the Lord Jesus Christ.

Wally had just "bumped into the Savior," as he liked to say, and was looking forward to learning more about the Son of God, who Grandpa James kept telling him was "the best friend a sinner ever had." Wally was only thrity-five years old, but had lived a wild life in Texas. He knew for certain that he was a great sinner, and wanted to hear more about the great Savior.

Before they left, John sat everyone down at the kitchen table and read from the Scriptures. Grandpa then prayed for a successful hunting trip.

As they headed out the door, Janet grabbed John one last time and pulled him aside. "I don't think this is about hunting down three wild dogs," said Janet.

"What do you think it is about?" asked John.

"I think this is about Wally's soul."

"I think you're right," said John as he thumped the KJV Bible he had in his jacket pocket.

Grandpa overheard the conversation and came closer to John and Janet. "What is needed here is prayer," said Grandpa. "God has arranged it so you have three days with Wally and Matthew, and we have three days, or more, with Marie. Let's use the time wisely."

John hugged Janet and his dad. "Janet," said John. "I left old Betsy over the mantle and would suggest you keep your own rifle handy, hidden and loaded until we get back." John gave Janet a peck on the cheek and headed out the door.

As Matthew followed on the heals of his dad, Janet snagged him and gave him a great big hug good-bye.

Psalm 91:1-11

He that dwelleth in the secret place of the most
High shall abide under the shadow of the Almighty.
I will say of the Lord, He is my refuge and my fortress:
my God; in him will I trust. Surely he shall deliver
thee from the snare of the fowler, and from the noisome
pestilence. He shall cover thee with his feathers,
and under his wings shalt thou trust: his truth
shall be thy shield and buckler. Thou shalt not be afraid
for the terror by night; nor for the arrow that
flieth by day; Nor for the pestilence that walketh in darkness;
nor for the destruction that wasteth at noonday.
A thousand shall fall at thy side,
and ten thousand at thy right hand;
but it shall not come nigh thee.
Only with thine eyes shalt thou behold and
see the reward of the wicked. Because thou
hast made the Lord, which is my refuge, even
the most High, thy habitation; There shall no evil
befall thee, neither shall any plague come nigh thy dwelling.
For he shall give his angels charge over thee,
to keep thee in all thy ways.

Chapter 37

The Hunt

"W hat is that?" asked Matthew, pointing to the blood stained tarp that covered the carcass of the lamb in the back of the wagon.

"That is something you don't need to worry about right now," said John, as he helped Matthew in and told him to stay by the front of the wagon.

"Is it alright if Eager keeps Matthew company in the front of the wagon?" asked John.

"His favorite place," said Wally with a smile.

Eager needed no encouragement to jump into the wagon and make himself comfortable next to Matthew, who immediately won his affection as he rubbed his ears and stroked his head.

"Now don't you go a spoiling my best hunting dog," Wally said, as he leaned over the rail to drop all of John's gear into the front of the wagon.

"Too late for that," said John with a wink.

"Well, I guess I have sort of been partial to Eager," admitted Wally.

Wally had invested untold hours in training Eager. Eager was not only a prize coon dog, he was also a tracker. A tracking dog is just what Wally and John needed on this hunting trip.

The whole Spice family spilled onto the front porch to watch the hunting party depart. Wally heard a rapping from the attic window and looked up to see Charlie waving good-bye with one-hand and binoculars in the other. Wally, John and Matthew waved back as they headed out of the farm and down the road.

From the Eagle's Nest, Charlie fixed his gaze on the hunting party as it finally disappeared from his field of view as seen through his new binoculars.

"I see you're using Tarnation to pull the wagon instead of your horses," John remarked.

Tarnation was an old mule that had reached the tail end of his life. Wally used him on his hunting trips and had kept him well exercised and fed.

For an old mule, Tarnation was in good shape and eager to be on an adventure. His days of mischief, and there were plenty of those in the past, were a distant memory. Mules, like men, mellow with time. Tarnation was not going to be any trouble on this trip.

"Well, John, Tarnation only needs to pull us about three miles, so not much of a workout for him."

John did not know what Wally's plan was, but he was absolutely sure he had one. Wally had been hunting all his life and had lots of experience with bears, mountain lions, coyotes, wolves and even wild dogs.

HEAVEN'S PROMISE - THE SPICE FAMILY CHRONICLES

The short journey to the Franklin Farm was uneventful and quiet. No one really felt like talking as they each considered what adventures might lay ahead.

"Whoa up there, Tarnation," said Wally as he drove his wagon into the Franklin farm.

"I will be right back," said Wally.

Wally headed to the front door of the Franklin Farm where he was met by Matilda Franklin. Matilda Franklin was Wally's aunt. John and Matthew watched as Homer, Wally's uncle, came to the door and shook Wally's hand. Heads nodded as Matilda Franklin gave Wally a hug, or at least she tried to.

Matthew couldn't help giggling as Wally bowed down so his aunt could give him a squeeze. Matilda was just less than five feet tall and her short arms barely reached Wally's shoulders.

Wally stayed on the porch as Aunt Matilda went back into the house and returned with a bag that she proudly handed to Wally.

Wally returned to the wagon. "Goober peas anyone?" he asked as he offered the bag to John and Matthew. Matthew grabbed a handful and hopped out of the wagon. John Spice did the same.

440 | Chapter 37

Wally then began to unhitch Tarnation from the wagon.

"John, fetch me that wooden saddle pack."

John went to the back of the wagon and pulled out the wooden contraption made up of oak spindles and leather cinches. The saddle pack was designed for a mule or horse and allowed for the storage of a couple hundred pounds of gear.

Tarnation was an old hand at packing gear, as hunting trips were a regular feature of Wally's life. He paid no attention at all to the fuss being made to get all the gear safely strapped and balanced on his back.

"Now comes the tricky part," said Wally. "Tarnation is used to pulling game out of the woods on a sled, but he has strong feelings about carrying anything dead on his back."

Matthew watched with interest as Wally produced a black sack that was especially made to go over Tarnation's head. "John," yelled Wally, "there is a feedbag full of oats in the back corner of the wagon; bring it here."

John fetched the bag and brought it to where Wally was coaxing and sweet-talking Tarnation. Tarnation was a smart old mule who knew that being blind-folded usually meant that what was going to happen next was something he was not going to like. His ears twitched and went back for a second but immediately returned to normal as John nuzzled the feedbag into his mouth.

Wally then went to the back of the wagon.

"Come here, Eager," Wally commanded. Eager knew exactly what to do as Wally pointed to the spot most likely to have been in contact with the dogs as they had greedily devoured his prize lamb. "Got it boy?" he asked. Eager backed up and sat at attention. "Good boy," said Wally, who knew that this meant that Eager had the scent and was ready to begin tracking down the three 4-legged criminals.

Wally then carefully re-wrapped the carcass and tied it up. He grabbed some sweet hay, along with a handful of weeds and dirt that he rubbed all over the tarp.

Wally then lifted up the package and carefully set it on top of the mule pack and tied it down. Tarnation barely noticed as he ate the last of the oats and used his tongue to lick up the remaining kernels.

"That was easier than I thought," said Wally as he took off his cowboy hat and wiped his brow.

Matthew had no idea what Wally was doing or what he was planning. He decided not to ask what they were going to be doing next.

Eager, with her nose to the ground, led the hunting party. Wally and Tarnation, loaded with all the gear, followed next. Matthew and John picked up the rear.

Wally had trained Eager to track based on his own unconventional methods. Eager had been trained to keep his nose on the trail of the scent with one eye on his master. As soon as he lost sight of Wally, he would sit patiently until Wally caught up with him. Eager was trained to never bark while tracking and to never, ever chase whatever it was he was hunting.

When Eager closed in on his target he would become agitated, and this was the clue that the target was close at hand. Once close, Eager was taught to stand and look in the direction of the target with his body in line with whatever it was they were hunting.

This training allowed Wally, John and Matthew to set the pace, not Eager. As Wally was fond of saying, "Most hunting dogs will run your legs off and leave you out of breath and hopelessly lost if you let them." This was not the case with Eager.

Wally had trained Eager well, and John took notice and admired the hundreds of hours that must have gone into training him.

Wally was also fond of saying that you can't train a rock, which was his way of saying that he had learned long ago not to spend his time trying to train a dumb dog. Eager was smart, and with that natural intelligence, a love and loyalty for his master, and great training he, was a wonderful companion and a great hunting and tracking dog.

It was not surprising that there was little conversation between the three hunters. Except for the occasional recognition of a familiar landmark, it was a quiet steady hike up into the Blue Ridge Mountains. Since almost all of the hiking was uphill, there was little breath left for conversation.

Matthew watched the sun slowly make its procession to a spot that appeared to be directly overhead. Wally was the first to notice, "I can't see my shadow anymore so it must be time for lunch." Without a word, the three all spotted the same grassy knoll under a giant maple tree. Wally gave Eager a whistle and he immediately returned to be with his master.

Wally tied Tarnation up near some grass. He fetched a dish from the pack along with a bag of dried strips of meat. He poured Eager a dish of water and set three large pieces of dried beef in front of him. Eager took a long drink and then sat down and began gnawing on the sticks of dried beef.

"Have some beef?" asked Wally as he handed John and Matthew a generous number of dried beef sticks.

"Thank you," said John and Matthew.

The beef sticks were tough and hard to eat. Once you had a chance to work on them for a bit, flavor of the molasses and brown sugar that—Wally had soaked them in before drying them—kept you determined to keep chewing.

"These are really good," announced Matthew.

"It takes a few minutes to come to that conclusion," said Wally, "but most do in the end."

The men began lunch tired and hungry. Now they were just tired. "A fifteen minute nap will do us all a world of good," announced Wally, who laid down in the moist, cold grass and immediately fell asleep.

Fifteen minutes seemed like eternity, as Wally's snoring was seismic. "Time to wake up Wally," John said as he gently shook the large man's shoulders.

Wally smiled and replied, "That was the shortest fifteen minutes I ever experienced."

John pulled out his pocket watch. "Fifteen minutes and 30 seconds," said John with a broad grin. "Did I snore?" asked Wally, "Marie says I snore, but I don't believe her."

John stroked his chin trying to think of a thoughtful response. Finally, he said, "Wally, you married an honest woman who would never tell a lie."

Wally smiled and then took his hat off and laughed as he slapped his knee with his cowboy hat. "That's why she wants ear muffs for Christmas."

"Ear muffs, now why didn't I bring my ear muffs?" John said as he joined into the laughter.

Matthew knew enough to just remain silent as he wondered if it was possible to fall asleep with his fingers in his ears. He was soon to find out that it wasn't.

The three hunters dusted themselves off as Wally gave the command for Eager to get back on the trail. Eager was not misnamed, as he enthusiastically fulfilled his role as the chief guide and tracker.

The rest of the afternoon was spent hiking further and further up the Blue Ridge Mountains. The three dogs they were trailing had made no attempt to cover their tracks and were heading straight up the mountain. This was a good thing.

All of a sudden, Wally lifted his hand up and said, "Whoa." He then patted Tarnation on the velvety soft part of his nose as he whispered into his ear, "Good boy." Wally then went to fish something out of the pack. He returned with a brand new pair of binoculars. He took them out of the leather case and focused the lens on the ridge that lay about a mile up the Blue Ridge Mountains.

"I remember hunting up here with my dad when I was just a kid," Wally said, "and if I remember right, there is a valley just below that ridge up ahead that slowly dips down about 500 feet. Two streams fill a small pond, and to the north of the pond is a rock out-cropping with a few small caves."

John saddled up next to Wally. "Here, take a look," said Wally, as he handed John the binoculars. John surveyed the ridge and spotted a three-point buck just coming over the ridge and heading down toward a highly wooded patch just south of the ridge.

"Ideal spot for wild dogs," said John, "plenty of water and lots of shelter."

"Yes," said Wally, "and a watering hole for lots of animals that would not expect to be ambushed by three wild dogs."

"Here, Matthew," said Dad, "take a look." Matthew had never viewed anything through binoculars and was excited by the new experience.

"Can you watch the stars with these?" Matthew asked.

Wally laughed, "That's why the Good Lord put them up there. Tell you what, Matthew," said Mr. McDaniel, "you remind me tonight, and I will let you try them out."

Matthew smiled and gave the binoculars back to his Dad, who returned them to Wally. Wally put the leather case away in the pack and returned with the binoculars hanging around his neck.

Chapter 37 | 447

Isaiah 40:26

*Lift up your eyes on high, and behold who hath created
these things, that bringeth out their host by number:
he calleth them all by names by the greatness of his might,
for that he is strong in power; not one faileth.*

Chapter 38

More Spaghetti

W hen Janet went to fetch Marie in the early afternoon, she found her waiting with bags and boxes of food. Janet protested, but Marie insisted that she wanted to help out by making some of the meals. Marie loved to cook. She also missed her very large family. She was clearly looking forward to being a part of the remaining Spice household for three or four days.

Janet arrived back at the farm with Marie and was greeted by all. Marie was a hugger, and in response, the Spice children had developed a hugging repertoire that was both hilarious and heartwarming.

Marie had no sooner entered the front door when she found herself being hugged in all directions. Rosemary said it was like a herd of leeches. Ginger tackled one of Marie's knees as Cinnamon hugged her just below the waist. Rosemary held her hand and gave her a kiss on the neck while Mark and Luke filled up the rest of the real estate.

Marie clearly loved the attention and gave as good as she received—hugging and kissing all the Spice children mercilessly, which got the younger girls giggling and running around the room, always returning for more.

Janet, who was watching this from just outside the kitchen, was about to referee when Anna came along side and persuaded her to let it be. "It's embarrassing," said Janet, whose Southern manners were slightly offended by the open display of affection.

"It's joyful," said Anna. Janet smiled and returned to the kitchen.

Marie settled into her room and immediately entered the kitchen where she insisted she be allowed to fix dinner. The children followed her into the kitchen, eager to know what was going to happen.

"What would you children like for dinner?" asked Marie.

The spontaneous shouts of "spaghetti!" were deafening but abruptly ended when Janet let out a loud whistle that everyone knew meant to be quiet.

"You kids go get the boxes of food in the back of the wagon, and bring them into the kitchen. Then I want you all to get about your chores and leave Marie alone for a while," Mom said.

Marie smiled.

"Would you like our help?" Anna asked.

"Not really," said Marie. "Why don't you and Janet find a quiet spot and read a book or something."

"A quiet spot," laughed Janet.

They all laughed together for a moment and then Janet and Anna left the kitchen in Marie's charge.

Marie was young and had much to learn about life, but the one thing she knew all about was the purpose of a kitchen. She was a gourmet cook looking for hungry appreciative subjects, and she was right at home.

Janet and Anna took the gift of time they had been given by Marie to settle themselves into the porch swing for a good long talk.

Upstairs in the Eagle's Nest, Charlie and Grandpa were having one of their chats about Heaven. Charlie was anxious to show Grandpa all the secret places he had discovered with his new pair of binoculars which had been hanging around his neck for about two weeks, until Mom insisted he take them off when he went to sleep. Mr. McDaniel had given Charlie the gift of exploration, and when you're bedridden, that is a gift to be treasured above all others.

"Look out with your binoculars and bring into focus the big maple tree next to the road that leads to Elkin. Can you see it?" asked Grandpa.

Charlie was busy trying to get it into focus, and finally said, "I can see it clearly."

"What do you notice about that tree?" asked Grandpa.

"It is big," said Charlie. Grandpa listened to all the details that Charlie noticed about the tree, viewing it through his binoculars. "I see a bird's nest!" concluded Charlie, excitedly.

"Now," said Grandpa, "without looking through the binoculars, can you see the birds nest?"

Charlie strained his eyes, and finally answered, "no, I can't see anything but a tree."

"Now look on the ground under the tree with your binoculars and tell me what you see," said Grandpa.

Charlie lifted up the binoculars to his eyes and looked. "I see lots of yellow and red leaves," said Charlie.

"And why is that?" asked Grandpa.

"Because it is the fall season, and during this time of year, most of the trees, except the evergreens, lose their leaves."

"That is right," smiled Grandpa.

Charlie let his binoculars dangle from his neck as he sat up straight in his bed, knowing that Grandpa was about to tell him something special about Heaven.

"God has a season for everything, Charlie. God has made a special time for things to happen in His creation. Can you think of some of those seasons that God has created for us?"

"Well," said Charlie, "I know about the four seasons of the year."

"What about the apple orchard?" asked Grandpa. "Can you go out just anytime and pick apples?"

"No," answered Charlie, "the apples get ripe in August and September."

"What about the wheat that your mom makes the bread from—can you go into a wheat field and harvest wheat anytime of the year?"

"No," answered Charlie.

"That's right, you have to wait until the spring time. And what about the bird's nest, Charlie? Does the mother bird sit on eggs that hatch every day?"

"No," said Charlie.

"That's right," said Grandpa. "There is a special time on earth for everything that happens, including nesting and hatching baby birds. God has a season for everything," repeated Grandpa.

"You know, Charlie, when your Grandmother and I were sailing to India on a schoonerk, there was a big storm when we were out in the middle of the ocean and no safe harbor within hundreds of miles. Weeks later, we arrived in the safe harbor of Bombay. We could not avoid the storm by just sailing into a safe harbor in the middle of the ocean. There was a safe harbor waiting for us but we had to patiently wait for it to arrive. You see, Charlie, there is a time and a season for everything that God has done on earth. Do you understand that?"

"I think so," said Charlie.

"So let me ask you a question, Charlie. Do you think God has a time and a season for Heaven?"

Charlie, cocked his head, as he was not sure of what his grandfather was trying to teach him.

"Charlie if we die before Jesus comes again to clothe us in our resurrection-glorified body, what will Heaven be like?"

"You mean in our spirit bodies?"

"Yes," responded Grandpa, "in your spirit body."

Charlie's eyes brightened, "It will be wonderful, Grandpa."

Grandpa smiled, "Yes, it will, but it will also be incomplete, like a beautiful painting that is not quite finished. You can enjoy it, but you can also see that it is going to be even more beautiful once it is finished. That is exactly what it is going to be like for us if we go to Heaven before the Lord clothes our spirit Body with our resurrection-glorified body. The spirit body can enjoy Heaven very much, but until we are clothed with our final glorified body, we will not be able to fully appreciate Heaven. Do you know why?"

Charlie shrugged his shoulders.

"The answer," declared Grandpa, "is that God has a time and season for Heaven, and it will be perfected at exactly the right time on God's calendar. And do you know when that is?"

"When Jesus comes back in the clouds and we get our new bodies, and then go back to Heaven with Him!" said Charlie, excitedly.

"That is exactly right. So what do we become when we are changed into our glorified body?" asked Grandpa.

"I don't know," answered Charlie.

"Charlie, we become the spotless and perfect bride of Christ. And we will have fellowship with Jesus in a way that we cannot have with our spirit body alone."

"God has two seasons for His children. Do you know what those two season are?" asked Grandpa

"One season is when we die and go to Heaven before Jesus comes back to earth to give us our glorified body," replied Charlie.

"And what is the second season of Heaven for those that belong to the Lord Jesus Christ?" asked Grandpa.

Charlie smiled, "I know the answer, Grandpa, but you say it so much better than I do."

"I don't know about that, Charlie, but since you would like me to tell you in my own words, I will.

"The second season of Heaven is when Jesus returns in the clouds and raises those that have died and those that are still alive into His presence, and when they arrive in His presence, they will have all been perfected by Jesus; clothed with a glorified, perfect body, to go along with a perfect soul and a perfect spirit that loves Jesus and wants to be with Him forever."

Grandpa opened his Bible and read the following verses for Charlie, as he underlined the verses in red and put a marker in each page.

"Now, Charlie, here is the challenge."

Charlie smiled; he loved mysteries and puzzles.

"You figure out which of these verses has to do with God's first season in Heaven, and which has to do with the second season. And when we get together tomorrow to continue our discussion of Heaven, I want you to tell me which verse goes with which season. OK?"

"Alright," said Charlie, eager to occupy the rest of the afternoon figuring out the answer.

2 Corinthians 5:6-8

Therefore we are always confident, knowing that, whilst we are at home in the body, we are absent from the Lord: (For we walk by faith, not by sight:) We are confident, I say, and willing rather to be absent from the body, and to be present with the Lord.

2 Corinthians 5:1-3

For we know that if our earthly house of this tabernacle were dissolved, we have a building of God, an house not made with hands, eternal in the Heavens. For in this we groan, earnestly desiring to be clothed upon with our house which is from Heaven: If so be that being clothed we shall not be found naked.

Revelation 21:4

And God shall wipe away all tears from their eyes; and there shall be no more death, neither sorrow, nor crying, neither shall there be any more pain: for the former things are passed away.

1 Thessalonians 4:13
But I would not have you to be ignorant, brethren, concerning them which are asleep, that ye sorrow not, even as others which have no hope.

1 John 3:2
Beloved, now are we the sons of God, and it doth not yet appear what we shall be: but we know that, when he shall appear, we shall be like him; for we shall see him as he is.

1 Corinthians 2:9
But as it is written, Eye hath not seen, nor ear heard, neither have entered into the heart of man, the things which God hath prepared for them that love him.

Romans 2:7
To them who by patient continuance in well doing seek for glory and honour and immortality, eternal life:

1 Corinthians 15:53
For this corruptible must put on incorruption, and this mortal must put on immortality.

1 Thessalonians 4:13
But I would not have you to be ignorant, brethren, concerning them which are asleep, that ye sorrow not, even as others which have no hope.

1 Peter 1:3

Blessed be the God and Father of our Lord Jesus Christ, which according to his abundant mercy hath begotten us again unto a lively hope by the resurrection of Jesus Christ from the dead

Titus 2:13

*Looking for that blessed hope,
and the glorious appearing of the great God
and our Saviour Jesus Christ*

When Grandpa was done reading, he handed Charlie his Bible with the pages all marked and asked him to spend the rest of the afternoon reading the verses he had just read. "And," said Grandpa, "you will be greatly blessed by reading the verses before and after the ones I have marked out for you."

"Is this the same Bible your Grandfather gave you for your inheritance?" asked Charlie.

"Yes, it is," said Grandpa as he carefully handed Charlie his worn out, falling apart Bible. "You know," said Grandpa, "people that read their Bible until they fall apart usually have lives that don't."

Charlie took the Bible and carefully began reading the passages that Grandpa had selected.

"Hey, Charlie," said Grandpa, "can I get you a mug of hot chocolate?"

"Yes, sir," Charlie beamed.

"Promise not to spill it on our Bible?"

"I double promise," said Charlie.

Charlie and Grandpa both bowed their heads, as they did after each of their get-togethers, and prayed that God would give them both wisdom and revelation.

Grandpa returned to the Eagle's Nest with the cup of hot chocolate and news that Marie was making spaghetti for dinner. It was going to be a wonderful day!

Ecclesiastes 3:1

To every thing there is a season,
and a time to every purpose under the heaven:

Chapter 39

Camping

W ally put his binoculars back in the case and was about to tuck them into the nap sack hanging from Tarnation's pack when he heard a dog bark. Wally quickly returned to the crest of the hill and began carefully surveying the valley below.

"Let's all be very quiet," said Wally. "John, move Tarnation and Eager out of sight." Wally continued as he slowly got down on his stomach, braced the binoculars between his elbows and began carefully peering down into the valley.

John went over to Matthew, who was having a little trouble keeping Tarnation from bolting. John took the reins and began sweet talking Tarnation as he moved him down the hill and out of the view of anything that might be looking up toward the crest of the hill. "Matthew," John said in a whisper, "stay very quiet."

John crouched as he approached Wally. "See anything?" asked John in a whisper.

"My eyes are not what they used to be," said Wally. "You wanna take a look?" he asked.

"Be happy to," said John, who lay on the ground as Wally slid backwards and handed the binoculars down to him. John re-adjusted the binoculars and systematically began scanning the valley below. He patiently waited for any signs of life. John put down the binoculars for a second as he rubbed his eyes; it was then that he saw, out of the corner of his left eye, some movement in the tall brush, down by the pond. John trained his binoculars on the spot and waited. "I see two dogs, now three," said John.

Wally returned, crawled back up the hillside, and got back down on his stomach. John handed him the binoculars and pointed out the spot where the dogs were seen.

"I see them," said Wally, as he crawled back down the hill.

John and Wally huddled up and began to come up with a plan. "If we go over the hill, we will spook them and it will take weeks to hunt them down," said Wally.

John surveyed the landscape and held his wet finger up to the wind. "They are going to be hungry again soon, and it is my guess that they will follow the same trail we used to track them," John said.

"Yes, and our scent is all over that trail, which will alert them to our presence."

"We need to find a place to put the bait that is upwind so they get the scent as soon as they come over the hill." Said John. "Then, we need to find a spot where we can catch them in a crossfire—someplace where we have some cover."

Matthew was the first one to spot a stump that was about twenty feet off the trail and about fifty feet off the crown of the brow of the hill. "Would that be a good spot?" asked Matthew as he pointed to the stump.

Wally looked around and decided that it would be a perfect spot to put the bait. "Now we just need to find some cover for ourselves that isn't too far away to take a good shot."

There was a small wooded area about 100 feet from the stump that looked perfect. The three hunters headed for the wooded patch and looked around. When they arrived on the spot, they noticed another wooded spot about 300 yards away.

"We can set up our artillery here, and camp out over there," said Wally, as he pointed to the grassy wooded area about 1000 feet away and fifty feet below the spot they had picked as their gunnery position.

They had about an hour of sunlight left and used that time to set up camp. "We don't want them to get wind of our bait until they come over the hill," said Wally.

The three hunters set up camp behind the second patch of trees—way out of sight and below the line of sight of the hill. If the dogs followed the same route back down to the farms, they would immediately smell the bait. And as long as they didn't get the scent of man, the hunters might get a clean shot at the wild dogs. The scent of man would send them back over the hill and into the woods on the other side of the pond, where they would not be found for weeks, if ever.

Just before the sun went down, Wally took the canvas tarp that wrapped the carcass of the lamb, threw it over his shoulder, and headed for the top of the hill. He then unwrapped the carcass, tied a rope to the back legs of the half-eaten lamb, and dragged it behind him as he walked the entire brow of the hill. Matthew and John came out of the clearing to watch how Wally baited the trap.

Wally dragged the carcass slowly over the path they had followed up the hill, ending at the tree stump. Next, he dragged the carcass to the spot where Tarnation and Eager had been, just hours earlier, and then back up and down the hill, covering all the places that they had walked or laid down.

Finally, Wally walked back down to the stump where he dumped the lamb carcass and took a stick to spread it out over the stump. He then walked about twenty more feet down the hill and straight over to the camp site where John and Matthew were watching with great interest.

"Do you understand why Wally is doing what he is doing Matthew?" asked John.

"Not really," said Matthew.

"Dogs have a powerful sense of smell and Wally wants them to smell, food, not humans. Once they get the scent of fresh meat, they will make a bee-line for it and then they will be in our target range," John said.

"I understand, Dad," said Matthew. "I was wondering why Mr. McDaniel brought the lamb carcass."

"Yes, and now you understand why."

Matthew nodded.

The three hunters retreated to their campsite which was a about quarter of a mile from the crest of the hill, and a good two miles away from where the wild dogs had made their dens, next to the pond, in the valley, just over the hill.

"We can relax here," said Wally. Matthew took the harmonica out of his pocket and put it to his lips. "Matthew," said Mr. McDaniel, "let's not play that just yet; dogs have ears tuned for high pitched sounds. Even with our elevation, and the distance, I don't want to take a chance." Matthew nodded as he put the harmonica back into his pocket.

John took care to get Tarnation settled out of site and began building a small camp fire. "The wind is blowing off the mountain." said John. "We just need to make sure we put the fire out completely before sunrise."

Wally produced a big bag of grain out of the mule pack that was now leaning against a tree in the middle of their new campsite. He poured a couple of cup-fulls into a feed sack and headed toward Tarnation.

John began unfolding the tent and gathering up the tent stakes. "Matthew, let me teach you how to put up a tent," said John, as he spread the canvas tent out on the smoothest, softest spot he could find. "Go ahead and put these poles together," said John, handing Matthew the tent poles.

By the time Wally returned, the tent was up and John was securing the tent stakes.

Wally announced, "Time to get your guns loaded and ready for the morning. We need to be up and in place before the sun, by my reckoning, those dogs will be looking for a meal just after sun up."

John and Matthew checked and loaded their guns and got all their ammunition ready for the next morning. John wrapped the guns in a blanket and tucked them into the side of the tent where they would not get wet. Wally went into the wooded area and scrounged up some firewood.

Just as the sun slipped over the horizon, John opened up a couple cans of beans and dumped them into an iron cook pot that he hung over the fire. As the light diminished, the three hunters each found a comfortable log to sit on and moved it as close to the warmth of the campfire as they could.

The smoky aroma of the bacon and beans created just the right atmosphere for the kind of conversation that usually passes between hunters as they huddle around a campfire.

After all the plans for the big morning hunt were discussed, Wally made himself comfortable against the tree he was leaning upon and asked Matthew if he would like to hear a tale told by a cowboy from Texas. Matthew, of course, was excited by the prospect of listening to a real life, cowboy story.

Wally then settled into his favorite cowboy story in which, guns blazed, cattle were rustled, wild horses were rounded up and saddle-broken, and horse thieves were given necktie parties with big crowds attending. There were shoot-outs and bank robberies, horse thievery and stage coach robberies. There were prairie fires and floods, outlaws and lawmen, and lots of newly made widows and orphans. Everything Matthew had ever read in one of his *Tales of the Wild West* dime novels was packed into Wally McDaniel's story.

By the time Wally finished his tall tale, Matthew and John knew it wasn't true, but it sure was entertaining. What John and Matthew did not realize is that there was more truth in Wally's wild stories than either of them could have dreamed.

Wally McDaniel had been the "worst in the west" cowboy for about two decades. He was just barely on the right side of the law most of the time and well outside the law on more than one occasion. By his own admission, the only reason he wasn't hung, on more than one occasion, is because they couldn't find a rope strong enough to string him up, and nobody was willing to waste a bullet.

Wally decided to move back to North Carolina after he had walked into a post office in Laredo, Texas, and noticed his picture on a wanted poster. It was for something he had not done, but since he had done worse, Wally decided not to mail his letter. He gathered his belongings, said good-bye to no one, and rode out of town. He kept riding until he was out of Texas. He then sold his horse and bought a train ticket to North Carolina.

Wally had cleaned up his story for the ears of John and Matthew in order to conceal the simple fact that Wally McDaniel had done some pretty terrible things in his life. Things he once bragged about were now carefully guarded secrets.

There was a long silence around the campfire as the pitch in the pinecones crackled and the embers flew upward in a cloud of grayish black smoke.

Romans 6:20-23
For when ye were the servants of sin,
ye were free from righteousness.
What fruit had ye then in those things
whereof ye are now ashamed? for the end
of those things is death.

But now being made free from sin,
and become servants to God,
ye have your fruit unto holiness,
and the end everlasting life. For the wages
of sin is death; but the gift of God is eternal
life through Jesus Christ our Lord.

Chapter 40

The Campfire Meeting

"**M**atthew, I want you to climb into the tent with your bed roll, and get some sleep," said John. Matthew was very tired and made quick work of getting himself into the tent where he immediately fell asleep. "That boy is so tired I doubt even your snoring could wake him up," quipped John.

"Snoring," said Wally, "what snoring?" The two men laughed as Wally stood up and poured John another cup of hot, black coffee.

"I have a question for you, John," said Wally.

John smiled as he sipped the piping hot cup of coffee. "I would love to answer any question you have, if I am able," said John.

"Oh, you're able all right; I am sure of that. You know, John, you and your entire family are the first seven-day-a-week Christians I have ever met."

"I can't take any credit for that," said John.

"What do you mean?" asked Wally.

John took another sip of coffee and thought for a moment how to best answer Wally. "You see, Wally, I am nothing special—just a sinner that God began to do a work in a long time ago. So, anything praiseworthy about me is really more about me diminishing into the background while Christ becomes larger and larger in the foreground."

Wally thought for a minute. "Is that going to happen with me?" asked Wally. "I mean, how does that work?"

"Wally, when you trusted in Christ as your Savior, what do you think happened?"

"Well, I felt like a giant burden went off my back... I mean... my past life, and sin and all that. Then, after a couple of days, I found myself doing some of the same stupid things I did before I trusted Christ. Is that normal?"

John laughed. "Unfortunately, that is normal; we are still sinners, Wally."

"I get that," said Wally, "but what happens next?"

"It is all about Heaven," said John.

"Heaven," said Wally, "I don't think I am ready to go to Heaven right now. I have a wife and a new child on the way."

John laughed again. "Wally, God has a work that He has begun in your heart, and mind, and soul—in order to get you ready for Heaven. Heaven is our great hope and our final and eternal destination."

"Tell me more," said Wally.

Wally had been to Texas and all the places in between Laredo and Elkin.

John had lived in India, and in the first twenty years of his life, he had visited five continents including South America.

"Have you ever seen someone dress up a monkey and put it on a chain?" asked John. "When I visited Italy, I ran across many organ grinders with a monkey dressed in a red suit with a funny little hat. The man would grind the organ and play a tune while the monkey would scamper and dance about. He'd go up to everyone that passed by, hold out his hat or a tin cup, and beg for loose change. The monkey would be rewarded when he returned with coins in his hat and a scrap of food," explained John.

"Oh yes," said Wally with a laugh, "I saw that act on the streets back in 1910 when I went to pick up Eager from a breeder in Charlotte."

"I have a cousin who is a missionary in Brazil," said John. Wally listened carefully, not really understanding where this conversation was headed or what it had to do with Heaven. "When I returned to North Carolina, from India, I made a one-year stopover in South America, where I spent almost a year ministering with my cousin in Brazil."

"Let me guess," said Wally, "this has something to do with monkeys?"

John smiled as he continued, "My cousin was ministering in a small village on the edge of a jungle forest, and those Capuchin monkeys, like the one you saw with the street pan handler, were all over the place. The kids in the village made pets out of some of them, and the rest were like barn cats—all over the place and into everything."

John continued, "The ones out in the jungle were more wary. They spent their time in large family groups of thirty or forty, swinging from trees, foraging all day, and sleeping under the stars at night. They ranged the entire forest and lived free and easy, as food and shelter were abundant. It wasn't perfect; once in a while one would fall prey to a panther, or some other predator. But on the whole, it was a pretty amazing life they lived in the habitat that God created for them. I used to watch them for hours and dream about what it would be like to be back in the garden before Adam sinned."

"I think I know where you are going with this John," said Wally.

John smiled as he continued. "Wally, you can take those little critters out of the jungle, dress them up, and put a chain on their neck, and they will perform in order to survive. But they know in their own little hearts—or brains, or wherever God stores that information—that they belong in the jungle, not chained to an organ grinder, dressed up like an English butler, and begging for coins."

Wally nodded as John continued. "Wally, before you trusted Christ, you probably felt pretty comfortable in this world; am I right?"

"Pretty much," replied Wally.

John continued, "But when you trusted Christ, He took up residence in you."

Wally interrupted, "Could you explain how that works?"

John paused as he reached into his memory for the addresses of the verses he wanted to share with Wally.

"Let's start with the testimony of the Bible and work backwards from there," said John.

"Fair enough," said Wally, who was genuinely interested in trying to figure out what these changes that taking place in his mind and heart were all about. He was interested to know if he was just imagining them, or if God was really doing something in his life.

John fished his New Testament out of his jacket and tried to find a spot by the campfire where there was enough light to read. "Here, let me help you with that," said Wally, as he got up and poked around the pack that was leaning against a nearby tree. "Here we are," said Wally, pulling the kerosene lantern out of the mule pack. "Now, where did I put that tin of kerosene?" he muttered. "Ah, here it is."

Wally filled the kerosene lantern half full and took it over to where John was settled in by the camp fire. He then poked a twig into the fire until it ignited and then quickly lit the wick. "That should give you enough light," said Wally.

John began thumbing through his Bible, bookmarking passages with leaves he picked up off the ground.

Wally and his wife, Marie, had trusted Christ as their Savior about three weeks earlier. The night that Wally repented and called on Jesus to save him was a night that neither Wally nor John would ever forget. Before Wally and Marie left the Spice home that following morning, John and his father, James, had prayed with Wally and Marie and had given them both a King James Version of the Bible. John had bookmarked the Gospel of John and encouraged them both to read that Gospel account at least a dozen times, until they were intimately familiar with every detail. They had promised that they would do exactly that, starting every morning for the next two weeks. John was about to find out if Wally had kept his promise.

"Wally, do you remember what happens in the thirteenth and fourteenth chapters of the Gospel of John?" asked John.

Wally scratched his head, "John, I am not sure, but ain't that where Peter gets the bad news about the rooster?"

John laughed, "Wally, you do have a way of keeping things simple."

"I am a simple man," said Wally with a broad smile that flickered across the camp fire.

"Wally, I would like you to tell me what you remember about that section of the Bible found in John thirteen and fourteen."

Wally scratched his head again, and after a brief pause, began to recount the two chapters in the Gospel of John.

"It all started with that shin-dig up in the attic in Jerusalem."

John interrupted. "You're referring to the last supper in the upper room."

"Yep, that's it," said Wally.

"Well," said Wally, collecting his thoughts, "after they eat the lamb and all the herbs and such, Jesus tells His disciples that He is going to be sacrificed in order that they can be saved. He tells them that every time they eat the bread, which represents His body that was broken, and drink the wine, which represents His blood which is going to be shed on the cross, they are to remember Him." Wally paused.

"That's right, Wally," said John. John thought for a minute in order to collect his thoughts and figure out how to best explain to Wally what this all had to do with Heaven.

"Do you know what happens right after Jesus tells Peter that he would deny him three times, and Judas Iscariot is filled with Satan and leaves to betray Jesus?"

Wally thought for a moment. "They all went out into the Garden of Gethsemane where Jesus prayed, and His disciples were so tuckered out, they all fell asleep. They all got woken up when that skunk, Judas, showed up with a posse and had Jesus arrested."

Wally paused. "I think that Judas fella kissed Jesus to let everybody know He was the one they were looking for. I think I would have punched him in the mouth and told him to go kiss a toad, but that's not what Jesus did. No, sir! And that's when Peter pulled out a knife and cut that fella's ear clean off his head. And as I recall, Jesus wasn't too happy about that poor fella losin his ear and stuck it back on, permanent like. That should have been a clue that they were dealing with the Son of God, but it didn't seem to faze them a bit, which tells me they were dumber 'an rocks and just determined to do something low down stupid."

John had never heard the account found in the Gospel of John explained quite like Wally explained it.

"Wally, I can see you have been reading the Gospel of John like you promised you would. That is good news; pardon the pun."

"Marie and I have been reading it together, and we have lots of questions. I figured we would invite ourselves over to share some of the delicious pie Marie made with the apples Janet gave her last week," said Wally.

"I am looking forward to it," said John.

John opened his Bible and leaned over to get the best light he could out of the kerosene lantern. He then read the following passage from the Gospel of John.

John 14:1-3

Let not your heart be troubled: ye believe in God, believe also in me. In my Father's house are many mansions: if it were not so, I would have told you. I go to prepare a place for you. And if I go and prepare a place for you, I will come again, and receive you unto myself; that where I am, there ye may be also.

John paused for a minute to let Wally think about what he had just read.

"Sounds like Jesus is saying 'so long, I will catch up with you later, and in the meantime, I am going to be getting your bunk house ready up in Heaven,'" said Wally.

"So what does that mean for those of us who are followers of Jesus Christ?" asked John.

Wally stroked his chin and answered, "Well, John, it means we are on our own until the boss gets back."

John sipped from his cup of coffee, and then replied, "Wally, let's say that Janet and I took off and left our nine youngsters on their own on the farm. When we returned, what would we probably find?"

Wally laughed large as he imagined the chaos that would ensue. "Well, if they are anything like I was when I was their age, you would probably return to a heap of ashes. And I imagine the herd would be culled down a bit."

John wanted to think that it wouldn't be that bad, but for the sake of making a point, he let Wally's bleak appraisal stand.

"So you agree that children need constant supervision?"

Wally lifted up the brow on his cowboy hat and gave John a broad smile as he spit in his hand and held it up, "I would swear to it." Wally said. John chuckled, as he had never had a conversation with a new believer that was as colorful and genuine as the one he was having with Wally McDaniel.

John repositioned his Bible for the maximum amount of light. "Now let me read you a couple more verses from the Gospel of John." Wally immediately became serious and was clearly paying attention.

Leaning over to get the best light, John said. "Now remember, said John, Jesus has just finished telling them that He is going to prepare a place for them in Heaven. Jesus told them flat out that He was going away."

Wally nodded, "Got that partner."

Then John read John 14:22-23, Judas saith unto him, not Iscariot, Lord, how is it that thou wilt manifest thyself unto us, and not unto the world?

Jesus answered and said unto him, If a man love me, he will keep my words: and my Father will love him, and we will come unto him, and make our abode with him.

John waited for the verses to sink in. "Do you understand what Jesus is telling His disciples, including you and me?"

Wally craned his neck and looked upwards at the starlit sky. "Sounds like Jesus is saying that He is going away, but in the meantime, the Heavenly Father and the Son of God are going to abide in us at the same time."

John smiled, "That is the miracle that happened to you the night you trusted in Christ. Christ was knocking at the door of your heart, and you welcomed Him in. He promised to come in and to stay with you forever. Only God can do that, Wally." John paused as Wally stroked his chin.

"Now let me ask you a question, Wally."

Wally nodded, "shoot partner."

John smiled, "Where does God and His Son live?"

Wally smiled, "I thought you were going to ask me something hard— they both bunk up in Heaven."

John figured this was not the time to tell Wally that God never slumbers or sleeps, and since he got the location right, John just moved along with the conversation. "So," said John, "if God the Father and His Son both live in Heaven, and they are also spiritually in you here on earth, then what do you think your heart and mind are going to start thinking about and longing for?"

"True North!" said Wally, and then exclaimed, "I get it! That's why I have started thinking more about Heaven and less about things down here on earth." John could not help but send up a whisper of praise to the Lord for the revelation that Wally had just received.

"Wally, the proof of purchase is the blood of Jesus," continued John. "And the fact that you're thinking about Heaven means you have the ticket to the Celestial City in your pocket.

"And one more thing," said John, as he turned the pages in his Bible and found the passage he was looking for, John 14:16-17, "*And I will pray the Father, and he shall give you another Comforter, that he may abide with you forever; Even the Spirit of truth; whom the world cannot receive, because it seeth him not, neither knoweth him: but ye know him; for he dwelleth with you, and shall be in you.*"

"Do you understand what this means, Wally?" asked John.

"Sounds to me like Jesus is sending the Holy Spirit to live in me forever," responded Wally.

"Now you know how seriously God loves you. He not only sent His Son to pay the penalty for your sins, but He also sent the Holy Spirit to both comfort you and lead you into His truth."

"Sounds like I got it made!" exclaimed Wally.

"That is exactly right," said John. "If God be for you, then who can be against you? The answer is that the whole world may be against you, but not to worry because Jesus tells us that, 'greater is He that is in you, than he that is in the world.'"

Wally thought for a minute and finally added, "So, the longer I live in this world, the more I become like a fish out of water."

John smiled, "I have never heard it put quite like that, but you're right, Wally. This world is no longer your home; you're just a pilgrim on the way to the Celestial City."

"I will give that some further noodling as I lay out under God's light show," said Wally, pointing upward.

John said goodnight and headed into the tent. Matthew was fast asleep, and not even Wally's snoring could wake him up. Wally's "log sawing" did keep John up for an hour or so. John used the time to pray that the hunger and thirst for the things of Heaven, that God had put in Wally's heart, would continue to grow.

1 Peter 2:9

But ye are a chosen generation, a royal priesthood, an holy nation, a peculiar people; that ye should shew forth the praises of him who hath called you out of darkness into his marvellous light;

Chapter 41

The Big Stink!

J ohn was up about twenty minutes before the sun peaked over the crest of the Blue Ridge Mountains. The first thing he did was make a small fire to heat up the coffee. He was willing to shake Wally awake, but decided that the wiser thing to do was to let the aroma of freshly brewed coffee do the job for him.

Matthew got up as soon as John stirred and was obviously anxious to begin the hunt. "We will be ready in a few minutes," reported John. "Grab some grain and go feed Tarnation." Matthew did as he was told.

Wally woke up to the smell of freshly brewed coffee and the anxious snorts of Tarnation, who was happy to get his nose into some sweet smelling barley and oats.

Wally didn't say a word, as he put his finger up to his mouth. "We need to stay very quiet," he whispered as he dug out his jacket, folded his bed roll and grabbed his gun. "Those critters will be on the move as soon as the sun comes over the mountain," Wally continued to whisper.

Matthew returned to the camp, slapping his hands together to get rid of the grain dust. "Matthew, we need to be very quiet," whispered John. Matthew nodded his head and went into the tent to retrieve his rifle.

The three hunters huddled around the camp fire. "Rifles all loaded?" asked Wally.

"Yes, Sir," said Matthew. John nodded in agreement.

They waited another minute, kicked dirt over the camp fire, and made their way to the rotten log, which they had decided the day before would be the best place to ambush the wild dogs.

The rotten log lay about sixty-five feet along a vantage point that was just about ten feet higher than the half-eaten lamb they had tied to a tree as bait. The kill zone was in an open area that would give the hunters the best chance of shooting the wild dogs without a chance for them to duck back into the underbrush.

The three hunters and Eager approached the rotten log that was to provide them cover and a steady spot to position their rifles.

"Keep low," whispered Wally as they approached the log. "Eager and I will take the spot on the right end of the log; John, you take the middle, and Matthew, you take the far end."

The three found their places and got comfortable. John and Matthew began lining up their sites with the bait that was tied about 100 feet below them. Wally leaned his rifle against the log as he pulled out his binoculars and began scanning the caves down by the small pond, that was about a quarter of a mile away.

John leaned over to whisper to Matthew. "Hunting is mostly waiting."

Matthew smiled and immediately went back to looking down the muzzle of his rifle.

The sun came over the crest of the mountain and began to warm up the three hunters, who welcomed the change with silent thankfulness. A breeze began to sweep over the mountain, sending the aroma of the lamb down wind and into the valley below.

"They are starting to stir," said Wally, who had spotted two of the three wild dogs with his binoculars. "Two mixed breeds about sixty pounds each," reported Wally. "Would you look at that!" said Wally. "I just spotted the alpha leader of the pack; he is a big one. Looks like he is half wolf and about 160 pounds if he is an ounce."

Wally slipped down below the log to talk to John and Matthew. "John, I will take out the leader, and you and Matthew take out the other two. John, you shoot the brown dog; Matthew, you shoot the black dog. But don't shoot until after I take my shot." John repeated the instructions for Matthew, making it clear that he was not to shoot until after Wally had taken a shot at the leader of the wild dog pack.

The three dogs drank from the pond and then began sniffing the air. The lamb bait was working. Within minutes, the three wild dogs were at the crest of the ridge, noses to the ground. The leader of the pack picked up the scent trail that Wally had laid the day before. Eager was on high alert. Wally stroked his head and gave him a command that sent Eager down to the ground. "Quiet," commanded Wally. Eager whimpered and then went silent. "Good dog," said Wally.

The alpha leader of the pack had found the scent and made a bee line for the bait. He got within about ten feet of the carcass and began to circle. The other two dogs were not so cautious and immediately began to ferociously tear into the lamb carcass. The leader of the wild dogs carefully approached the carcass. And after snapping and snarling at the other two dogs, finally found the prime spot for feeding. Within a few minutes, they were all eating lamb. Wally wanted them to be thinking about nothing but eating, and so he gave them a couple of minutes to feast on the breakfast that the three hunters hoped would be their last meal.

Wally raised his rifle and set his sights on the target. He was just about to squeeze off the first shot when something no one could have ever imagined, happened.

A skunk exited the log, raised his tail, and sprayed Wally right in the face. Wally shrieked as he pulled the trigger on his gun. The shot went up in the air and missed the wild alpha wild dog by a mile.

John and Matthew immediately began shooting and killed two of the three wild dogs. The leader of the pack took off down the Blue Ridge Mountains and was out of rifle range in just a few seconds.

Eager took off like a shot after the skunk and returned a minute later smelling worse than his master.

John and Matthew immediately distanced themselves from Wally.

The skunk had sprayed Wally in the face from less than a foot away. Wally immediately stood up and told John and Matthew to keep their distance. An order that John and Matthew had no intention of disobeying.

"John," said Wally, as he wheezed and rubbed his eyes, "I want you to start the fire and pack up Tarnation so we can get out of here quickly." John began doing as he was told without a word. "Matthew," continued Wally, "I want you to fill the bean pot with water and put it on the fire."

"Yes, Sir," said Matthew.

"Then," he continued, "find me as much moss and compost as you can, and heap it by the fire."

Wally then took off his hat and his jacket. He unsheathed his knife and cut a patch of cloth out from the inside of his jacket. He then dropped the remains of his jacket and hat next to the rotten log as he moved down to the other end of the log, where he leaned up his rifle.

Wally waited for John to get the fire started and for Matthew to put the iron pot, full of water, in the fire. When Matthew finally returned with a heap of moss and composted soil, Wally made his way slowly to the campfire. John and Matthew began stowing all the gear in preparation for the trip back home.

Wally put the patch that, he had cut from his jacket, in the pot of water and waited for it to get warm. Within a few minutes, he pulled the wet rag out of the fire and began to wipe down his hands, face and neck. He then grabbed the moss and compost and smeared it all over his face and neck and hands. He let it set for a minute and then washed it off with water.

"John," Wally yelled, "I have an old horse blanket in the mule pack; fish it out and throw it over here."

"You doing any better?" asked John as he rustled through the gear and finally found the horse blanket, which he threw over to Wally.

Wally did not answer. Finally, Wally picked up the horse blanket and draped it over his head and shoulders. "John, find me about six feet of rope." John returned in a few minutes with the rope. Wally used the rope to tie the blanket at his waist. "It's cold and I don't want to freeze to death," Wally reported to John and Matthew, who were looking at Wally as he lashed the horse blanket snuggly around himself.

"One more remedy," said Wally as he poured the water on the fire and put it out. Wally then reached into the fire and pulled out a handful of ashes. He smeared them all over his head, hands and neck and then asked Matthew to throw him his canteen.

A minute later, Wally splashed water into his eyes and headed toward his rifle that he had leaned up against the rotten log. Wally took the rifle and wiped it down with the wet rag that was soaked in ashes. He then sat on the log and called for John and Matthew.

"We got a problem fellas," said Wally.

"Yes," said John, "but nothing a hot soapy bath won't fix."

Wally laughed, "Me smelling like a skunk is not the problem. The problem is that wild 160-pound terror that we just sent down the hill. One of our neighbors is going to be losing a calf or a lamb before noon and we can't do a thing about it."

"Actually, Wally," said John, "there is something we can do about it."

Wally acted surprised. "I don't get your meaning, John. What on earth can we do about it—stuck up here ten miles from the closest farm?"

John looked at Wally and said, "Wally, you got some things to learn about being a child of God." Wally straightened up and gave John a quizzical look. John smiled and bowed his head and lifted up his hands.

"Heavenly Father," said John, "we have gotten ourselves in a fix down here, and we need your help. We know you have been watching all this, knowing we were not going to figure this out on our own. Thank you, Father, for your patience with us. We are sorry we didn't take this to you before we all went off, half-cocked. We ask you now Father to intervene to protect the livestock from the wild dog that is headed toward one of our neighbors, as we are speaking to you. We ask that you protect our neighbors and give us wisdom and favor as we track this vicious animal down. And Lord, we want to ask you to help Wally not get sick from the skunk odor, and increase his faith. We ask all this in the name of our Savior, The Lord Jesus Christ, Amen."

John looked up just in time to see Wally unfold his hands and open his eyes. Wally gave John a half grin as he asked, "Do you think the Lord has time for our little problem?"

John smiled and confidently responded. "Wally, I have seen smaller prayers than this answered in amazing ways. I think the Lord has something to teach you that will encourage you to take everything to Him in prayer, no matter how small you may think it is."

Wally shook his head, "OK, John. I am new at all this and never really thought of relying on anybody but myself."

John laughed out loud. "And look at where that has gotten you!" Wally smiled and then joined in the laughter.

Eager was busy pawing his eyes and rubbing his muzzle and chest in the grass. "Come here, boy," commanded Wally. Eager cautiously approached Wally, who finally coaxed him close enough to wipe down his face with the wet ash soaked rag. "That will give you a little relief," said Wally.

"What's the plan, Wally?"

Wally thought for a minute and finally said, "finish packing up Tarnation while I dig a hole and bury that lamb carcass; we don't want any other critters up here to get a taste for lamb."

Wally asked Matthew to fetch the shovel and throw it over in his direction. Matthew did as he was told. "John," said Wally, "I hope the skunk odor does not interfere with Eager's ability to track that killer dog down the hill.

John and Matthew finished packing up all the gear, feeding both Eager and Tarnation and putting out the campfire.

Wally spent the next thirty minutes digging a hole and burying the two dead dogs, along with the lamb carcass.

An hour after Wally had been skunked, the three hunters, Eager the dog, and Tarnation the mule made their way down the hill. Eager led the way, following the scent of the wild dog; Wally brought up the rear, being careful to keep his distance from John and Matthew, who were happy to be breathing clean, fresh air.

Matthew 7:7-11

Ask, and it shall be given you; seek, and ye shall find; knock, and it shall be opened unto you: For every one that asketh receiveth; and he that seeketh findeth; and to him that knocketh it shall be opened. Or what man is there of you, whom if his son ask bread, will he give him a stone? Or if he ask a fish, will he give him a serpent? If ye then, being evil, know how to give good gifts unto your children, how much more shall your Father which is in heaven give good things to them that ask him?

Chapter 42

The Show Down

A t the Spice Farm, the day had begun a little earlier than usual. Marie McDaniel was an early riser and could be found, just before the sun came up, making coffee and preparing flaky corn meal muffins in the Spice family kitchen.

The clatter woke up Janet, and within minutes, the two women were enjoying each other's company around the kitchen table.

Moments later, Ginger came sauntering into the kitchen, dragging her blanket behind her. Marie turned and opened her arms, and as soon as Ginger made contact with Marie's beaming smile, she made a bee line for her lap, where she spent the next sixty minutes making herself comfortable.

James and Anna were the next to arrive. They both helped themselves to a cup of coffee and then made their way up the stairs to visit Charlie, taking with them a bowl of cereal, a mug of hot chocolate, and a corn muffin drowned in butter and honey.

Janet was determined to use her time with Marie to answer questions that she knew she must have as a brand new child of God.

Janet was right, Marie had lots of questions.

"How are you and John the Apostle getting along?"

Marie cocked her head and looked a little puzzled. "Your Bible study," added Janet.

Marie laughed. "Pretty good," she said, as she sipped her cup of black coffee. "I don't know how Wally stands his coffee black, but I am determined to learn to like it."

Janet got up from the kitchen table and returned with a small pitcher of cream and a heaping table spoon of honey.

"You can learn to like black coffee at your house, but while you're in my house, you will learn to like coffee with cream and honey."

Marie laughed, "That won't be too hard," she replied, as Janet returned the creamer and the tablespoon to the kitchen sink.

"I do have a few questions," said Marie. Janet returned to the table with her Bible and opened it up.

Marie waited a minute, and then said, "I am wondering about some of the things I used to think were pretty important to me." Marie halted. Janet kept silent and allowed Marie to form and finish her thought.

"Well, what I mean is that some of the things I really desired seem like they are not as important, but I still have a desire for them."

Janet took a sip of coffee and hazarded a guess. "You mean like a big, fancy house and lots of expensive furniture?" Janet asked with a smile.

"Yes, and fancy clothes and jewelry." Marie added.

Janet paused and then asked Marie a question. "Marie do you like to garden?"

"No, Janet, I don't like to garden; I love to garden!" said Marie. "I love growing herbs and spices for the meals I prepare. And I love planting tiny seeds and watching them sprout up into beautiful plants."

Janet set her cup of coffee down, placed her elbows on the table, and rested her chin between her two open hands. "Marie, your life is like a garden." Marie was intrigued by the metaphor and tilted her head forward in silence.

Janet looked at Marie and asked, "What do you call the plants that just grow up in your garden without you ever having to even plant a seed?" Marie was puzzled.

Janet let a little time pass and then answered her own question. "We call them weeds." Marie nodded her head and laughed.

Janet continued, "Ever notice how they just show up as uninvited and unwelcome guests of our garden? They suck the nutrients out of the soil and get watered right along with the plants we are trying to grow."

"Yes, I spend a lot of time in my garden, pulling out the weeds," replied Marie.

Janet continued, "Our lives are like a garden full of weeds. But instead of pulling out these weeds, we water them, fertilize them, and encourage them to grow. These weeds have names like anger, pride, covetousness, gossip, slander, jealously, spitefulness and lying, just to name a few."

Janet paused and then added, "Now, some people don't like to gossip, so they are constantly trying to pull out that weed in their lives, while they are watering and fertilizing the weed of pride. Some people have the weed of anger under control while the weeds of covetousness and greed are growing out of control."

Marie listened and then added. "Like the Bible says, we are all sinful, and if we say we aren't, we are lying."

Janet was impressed, "That's right, Marie; we all struggle with sin."

Janet could tell that Marie was thinking about it as she turned in her Bible to the Apostle Paul's letter to the Galatians and read Galatians 5:22-23, "*But the fruit of the Spirit is love, joy, peace, longsuffering, gentleness, goodness, faith, Meekness, temperance: against such there is no law.*

"Marie, what do you think happened to your garden when you trusted the Lord Jesus Christ as your Savior Janet asked?"

Marie thought about the verse Janet had just read and answered, "I think He plants the seeds of love and joy and peace and the rest of the things you mentioned."

Janet smiled, "Well, you're on the right track, but there are not *many* seeds that the Lord plants—He only plants *one* seed as it were."

Marie was confused, "I don't understand. Do you mean that the Lord just picks out one of the fruits of the Spirit and plants it in my life?"

Janet chuckled, "To look at some Christians, you might think that was true." Janet paused and then read the passage again as she emphasized the point she was trying to make. *"But the fruit of the Spirit is love, joy, peace, longsuffering, gentleness, goodness, faith, Meekness, temperance: against such there is no law.*

Marie brightened, "I understand now; all those beautiful qualities come from the one seed the Lord plants in my garden."

"Yes," said Janet, "they all come from the Holy Spirit who now lives in you, every single one of them."

Janet and Marie both paused as they sipped their coffee.

Just then, Anna entered the room, poured herself a cup of coffee and asked if she could join Janet and Marie. Both women beamed at the prospect and invited her to be a part of their conversation.

Anna listened as Janet continued to explore the garden metaphor with Marie.

Marie had lots of questions. "Since the Lord has sent the Holy Spirit to live in me, why am I still dealing with the weeds in my garden?"

"That is a very good question, Marie, and I think Anna might like to answer that for you," Janet said.

Anna had been listening attentively and silently praying that Marie might understand the important lesson that Janet was trying to teach her.

Anna took Marie's hands and patted them gently. Ginger, who was asleep in Marie's arms, woke up for a few moments as she snuggled into another comfortable position and nodded off again.

Anna began, "God allows the weeds of sin to remain in our life because He wants us to learn to hate sin, as we see what it does to us and to Him, from His point of view. He allows us to struggle with sin, not because we can ever overcome it, but because He wants us to understand that on our own, we *cannot* overcome it. We are commanded to wage a battle and to struggle against the weeds of sin that grow so effortlessly in the garden of our life."

Marie thought for a moment, and then asked, "How do I do that?"

"Now *that* is the question I was hoping you would ask, Marie," said Anna as she slid the Bible out from under Janet's nose and began rustling through the pages.

Just then, Rosemary came into the kitchen hoping to be fed breakfast. "Come here, Honey," said Janet, not wanting to upend the moment with the duties of making breakfast. "You go milk Six-Pints, and when you're done, I will make you breakfast."

"OK, Mom," said Rosemary, as she went back to her room to put on her jacket, then headed out the kitchen door to milk the goat.

"Here it is," said Anna as she put on her glasses and began to read from Paul's letter to the Ephesians.

Ephesians 6:10-18

Finally, my brethren, be strong in the Lord, and in the power of his might.Put on the whole armour of God, that ye may be able to stand against the wiles of the devil. For we wrestle not against flesh and blood, but against principalities, against powers, against the rulers of the darkness of this world, against spiritual wickedness in high places. Wherefore take unto you the whole armour of God, that ye may be able to withstand in the evil day, and having done all, to stand. Stand therefore, having your loins girt about with truth, and having on the breastplate of righteousness; And your feet shod with the preparation of the gospel of peace; Above all, taking the shield of faith, wherewith ye shall be able to quench all the fiery darts of the wicked. And take the helmet of salvation, and the sword of the Spirit, which is the word of God: Praying always with all prayer and supplication in the Spirit, and watching thereunto with all perseverance and supplication for all saints;

Anna paused and looked up at Marie. Marie thought about the verse and then said, "It sounds like I am in a battle."

Janet smiled, "Marie, you're not just in a battle, you're in a war."

Anna rustled through the Bible and found the verse she was looking for. "Marie, you asked a good question; you asked 'how do I do it?' And the answer is that you can't do it, but God can do it *in* and *through* you. Just like you couldn't save yourself from the wrath of God, you cannot live the Christian life without the Spirit of God dwelling in you. You simply cannot do it without His help."

"Sounds a little discouraging," remarked Marie.

"Yes, it is very discouraging and also very encouraging at the same time. We want to please the Lord and do what is right, and we are constantly doing the things that displease Him, and constantly going to Him and asking for His forgiveness and grace. The good news is that He is eager to help us," Anna replied.

"Marie, here are two passages you should commit to memory—both found in 1 John," said Janet.

1 John 2:1

My little children, these things write I unto you, that ye sin not. And if any man sin, we have an advocate with the Father, Jesus Christ the righteous:

1 John 2:15-17

Love not the world, neither the things that are in the world. If any man love the world, the love of the Father is not in him. For all that is in the world, the lust of the flesh, and the lust of the eyes, and the pride of life, is not of the Father, but is of the world. And the world passeth away, and the lust thereof: but he that doeth the will of God abideth forever.

Janet realized that an hour had passed and it was time to prepare breakfast for the Spice family.

"Let me summarize this for you, Marie," said Janet. "God has planted a desire for Heaven in your heart, in your garden. He expects you, and will aid and assist you, in watering and tending that planting so that it will grow and increase all through your life. You are now a pilgrim here on this earth. This earth is no longer your home, it is just a place where you're waiting and hoping to go to be with your Savior. Heaven is not only your hope here on earth, it is your final destination.

"One day you will either die or the Lord will come and gather you to Himself without you dying. Either way, you will go to be with Him in Heaven, the very place that He is preparing for you to live in. When that happens, all the struggles and evils of this world, and the sin that remains in you, will vanish in an instant. You will be perfected in righteousness by the same Lord that died, in order that you might have fellowship with Him in Heaven."

As Janet searched for the words to complete her thoughts, she heard a blood curdling yell that sent shivers up her spine. Ginger woke from her nap with a cry.

The normal thing to do in a situation like this would be to investigate the problem. But Janet had been trained from her youth by her father to think strategically and not do what everybody else thought was normal.

"Oh dear," said Anna as she headed toward the window to see what in the world was going on.

Janet immediately stood up and rushed into the living room where she reached for the loaded rifle that hung above the fireplace. When she returned to the kitchen, Marie was trying to comfort Ginger, and Anna was down on her face praying for deliverance.

Whatever this was, it was not good.

Janet did not waste a second tending to Marie or inquiring of Anna. She simply rushed to the kitchen door and surveyed the situation from the sight of her rifle. What she saw would have had her shaking in her boots had she given herself even a few seconds to think about it.

Rosemary was swinging the milk bucket at the biggest, most ferocious dog that Janet had ever seen. Just then, the bucket slipped out of Rosemary's hand as the dog began to lunge at Six-Pints, the goat.

At this point, Scruffy came at full speed around the barn. She was half the size of the killer dog that was about to dispatch the Spice family milk goat, but that did not deter Scruffy. She ran full speed at the wild dog and temporarily knocked him off his footing. The dog immediately got back up on his feet and went for Scruffy. He was just about to put Scruffy's jugular between his vice-like jaws when the shot rang out.

The wild beast slumped to the ground, motionless, as Scruffy got back on his feet and began circling the killer dog, growling and snarling at the lifeless killer.

Rosemary rushed into her mother's arms, weeping. Marie peered through the kitchen window, holding Ginger, who was crying her eyes out. Anna had gotten off her knees and was thanking the Lord for the deliverance she had just been praying for seconds earlier.

Everyone retreated to the kitchen, except for Scruffy and Janet.

Janet carefully walked toward the beast, who was lying lifeless on the ground, with her eyes still looking through the rifle sight. *Were there more?* she wondered.

A moment later she was standing over the beast and without poking the animal, something she had been taught not to do, she put a bullet through the head at six inches. "Now I know you're dead," she whis pered to herself.

Janet immediately went back to the kitchen and made sure everyone was accounted for. "Then she loaded John's Colt pistol, gave it to James and reloaded the rifle.

She gave instructions for no one to leave the home until she and Grandpa had returned to the house.

James held the pistol while Janet kept the rifle in shooting position. The two began with a search of the barn and then circled the property to make sure that the beast that had terrorized the Spice Farm was a lone killer and not a part of a pack.

After carefully investigating the entire farm, both were satisfied that there was no imminent danger.

While Janet returned to the kitchen, James fetched a shovel and a rope. He tied the rope around the dead dogs back legs and drug him out into the orchard where he began to dig a large hole. He knew that John was going to want to take a look at this beast, and so he didn't bury it.

When James returned to the kitchen, he was greeted with a hundred questions by Mark and Luke, who were determined to view the remains of the killer dog. Grandpa realized that they were not going to stop badgering him until he allowed them to view the remains, he insisted that none of the other children go near the orchard to view the body.

It all happened in less than a minute, and yet the impact on Marie would last a lifetime.

She witnessed a grandmother whose first instinct was to go to her knees in prayer, and a mother whose first instinct was to courageously face the killer.

Marie wondered what she would have done under the same circumstances. After giving it some thought, she came to the conclusion that she was going to learn to do two things amazingly well.

She was going to learn to pray and she was going to learn to shoot like a man. She further decided that Janet and Anna were going to assist her in meeting these two goals, starting immediately.

The Spice family all gathered together in the kitchen for a time of thanksgiving, and then all reported to the living room for a season of prayer.

There was much to be thankful for—Rosemary might have been mauled or killed by the feral dog; Six-Pints might have been killed or badly injured, and the killer dog might have escaped to return another day, leaving the Spice family in a constant state of siege.

Yes, there was much to be thankful for, and most of it was repeated at least twice, as each member of the Spice family thanked their Heavenly Father in their own unique way—starting with Ginger, who said it best. "Thank you, Daddy, for loving us, and our goat. Amen."

2 Samuel 22

And he said, The Lord is my rock, and my fortress,
and my deliverer; The God of my rock; in him will I trust:
he is my shield, and the horn of my salvation, my high tower,
and my refuge, my saviour; thou savest me from violence.
I will call on the Lord, who is worthy to be praised:
so shall I be saved from mine enemies.

Chapter 43

Returning Home

T he hunting party was on the trail traveling as fast as they could manage down the winding paths of the Blue Ridge Mountains. Eager ran ahead about 100 feet as he followed the scent of the wild killer dog. John and Matthew hurried along as they talked about the events of the morning.

"I thought hunting would be fun," said Matthew.

"Hunting must have a purpose, Son, and it is usually not fun. I can remember the time I shot and killed a three-point buck, not five miles from here. It was a beautiful animal, and I hated to kill it," said John.

"Why did you shoot it?" Matthew asked.

"I shot it to feed your Mom and all your brothers and sisters, including you." John replied. "We had run out of provisions and had no money to buy food; everyone was getting tired of eating corn muffins and drinking goat's milk. We needed some protein in our diet, and we needed it badly," concluded John.

"I didn't like shooting the dog," said Matthew as he hung his head and looked at the ground.

John put his arm around Matthew as they moved into a relatively flat meadow, just above the road that would lead them home. "I am glad you didn't like shooting the dog this morning," said John. "But sometimes a man has to do things he doesn't like to do, for the safety and welfare of his family. So, the question is not whether you like it or don't like it. The question is, 'Are you going to be a man and do the right thing for your family, friends and neighbors?' And this morning you proved that you were a man willing to put the welfare of your family above your personal feelings, and for that I am very proud of you," said John, as he gently patted Matthew on the back.

"Almost home," yelled Wally.

"Yep," echoed John.

As soon as they got on the road, they traveled as fast as they could back to Uncle Homer and Aunt Matilda's farm to re-hitch Tarnation to the Wagon. Eager walked ahead and went right past Wally's uncle's farm.

Wally gave a loud whistle and Eager immediately returned to his side. "You stink to high Heaven," said Wally. Eager agreed as he whined and pawed his snout.

"You stay right here," Wally pointed. Eager sat down obediently and waited for his next instructions. The two men and the boy led Tarnation to the wagon and quickly hitched him up.

"Eager is on the fresh scent of that killer dog. Looks like he is headed down the road," said Wally as he stowed his gear in the wagon.

"You two ride in the back," instructed Wally, grabbing a handful of grain and heading toward Tarnation. "We don't have time to dilly dally," continued Wally as he allowed Tarnation to lick up the remains of the grain off his sticky fingers.

Wally quickly moved to the wagon, jumped into the driver's bench, and gave a loud whistle that released Eager to continue the hunt. This was followed by a loud command that got Tarnation moving as fast as a mule can move.

Wally knew that the killer dog had a big head start. That was not going to stop him from pursuing the killer at full speed.

The threesome followed Eager past one farm after another. Wally looked worried.

Wally turned his head and shouted, "John, you and Matthew get your rifles loaded and ready."

Just then, Eager turned into the path that led to the Spice family farm. "Looks like that critter is at your farm."

A chill went up the spine of John, who could not help imagining the carnage that animal could have reeked on his family.

As the wagon turned into the farm, John and Matthew jumped out and began running toward the front door with their rifles in hand and ready to shoot.

Just At that moment Janet rose out of the front porch swing, waving her rifle over her head and smiling. "Everything is good here!" she yelled.

John and Matthew slowed their pace as they jogged to the front porch, a little out of breath.

"We have had quite a morning, John," Janet said. John and Janet hugged as Matthew watched the rest of the Spice family emerge from the front porch.

Ginger, looking for someone to hug, headed straight for Wally. "Hold it Ginger; I love you, but don't come any closer." Ginger was not deterred as she ran and leaped into the arms of big Wally.

"You are now an official little stinker," said Wally as he laughed at the predicament and put Ginger back on the ground. Just then, Marie began to sprint toward Wally. "Hold it, Marie," said Wally. Marie wasn't listening as she closed the distance between them, grabbed Wally with both hands around his neck, and pulled him in for a barrage of kisses.

"I smell like a skunk!" protested Wally.

"No," said Marie, "we both smell like skunks, and I don't care." Marie paused from kissing just long enough to face her husband and look into his dark brown eyes. "And do you know what else big fella?" she said affectionately, with a smile of rugged determination.

"We're both going be soaking in the water trough and burning our clothes." Wally replied with a humorous grin.

Marie laughed at the thought of it, and then answered, "You're going to buy me the best rifle you can find, and then you're going to teach me how to shoot like Janet."

Wally was completely taken back. Was this the same "indoors prim and proper" Marie he had dropped off at the Spice Farm?

"I will buy you the best rifle in North Carolina," reported Wally, who was delighted at the prospect and wondered what miracle had brought about this transformation. Wally then continued, "But teaching you to shoot like Janet Spice? Honey, I can't even shoot like Janet Spice."

"You should have seen her, Wally," said Marie as she began to tear up, "she was amazing!"

Wally had half figured out what had happened but was anxious to get filled in on all the details. This was not going to be difficult, as the only thing Marie did better than cook spaghetti was talk. "C'mon, we are stinkin' up the place. Time to go home and soak in vinegar," Wally instructed.

Ginger watched as Wally and Marie waved good-bye and headed home. Ginger then made a beeline for her mom before she could do anything about it.

"I'm a little stinker!" shouted Ginger.

Janet held her at arm's length as she instructed Rosemary to bring her a wet wash cloth and a small blanket. Ginger was stripped, washed and soaking in a tub within fifteen minutes.

James escorted John and Matthew to the grave site of the killer dog. "Tell me what happened here this morning, Dad," queried John.

"What happened here today was a display of God's protective hand over the Spice family, a display of instant intercessory prayer by your mother, and a display of the best 'dog gone and done died' shooting in all of North Carolina," James replied with a smile.

As they arrived at the grave site where James had carried the dog, a chill went up and down John's spine as he viewed the body of the dead monster. "What is it, Dad?"

"I don't know for sure, Son. I have never seen such a creature."

"Looks like some sort of wolf mongrel mixed up monster," John whispered as he stood over the grotesque remains of the animal. "Clean head shot."

"It had to die instantly or it was going to maul and kill Six-Pints or Rosemary."

"It attacked Rosemary?" John asked.

"It was certainly on its mind," answered James.

"Thank the Lord for Janet," said John.

"I do every night, and I am sure you do, too," said James.

"I do, Dad," said John with a somber smile, "I really do."

There was no "getting back to normal" for the remains of that day. All of the chores except the absolutely essential ones, were suspended as the Spice family gathered in the living room to have a family pow-wow, rehearsing the events that had just unfolded.

James entered the room carrying Charlie, who still had his binoculars around his neck. "I saw it, Dad," said Charlie, as he was carefully placed into his wheelchair and rolled over next to Rosemary.

Rosemary, who was stroking Scruffy, sat up and gave Charlie a hug and then went back to scratching Scruffy around her ears.

Rosemary and Scruffy had forged a bond together that morning that would last until the day Scruffy died. The incident had left Scruffy with an open wound around her neck, which Rosemary had been nursing with tender loving care all morning. Rosemary had made Scruffy a home-made bandage and carefully wrapped it around her neck. The torn white sheet was stained red as a badge of Scruffy's courage. Scruffy licked Rosemary's hand as she curled up at her feet, looking up at the rest of the Spice family with her warm brown eyes.

"I saw the dog attack Six-Pints!" Charlie said excitedly.

"I want to hear all about it, Charlie, but first we have some business to do with the Lord," Dad said.

John reached for his Bible and turned it to Psalm 91. The family quietly listened as John read.

Psalm 91:1-11

He that dwelleth in the secret place of the most High shall abide
under the shadow of the Almighty. I will say of the Lord,
He is my refuge and my fortress: my God; in him will I trust.
Surely he shall deliver thee from the snare of the fowler,
and from the noisome pestilence. He shall cover thee with
his feathers, and under his wings shalt thou trust:

his truth shall be thy shield and buckler.
Thou shalt not be afraid for the terror by night;
nor for the arrow that flieth by day; Nor for the pestilence
that walketh in darkness; nor for the destruction that
wasteth at noonday. A thousand shall fall at thy side, and ten
thousand at thy right hand; but it shall not come nigh thee.
Only with thine eyes shalt thou behold and see
the reward of the wicked. Because thou
hast made the Lord, which is my refuge,
even the most High, thy habitation; There shall
no evil befall thee, neither shall any plague come nigh
thy dwelling. For he shall give his angels charge over thee,
to keep thee in all thy ways.

John finished reading this passage, and the family was silent for a few minutes as they each thought about what this day had brought and taught them.

Charlie broke the silence with a question.

"Dad, could you tell us about your hunting adventure with Mr. McDaniel and Matthew? What happened?"

John smiled as he relayed the events that led up to his return home.

The family laughed at the story of big Wally McDaniel and the little skunk that ruined his day. Ginger began giggling as she somehow sensed that she had become entangled in that story in a way no one expected.

Ginger had just gotten out of her bubble bath. Janet had held her nose as she poured in a generous portion of rose water and a half bottle of lavender bath salts that her Aunt Ida had sent her last Christmas.

Ginger was partially smelling like the queen of England's parlor, and partly like something that made you want to rub your watery eyes. The pungent odor of skunk, and rose-water laced with lavender, swirled around the living room.

John rose and picked up Ginger, gave her a big kiss, and set her on the fireplace hearth next to Anna. He was hoping the vapors would rise up the chimney before everyone's eyes started to water. It turned out to be a good plan, and soon no one in the room was distracted by the "little stinker's" aromatic presence.

John finished telling the story of the hunting adventures of Wally, Matthew and himself. John made sure to heap bountiful praise on Matthew, noting his steady aim and bravery in the midst of the skunk fiasco.

"Janet," concluded John, "I think Matthew has the makings of a crack shot that might give you some competition."

"Oh, Dad," said Matthew, "I could never shoot as well as Mom."

"Says who?" Janet piped up, determined not to let the moment pass without adding her good opinion of Matthew's sharpshooting prospects.

James told the story from his vantage point, "I was upstairs with Charlie when, through his binoculars, he spotted the wild dog invading the farm. I ran downstairs, looking for the rifle above the mantle. But by the time I got there, it was gone. The next thing I heard was a shot. I don't know what happened next."

Charlie was the next to speak up, "I saw it all, Grandpa. The wild dog was going after Six-Pints, and Rosemary started swinging at it with the milk pail. Then the milk pail slipped out of her hand and went sailing off toward the barn."

"Then what happened?" asked John.

"Well, that dog faced off with Rosemary, and I thought it was going to attack her; that's when I started praying for Rosemary."

Janet began to tear up as she listened to the drama, that she had played a part in, being described from different vantage points.

"I was scared, Dad," said Rosemary. "That dog was not a normal dog, it made me really afraid." Rosemary leaned down and stroked Scruffy as John considered again the tragedy that could have been.

"And then what happened Rosemary?"

"I don't know; the dog just turned around and attacked Six-Pints. That's when Scruffy came around the corner of the house and took a run at the wild dog. I ran to the barn to get a pitch fork, and that's when I heard the shot."

As John imagined more outcome that could have easily attended this drama, he was overcome with gratitude towards God. As John listened to the stories of his children giving their unique testimonies to the events of that morning, he became convinced of one thing. The one thing that held the entire story together, started with the prayer of his mother.

"Dad, I want you to start the Spice family prayer chain, and I will put in the last word of praise," John said.

James got out of his chair and on his knees, folded his hands together, and lifted up his head with eyes wide open. Everyone else in the family followed their grandfather's example.

The prayers were not long, and they didn't sound like the prayers you hear in most churches. The prayers that rose to Heaven, on that late morning in the Spice family living room, were sincere and emotion packed cries of thanksgiving and praise.

John listened to all the prayers of the family, giving plenty of time for each one to thank God for preserving their family in a moment of crisis, that they would never forget.

When it came time for John to conclude the prayer meeting, he was convinced of two things that made him very joyful: He served the only true God—who loved and cared for him and his family in ways the rest of the world would never know. And, he had a family that knew how to pray.

Mark 16:15
*And he said unto them, Go ye into all the world,
and preach the gospel to every creature.*

The Shadow of a Wooden Cross

The shadow of a wooden cross,
A rising Son displayed.
On that spot and on that day,
An Ancient debt was paid.

Prophetic WORD, merged with flesh,
With love bound to a tree.
There Justice met with mercy,
For all the world to see.

Divine the name of Him who hangs,
With emblem wounds of glory.
Page of light that turned the night,
Into another story.

Joy was mixed with Agony,
That day upon the tree.
Reflecting on the Book of Life,
My Savior thought of me.

Holy Holy Holy is the great I AM,
Providing for Himself that day,
The perfect spotless Lamb

Love deep and wide and full and free,
Love priceless and apart.
Love stained with crimson hues and tears,
Has entered human hearts.

Look up dear soul and fix blind eyes,
Upon the Savior's tree.
And you will find as others have,
He makes the sightless see.

An unexpected resting place,
Was found beneath that tree.
Where all my burdens came undone,
And I found liberty.

Written for those who love Jesus, by CJ Lovik

A FREE PREVIEW OF
HEAVEN'S REST

GET YOUR COPY NOW AT:
www.lighthouse.pub

© 2019 C.J. Lovik
All rights reserved

Introduction

THE *Saints Everlasting Rest* by Richard Baxter stands alone as one of the stellar witnesses to the reality and ultimate motivations for treading the pilgrim path in order to arrive safely in Heaven's Rest.

Unfortunately, it is not widely read today. One of the reasons this amazing book is rarely read by Christians is because it is dated and difficult for most people to read.

It is with this in mind that I offer an original rendering, inspired by the first chapter of *The Saints Everlasting Rest*.

The book you are about to read is original with me. It is not a paraphrase or translation, but it does build on the outline of the book originally written by Baxter. I have also included a few inspirational quotes by Baxter.

So while this book is original with the author, it owes its rebirth to Baxter. This is a work launched by one saint and now rewritten for another generation, in order to reveal the timeless truths of Scripture.

May you be blessed and encouraged as you read this short book.

– C.J. Lovik

Chapter 1

The end of evil
...and the end of grace

Hebrews 4:9-10

There remaineth therefore a rest to the people of God. For he that is entered into his rest, he also hath ceased from his own works, as God did from his.

I cannot fully comprehend the complete meaning of the "rest" that Apostle Paul speaks of in his letter to the Hebrews.

Nevertheless, we may nibble around the edges of this sweet manna that has come to us from Heaven, by God's intentional, if not fully illuminated, revelation.

What does it speak to the soul? What does it say to one who has found genuine, but mostly unrealized, rest in the work of Christ's Cross?

Rest! What is this "rest" that Jesus proclaims as he beckons those who are weary and burdened to come to him and receive? (Matthew 11:28)

Something comes to an end just before this most anticipated rest is completely and fully realized. Do you know what it is? It may surprise you!

A STORY OF GRACE

The bucket quickly swished up the creek water and captured a small fry, moments before it would be swallowed by a larger trout.

Joshua, who scooped up the fingerling, decided that he would keep it alive and transport it to the pond in his back yard, a couple miles away.

Joshua's rescue plan posed two challenges. The first was that the bucket he used to capture the trout had a leak.

The second problem was that all the bouncing up and down in the back of his dad's pickup truck would surely slosh all the water out of the bucket before they reached home. What to do?

Joshua thought about the problem and came up with a solution. He filled his lunch thermos with creek water and carefully positioned himself, with his bucket and wiggling passenger, in the bed of his dad's pickup.

Joshua pressed the bucket between his knees as the old truck rumbled down the bumpy dirt road. He found himself fully engaged in preventing water from slosh

A FREE PREVIEW OF **HEAVEN'S REST**

ing out of the bucket and, at the same time, adding water as needed.

The two-mile journey seemed an eternity, but Joshua and his small trophy arrived safely home. It took Joshua only a minute to take the bucket down to the pond and gently pour the agitated trout into its new nursery.

WHEN GRACE IS NO LONGER NECESSARY

This very imperfect illustration does manage to teach a lesson in grace.

While the first act of grace was evident in the rescuing of the small trout; the second act of grace was achieved, not by one work, but by many means: the constant resupplying of the water, the balancing of the bucket, and the quick hands preventing the life-giving water from escaping the bucket.

When the trout left the confines of the bucket and entered the five-acre pond, the means of grace ended for the small fish.

> When we enter God's final rest, the means of grace cease, as they are no longer necessary.

The angels who had been assigned to preserve our welfare, report for new duties. All the circumstances that God surrounded us with to keep us from destroying ourselves, immediately cease.

The vexations caused by our daily pilgrimage through the nasty **now-and-now** come to an abrupt conclusion.

All the thousands of means of grace—some realized, most hidden—supplied so readily and abundantly by our Savior, suddenly and forever cease. Is that possible? The answer is a resounding **yes**!

But it is only possible for those who enter His rest. The means of grace come to an end for those who enter God's rest!

FREEDOM FROM EVIL

The little trout rescued by Joshua found itself in a safer place, but not one without dangers. The ducks in Joshua's pond are unreliable vegetarians who would like nothing more than to garnish their diet of green veggies with a tasty wiggling tidbit.

The pond is also frequently visited by Egrets and King fishers who are skillfully designed to eat small unsuspecting fish.

We who enter God's rest do not go from a bad place to a better one with fewer dangers. **No!** We enter a rest that is designed to forever keep us perfectly free from all evil and evils.

John Bunyan captured the twinkling rays of this truth in **Pilgrim's Progress**. Listen to the words of Bunyan's character, Christian, as he explains to Pliable that their destination, the Celestial City, is free from anyone who would wish them harm.

Pliable asks, "And what company shall we have there?"

Christian replies, ". . . you shall meet with thousands and ten thousands that have gone before us to that place; none of them are hurtful, but loving and holy . . . "

The rest reserved for the saints is free from all evil!

This does raise a question. If the means of grace ends and I am to enter a place that is free from all evil, what am I to do in such a place?

Something needs amending. There must be unfinished business since I am presently unfit for such a holy place.

We are all sinners, saved yes, but still a sinner.

Without some drastic change, Heaven would not be fit for you or me, or we for Heaven. We have been treading our way on this Earth, trading on the perfect righteousness of Christ. And while it is true that some of His mind is in us, we are still ill suited for Heaven.

Let's be honest, our flesh still wars mightily against all that is God and good. And we still sin.

It is only God's preserving and enabling Spirit, the good intentions of God for you, and the ever vigilant persevering hand of the Savior that has kept us from sliding down the hill upon which the Savior's cross stands as our only hope.

Once begun, the slide down is not inconsequential. The welcoming, often-traveled, path tumbles down to an irretrievable entrance into a grave, which is the doorway to an eternal Hell.

In a word, if all means of God's good grace end, and I am now to enter a place of perfection, I have a real dilemma.

To put it plainly, I am unfit for the place and could never hope to enter into its sanctuary without some intervening miracle.

Full book available at
www.lighthouse.pub

CHECK OUT OUR WEBSITE FOR OTHER TITLES!

www.lighthouse.pub

2019

From the editor of the critically acclaimed and recently republished Pilgrim's Progress, author and editor C.J. Lovik brings a unique contribution to the retelling of this classic tale. Lovik brings a fresh and unique view, allowing for a modern audience to read and understand, yet preserving the deep and beloved truths of Bunyan's timeless tale.

2015

Comical yet kindhearted Theodore A. Bump learns an important lesson about God's love in Theodore Bump, What's in your trunk? A delightful story told in rhyme and pictures. Theodore's eagerness to help the world's hungry people takes him down some unusual paths; he tries shipping a trunk full of food to the needy.

2015

Rest! What is the "rest" that Jesus proclaims in the Book of Matthew as he beckons the weary and burdened to come to him? What is Heaven? How do we get there? What will we do there? What happens when we no longer need the grace of God? These questions, along with many others, are addressed in this brief but powerful book by writer C.J. Lovik.

2016

The story of the life of Jesus, as told by four separate biographers, weaves together a harmonized story that accurately portrays the life of Jesus Christ. This book displays the miracle of the four separate accounts, as they each stand without contradiction or discrepancy. Writer C.J. Lovik masterfully overlays these harmonized stories into a single account of the life of the Savior.

www.lighthouse.pub

Visit our website to purchase books, DVDs, and otherChrist-centered media, and to preview upcoming titles.

Check out these amazing resources, and begin your journey to a closer relationship with our **Lord and Savior!**

"Life, life, eternal life!" - John Buynan, The Pilgrim's Progress

www.lighthouse.pub